MEMORY AND THE MOVING IMAGE

MEMORY AND THE MOVING IMAGE

French Film in the Digital Era

Isabelle McNeill

EDINBURGH UNIVERSITY PRESS

© Isabelle McNeill, 2010, 2012

First published in hardback by Edinburgh University Press 2010

Edinburgh University Press Ltd
22 George Square, Edinburgh EH8 9LF

www.euppublishing.com

Typeset in 10/12.5 pt Sabon
by Servis Filmsetting Ltd, Stockport, Cheshire,
and printed and bound in the United States of America
by Edwards Brothers Malloy

A CIP record for this book is available from the British Library

ISBN 978 0 7486 3891 8 (hardback)
ISBN 978 0 7486 4942 6 (paperback)

The right of Isabelle McNeill
to be identified as author of this work
has been asserted in accordance with
the Copyright, Designs and Patents Act 1988.

CONTENTS

ILLUSTRATIONS

ACKNOWLEDGEMENTS

I am grateful to the Centre for Research in the Arts, Social Sciences and Humanities (CRASSH) in Cambridge for the Early Career Fellowship that helped me to complete this book, as well as to the research fund at Trinity Hall and travel grants from Corpus Christi College for helping to fund essential research trips to Paris. I am also grateful to Trinity Hall, the Department of French and the Newton Trust at the University of Cambridge for granting me research leave. The book is based on my doctoral research, which was made possible by the Arts and Humanities Research Council, to whom I am very grateful. I would also like to thank Esmé Watson, Máiréad McElligot and Sarah Edwards at Edinburgh University Press for all their help, support and patience. Thanks to Yoram Allon of Wallflower Press and editors Andrew Webber and Emma Wilson for granting me permission to use material in Chapter 4 published in an earlier form in *Cities in Transition: The Moving Image and the Modern Metropolis* (London: Wallflower, 2008). Many thanks to the filmmakers Zabou Breitman and Yamina Benguigui for their time and input, and to Agnès Varda and everyone at CinéTamaris, Bizibi Productions, Bandits Productions, SND Groupe M6, Argos Films, Les Films du Losange and Michael Haneke for their kind permission to reproduce images from their films. Thanks also to Sarah Cooper, Ian James, Patrick ffrench and Tim Murray for their careful readings of my work and insightful comments. I am especially grateful to two wonderfully supportive interlocutors: Emma Wilson for years of generous, astute guidance and stimulating discussion and Gerard Duveen for many inspiring conversations. Discussions with Will McNeill, Olly Otley and Hugo Azérad have also been helpfully thought-provoking and I am grateful to Gillie McNeill for a neuroscientist's perspective. Finally, my humble and deeply heartfelt thanks go to Jean-Baptiste Fourcade and to Gillie McNeill for their unwavering support, love and encouragement.

For Gerard, always remembered, and for Benedict, who is the future.

INTRODUCTION: FILM AND MEMORY
IN CONTEMPORARY FRANCE

A recurring image in Jean-Luc Godard's eight-part video series *Histoire(s) du cinéma* (1989–98) shows a man and woman staring intently at a film projection, taken from an early film by Ingmar Bergman, *Fängelse* (1946). Along with shots of James Stewart peering voyeuristically through a zoom lens in *Rear Window* (Hitchcock, 1954) the image is developed through the series as a figure of cinema's gaze upon history. Citing a line from Alain Resnais' *Hiroshima mon amour* (1959), the sequence of titles inscribed upon the *Fängelse* image as it appears in chapter 4B of Godard's series evokes a failure of witnessing that contrasts with the couple's absorbed gaze: 'tu n'as rien vu' (you saw nothing). The juxtaposition recalls the original context of the words in the Resnais film, where a French actress, visiting Hiroshima, claims to have seen it all and her Japanese lover reminds her that she has in fact seen nothing, because she has not witnessed the cataclysm designated by the word 'Hiroshima'. Godard then multiplies the signs of historical violence in his rendering of the critique by following Hiroshima with the inscriptions 'Leningrad', 'Madagascar', 'Dresde', 'Hanoi' and 'Sarajevo'. The words superimposed on the image of James Stewart in *Rear Window*, 'les signes parmi nous' (the signs among us), also form the title of the episode, another inscription that appears repeatedly throughout the series. It implies, particularly when juxtaposed with the subsequent image of Hitler giving a speech, that cinema's signs can be read historiographically but also that cinema has often failed to read the signs of history.

The Memory of Cinema

I open with these images because they show that the *Histoire(s)* series, as its polyvalent title suggests, is as much a cinema of history as a history of cinema. The filmic collages of clips, photographs, paintings, music, quotations and commentary evokes a complex vision of cinema, variously depicting it as fallible witness, implicated observer and powerful instrument of historiography. The underlying premise is that cinema's own history is bound up, for better or for worse, with the history of the twentieth century, the multiple stories of each having shaped and become entwined in the other. In this book I want to explore just such an intertwining of the memory of history and the moving image. I will investigate the ways in which cultural objects and the human experience of the past in the present are linked, through the workings of memory in and between people. This exploration will take as its focus a sample of French films, a multi-installation exhibition and a CD-ROM, spanning the turn of the millennium and taking the discussion forward into the twenty-first century. Each of the works discussed, in its own way, attempts to capture, call up or confront the past. In so doing they raise compelling questions about the interrelation of moving images and memory. How can films show the processes and mechanisms of memory? And what do the processes and mechanisms of moving images *do to* memory? Film is a communal medium and always provides some kind of shared point of experience in both making and viewing. Moving between apparatus, editing and spectator I want to explore how these collective artefacts and experiences are involved in the dissemination and transmission of memory. As French film critics Serge Daney and Ignacio Ramonet suggest here, the accumulation of filmed sounds and images across the twentieth century provides an extraordinary cultural archive:

> L'ensemble de ce qui a été filmé depuis le début du siècle (macro ou micro-histoire, événementielle ou pas, document ou fiction) constitue aujourd'hui, de fait, une *archive* considérable [. . .]. Depuis longtemps, le rapport des peuples à leur passé – leur mémoire – ne se distingue plus très bien de leur rapport à cette archive (leur 'mémoire filmique' en quelque sorte). (Ferro 1993: 63)

> (The totality of everything that has been filmed since the beginning of the century (macro or micro-history, descriptive or not, documentary or fiction) now in fact constitutes a remarkable *archive* [. . .]. For a long time now, people's relation to their past – their memory – has ceased to be clearly distinguishable from their relation to this archive (their 'filmic memory' in a sense).)[1]

Such a memory bank represents the past in a huge variety of ways, from the ideological to the sartorial, whether overtly, incidentally or insidiously. Far from gathering dust, it is an 'archive' that is continuously being reshuffled, reviewed (in the cinema, on television or on DVD) and recycled. From Godard through Sergio Leone to Quentin Tarantino, even in very recently made films the sounds and images of cinema's past return endlessly in the form of visual references or direct citation. It has become impossible to deny that our memories are now, in a very real sense, filmic.

Laura Mulvey highlights this return of 'old' cinema in her work on new viewing technologies. She describes the twentieth century's accumulation of film in terms of a parallel universe made particularly accessible by DVD:

> At the end of the twentieth century, new technologies opened up new perceptual possibilities, new ways of looking, not at the world, but at the internal world of cinema. The century had accumulated a recorded film world, like a parallel universe, that can now be halted or slowed or fragmented. (Mulvey 2005: 181)

As Mulvey points out, just as the traditions of cinema theatres and celluloid seem to be waning, the preservation of and nostalgia for these practices is keener than ever. The immense popularity of DVD has led to a high number of re-releases, while digital technologies have made quotation and compilation relatively easy. The contemporary enthusiasm for restoring 'classics' and revisiting cinematic history has fostered new technologies that create a zone where individual cinephilia mingles with an audiovisual archive. The historian Eric Hobsbawm writes of 'a twilight zone between history and memory', a 'no-man's land' where individual memory extends through family traditions into the relatively dispassionate, public sphere of history (Hobsbawm 1994: 3). Mulvey picks up on this idea and suggests that film has become a material record of this liminal territory:

> On celluloid, personal and collective memories are prolonged and preserved, extending and expanding the 'twilight zone', merging individual memory with recorded history. (Mulvey 2005: 25)

The spectator may now dip almost at will into moments of cinematic time, both within a given film and in the mass of films that make up cinema's history. The body of cinema is potentially a part of the cultural memory of even very recent generations of spectators. But new technologies not only have an impact on viewing practices, they also raise questions about the very nature of film and cinema and its function as witness of history and archive of collective memories. A significant strand running through this book seeks to address the impact of digital modes of production on the mnemonic role of film, if indeed we can call it 'film' now that it has dispensed with the need for a photo-reactive pellicle.[2] From chemical traces to pure code, does the medium affect the memory? Does digital manipulation always correlate to a distortion of memory or are there ways in which digital imaging can allow us to rethink the operations of memory? In 2003 the theme of an international symposium, held by the Screen Studies Group at the University of London, asked whether the digital revolution signalled the end of cinema and posed the questions of ontology and authenticity in digital filmmaking.[3] The diverse selection of papers made clear the need for film studies to respond to and account for the changing forms and increasingly hybrid character of what was once thought of as simply 'cinema' or 'film'.

Well over a century since the Lumière brothers first held a public showing of the cinematograph, the cinema has been pronounced dead. Though we still watch things that are known, at least in the UK, as 'films', more often than not we watch them on a small screen in an almost infinite variety of viewing situations, from family sofas to aeroplane flights. For Chris Marker this viewing on a small screen, which is becoming ever smaller with the proliferation of portable devices and internet downloading, is merely a haunting memory of what cinema really was: the experience of sitting in darkness, looking up at a projection on a huge screen:

> Godard l'a bien dit, comme il lui arrive: le cinéma, c'est ce qui est plus grand que nous, sur quoi il faut lever les yeux. En passant dans un objet plus petit et sur quoi on baisse les yeux, le cinéma perd son essence. On peut s'émouvoir sur la trace qu'il laisse, [. . .] on peut voir à la télé l'ombre d'un film, le regret d'un film, la nostalgie, l'écho d'un film, jamais un film. (Chris Marker, 'Cinéma' zone of *Immemory* (1988))

> (Godard has put it well, as he often does: cinema is that which is bigger than us, something we have to look up to. In its transition into a smaller object, something we look down at, cinema loses its essence. One can be moved by the trace it leaves, [. . .] on TV one can see the shadow of a film, the pining for film, the nostalgia for or echo of a film, but never a film.)

In this book my focus is on the period that follows the officially designated centenary of cinema in France.[4] It is therefore in the aftermath of cinema's coming of age as well as its 'death' that these films are situated. A video series made for television, Godard's *Histoire(s) du cinéma* seems to mark this moment. The inclusion of a CD-ROM, Chris Marker's *Immemory*, and Agnès Varda's exhibition *L'Île et elle* (2006) in my discussions reflects a move away from our conventional notions of film, even in its digital forms. Such deployment of filmic visual media is increasingly becoming mainstream, reflecting the important cultural and commercial position now held by video games and, as internet bandwidth increases, multimedia websites. However Godard's, Marker's and Varda's experiments beyond the traditional boundaries of cinema provide self-reflexive examples that encourage reflection upon the shifting relations between technology and the filmic. While not all the works I have selected are as experimental, they are all products of a particular, transitory period in moving image production, between cinema's past and the future of visual culture. As cinema commemorates its history or mourns its demise, the moving image texts I will discuss in this book appropriate cinema's forms, in highly varied ways, for their own commemorations of the past.

Remembering History in France

The 'century of cinema' was also something of a century of memory in France. As the nineteenth century moved into the twentieth, just as cinema was coming into its own, France saw the emergence of Marcel Proust's literary memory edifice, *À la recherche du temps perdu*, as well as philosopher Henri Bergson's groundbreaking and influential investigations into memory, time and consciousness. Proust, with his dense and poetic analyses of the minutiae of the narrator's experiences of time and memory, may well be the most directly influential thinker on memory in France. With his concepts of involuntary and voluntary memory, Proust gave a renewed and intensely subjective vitality to the Aristotelian distinction between *mnēmē* (a feeling) and *anamnesis* (an effort to recollect).[5] His famous account of an involuntary mental transport back to a childhood world, triggered by the taste of a Madeleine cake drenched in tea, is a ubiquitous reference point for French (and other) writings on memory to this day. A source of inspiration for Jean-Luc Godard and most particularly Chris Marker, Proust's thought and writings are part of the cultural foundations that make contemporary filmic explorations of memory possible and as such will often be revisited in the course of this book. Although it has been persuasively argued that Proust was not in fact influenced by Bergson (see Megay 1976), there are elements of resonance between their works, notably in the idea that memory is constantly implicated in our perception of the world. Bergson posited perception as inextricable from memory, which always forms and informs it. His theories were revisited by Gilles Deleuze in 1966 in a brilliant distillation of *Le Bergsonisme* (Deleuze 1998) and, more recently, in his two-volume philosophical investigation of the medium of cinema (Deleuze 1985). Bergson famously rejected the cinema, which seemed to him to incarnate the falsifying conception of time that had, he argued, incessantly hindered Western philosophy. Deleuze's re-reading of Bergsonism to account for cinematic time in radical new ways forms a contemporary connecting thread between the cinema and Bergson's philosophy. In conjunction with Deleuze, then, Bergson's theories of time and memory will also inform my exploration. In a similar period to Proust and Bergson, the work of Sigmund Freud was emphasising the importance of memory in relation to the unconscious. The concept of a present haunted by traces of the past, whether at an individual or a social level, was increasingly becoming common currency, and as the passing century brought with it violence on an unprecedented scale, the notions of trauma, commemoration and exoneration developed a vital social significance.

The other end of the twentieth century saw a renewed burgeoning of collective fascination with memory in France. This conceivably has its roots in the 1970s when France collectively began to revisit and rethink its role in the Second World War. Henry Rousso, in his study of the impact of the Vichy period on France's national self-image and engagement with its past, discerns, from the mid-1970s onwards, an obsession with uncovering the sins of the past, as a counterpoint to long post-war years of *refoulement* (repression) (Rousso 1987). As Eric Vigne puts it:

> La France, lorsque paraît l'ouvrage d'Henry Rousso, s'est installée depuis quelques années dans une crise de mémoire nationale dont elle n'est, aujourd'hui, toujours pas sortie: elle vit dans une véritable obsession, celle du régime de Vichy, passant comme d'un excès d'oubli, dans les années cinquante, de ce que furent ces quatre années noires (1940–1944), à un excès de remémoration. (Vigne 1997: 92)

> (When Henry Rousso's book came out, France had for several years been undergoing a crisis of national memory, which even to this day the country has not put behind it: France is experiencing a real obsession with the Vichy regime, moving from an excessive forgetting, in the 1950s, of the four dark years (1940–1944), to an excessive remembering.)

Rousso recognises the role of cinema in the 'breaking of the mirror', noting in particular the importance of the Marcel Ophüls film *Le Chagrin et la pitié* (1969), a four-hour documentary that used archive footage alongside contemporary interviews with both resistance fighters and collaborators. Originally made for the Office de Radiodiffusion-Télévision Française (ORTF), it was banned by the state for television screening, though it was eventually shown in cinemas in Paris in 1971. That Rousso accords it a key role in France's crisis of memory in relation to Vichy is a sign of cinema's powerful implication in the way societies remember their pasts.

The reassessment of a dubious period of France's past during the Second World War may have been a driving force behind the surge of interest in the concept of 'memory'. When faced with the marked absence of histories of collaboration and anti-Semitism in France, what terms other than 'collective forgetting' or 'amnesia' could describe this gap in official narratives, particularly when it involved a dormant sense of shame or confusion for so many individuals and groups? Though it had its concrete manifestation in facts and figures, here was a hidden history, emotive, often private and yet central to the shared past of the nation – its repressed unconscious, to pick up on Rousso's use of the word *refoulement*. Memory, rather than history, must have seemed a more appropriate term to describe the process of uncovering that was sparked off in the 1970s. Memory in turn became a new kind of model for historians, one that took account of the fissures in official histories and the mythification that takes place through the cultural dissemination of historical interpretation. At the forefront of this was Pierre Nora's collaborative project *Les Lieux de mémoire* (sites of memory) (1984–92). The seven-volume collection of essays undertook a study of the places, concepts and objects around which cultural meaning had crystallised and accumulated in France, such as Jeanne d'Arc, the café or the Larousse dictionaries. As such it was effectively intended to be a study of France's cultural and political memory, rather than a traditional history. The impact was huge, effectively popularising the very notion of a cultural memory. By the time Gallimard launched a new paperback edition of the volumes in 1997, the title of the review in *Le Monde* – 'Mémoire d'une nation' – had become a cliché. As the author of the article remarks, Nora had invented 'une notion dont on n'imagine plus qu'on n'ait pu l'ignorer' (a notion we now cannot imagine not knowing) (Catinchi 1997). Jacques le Goff's *Histoire et mémoire* was published midway through the work on *Les Lieux de mémoire*. Le Goff rejects any conflation of history and memory or the privileging of the latter over the former, remarking that 'des tendances naïves récentes semblent presque identifier l'une avec l'autre et même préférer en quelque sorte la mémoire, qui serait plus authentique' (recent naive tendencies seem almost to identify one with the other and even somehow to prefer memory, which would be more authentic) (Le Goff 1998: 10). None the less, the collection and publication of his essays, originally entries for an Italian encyclopaedia, showed that as a historian he took the subject of memory seriously: 'la mémoire collective fait partie des gros enjeux des sociétés développés et des sociétés en développement, des classes dominantes et des classes dominées' (collective memory is among the high stakes of developed and developing societies, dominant and dominated classes) (p. 174).

By 2000, Larousse, whose dictionaries had themselves been sites of memory for Nora's project, had brought out a new series of reference books entitled 'La Mémoire de l'Humanité' (the memory of humanity), including one called *Les Objets racontent l'histoire* (history told by objects), a lavishly illustrated collection of two-page essays each focusing on a significant object from world history, for example fragments of the Berlin Wall, or Napoleon's crown. Its preface demonstrates how Nora's terminology had become part of everyday vocabulary, used without any explicit reference to the original project:

> Les objets de ce livre sont presque tous des 'lieux de mémoire' de notre histoire, des éléments d'une mythologie collective, voire d'une légende, qui ont permis d'enraciner une époque dans notre souvenir. Le choix que nous avons fait est donc forcément arbitraire et subjectif. Il relève de notre propre sensibilité, de notre propre imaginaire. (Baylac and Garrigues 2000: 6)

> (The objects in this book are almost all 'sites of memory' of our history, elements of a collective mythology, or even a legend, which enabled an era to take root in our memory. Our choices are therefore necessarily arbitrary and subjective. They spring from our own sensibility and imagination.)

As this extract shows, the popularisation of memory as an alternative model to history drew on what might be termed a postmodern notion of truth, which conceives it as essentially refracted through subjectivity. In other words, it is possible to study the past but we must take into account how that past is framed and appropriated in the present through the desires and idiosyncrasies of individuals and groups. For the editors of *Les Objets racontent l'histoire* this 'subjective history' enables the participation of the reader, who can then fit his or her own individual past into the picture:

> À leur façon, ils nous racontent l'histoire, mais ils racontent aussi notre façon de percevoir l'histoire, de nous la représenter. Dans cette représentation subjective de notre histoire, nous espérons que nos lecteurs retrouveront un peu de leurs propres images et peut-être de leur passé. (p. 7)

> (In their own way, they tell the story of history, but they also tell of our way of perceiving history and of representing it to ourselves. In this subjective representation of our history, we hope that our readers will find some of their own images and, perhaps, something of their own past.)

THE COLONIAL FRACTURE AND MULTIDIRECTIONAL MEMORY

At the start of the twenty-first century, then, 'memory' was sitting on France's coffee tables, posited as a means of drawing anyone into history, whether that of France or of other countries. Yet while the troubled history of Vichy and the Second World War had taken hold within collective memory, the complexity of France's relation to its colonial past had received much less in the way of critical attention in the public domain. Even as Pierre Nora's seminal project drew attention to the unreliable, human element of historical representations of the past and to the role of official discourses in constructing and delimiting collective memory, the choice of 'sites of memory' in his project all but excluded the colonial past. Indeed, Nicolas Bancel et al., in their introduction to a volume addressing the 'colonial fracture' in French national identity, conclude justifiably that, 'dans le travail essentiel et fondateur que représentent les *Lieux de mémoire* [. . .] la "part coloniale" de l'histoire de la France est minorée, presque oubliée' (in the essential and foundational work represented by *Les Lieux de mémoire* [. . .] the 'colonial share' of the history of France is marginalised, almost forgotten) (Bancel et al. 2005: 15). It is only in more recent years, largely since the millennium, that the kind of obsessive excavation Rousso associates with the commemoration of Vichy in the 1970s and 1980s has begun to emerge with relation to this other problematic strand of French history.

The spectre of Algeria looms large in this collective repression of the past, as well as in the subsequent resurgence of memory. Unlike the distant colonies of Senegal or Indonesia, or the protectorate of Tunisia, Algeria was directly dependent on the French Ministry of the Interior and had been considered French soil for 130 years. Yet despite being part of the Republic, its Muslim citizens were not given equal rights (Stora 1991: 18). Historian Benjamin Stora argues that the Algerian war of independence (1954–62) is 'le nœud gordien de tous les retours forts de mémoire de ces dernières années' (the Gordian knot of all the powerful resurgence of memory in recent years) (2007: 50). Even though, as Stora points out, more than 2,500 books about the Algerian war appeared in France between 1962 and 1982 (p. 16), these texts, mostly written during the 1970s, tended to focus on the perspective of French veterans of the bitterly violent war, or the nostalgia of former colonials. Nostalgia, both for an image of France as a great colonial power and for former colonies as idealised spaces of otherness, has been seen as an important factor in the failure to integrate both the negative aspects of colonialism and the rupture of decolonisation into collective memory. Moreover such nostalgia has often pervaded official discourses: 'la France [. . .] est pratiquement le seul pays européen à s'être délibérément rangé du côté d'une "nostalgie coloniale" et de l'oubli institutionnalisé, tentant de dissocier histoire coloniale et histoire nationale' (France [. . .] is practically the only European country to have deliberately settled on the side of 'colonial nostalgia' and institutionalised forgetting, attempting to dissociate colonial history and national history) (Bancel et al. 2005: 14). At the same time, the emphasis on the Algerian war at the expense of a longer and more extensive sense of colonial history means that from the 1960s, 'une mémoire de vaincus s'est diffusée dans l'espace public pendant vingt ans' (the memories of the vanquished spread across the public domain for twenty years) (Stora 2007: 16), effectively sidelining alternative perspectives. As Stora shows in his eponymous essay, 'une mémoire (de guerre) peut en cacher une autre (coloniale)' (one memory (of war) can conceal another (of colonisation)) (Stora 2005).

These forms of collective evasion of the difficult and complicated truths of France's colonial history mirror the process charted by Rousso with relation to the Second World War and Vichy, wherein mythologising narratives and state censorship emphasised one aspect of history (resistance) at the expense of another (collaboration). It is noteworthy that Bancel et al., in describing the increased attention given to colonial and postcolonial history in the 2000s, pick up the same psychological terminology of *refoulement* used by Rousso, demonstrating the extent to which the idea of memory, as opposed to the supposedly neutral narratives of history, now inflects socio-historical analysis and discussion in France: 'cette apparition sur le devant de la scène de la "question coloniale" [. . .] n'est pas un accident, un hasard, mais bien le symptôme d'un "retour du refoulé"' (the fact that the 'colonial question' has taken centre stage [. . .] is not random, or an accident, but rather the symptom of a 'return of the repressed') (2005: 10). Significantly, however, this process of confrontation with problematic aspects of the past is still ongoing at the time of writing, producing tensions that are often described in the language of military conflict, such as 'la guerre des mémoires' (the war of memories) (Stora 2007) or a 'champ de bataille mémoriel' (battleground of memories) (Bancel et al. 2005: 23), as though echoing the haunting presence of the Algerian war. An example of this continued tension can be found in the now-infamous law of 23 February 2005, requiring French history teachers to transmit the 'positive role' of the French presence abroad and particularly in North Africa, which was finally repealed in 2006 after fierce public debate.

As was the case with Vichy, films are also playing a role in this return of the repressed and the resulting commemorative battleground. Martine Beugnet suggests that several recent films have gone towards breaking the 'long-lasting silence' surrounding France's 'dirty war' (the Algerian war of independence), citing as examples *Mon colonel* (Laurent Herbiet, 2006), *La Trahison* (Philippe Faucon, 2006) and *Nuit noire, 17 Octobre 1961* (Alain Tasma, 2005) (Beugnet 2007: 227). Guy Austin has also observed this 'recent, belated glut of French films on the Algerian War' (2007: 531). However, Stora notes that very few films have dramatised not only the Algerian war but the broader context of colonial history. He argues that it is possible to 'mesurer la périphérie de l'histoire coloniale par un regard sur les images de cinéma' (measure the periphery of colonial history by looking at the images in cinema) (Stora 2005: 59). In a later discussion, after the release of the films Beugnet mentions, Stora notes that *Mon colonel*, which confronts head on the use of torture by the French during the Algerian war, disappeared very quickly from cinemas after its release, while Rachid Bouchareb's hugely successful *Indigènes* (*Days of Glory*, 2006) blocks out many of the more problematic aspects of history, such as the Sétif massacres in 1945, the Madagascar massacres in 1947 and decolonisation (Stora 2007: 55). Though films such as *Mon colonel* are no longer censored as *Le Chagrin et la pitié* was in the 1970s, the implication is that the level of commercial success of films that confront France's problematic history is an indicator of a collective readiness (or lack of it) to integrate the events portrayed into collective memory. We should be wary of over-simplifying the factors leading to a film's commercial success, which cannot be attributed in any straightforward way to public resistance or acceptance but rather to many variables at each stage of the system of production, distribution and exhibition. None the less, a certain 'timeliness' may well have contributed the limited success of *Mon colonel* and the particular triumph of *Indigènes*. Of the latter, Alec Hargreaves has argued persuasively that 'it is practically certain that the film could not have been made a few years earlier' (2007: 205). Stora recognises that *Indigènes*, which depicts the role of 'indigenous' colonial soldiers drafted into combat in the Second World War, played an important role in bringing about a national consensus, acknowledging the role of colonial troops in the liberation of France (2007: 56). Indeed the film helped bring to light the injustice whereby veterans of the colonial armies had been receiving only a small portion of the war pensions received by veterans in France. As Hargreaves points out, it was in part a private screening of the film for President Jacques Chirac that led to the official decision to remedy this injustice, the announcement of which was then timed to coincide with the release of the film on 27

September 2006 (2007: 204). Yet this was not a sudden consequence of the film but rather grew out of various events and factors that themselves conditioned the making of the film (see Hargreaves 2007 for a full analysis). For me, these examples indicate the complexities of cinema's relationship to collective remembering. Far from being a straightforward reflection of shared visions of the past, films variously participate in, mediate and negotiate both the official discourses of the state and the often conflicting waves of public sentiment that flow in between the memories of individuals.

It is in the context of the ongoing struggle to integrate France's colonial past that two of the films examined in this book are explicitly situated. Yamina Benguigui's *Mémoires d'immigrés: l'héritage maghrébin* (1997) is a documentary trilogy that bears witness to the memories of generations of North African immigrants who arrived in France as an imported labour force after the Second World War. The films illuminate the colonial history underlying the immigrant community in France and confront France's unacceptable treatment and reception of these 'human resources'. Crucially, Benguigui's films appear to share with Benjamin Stora the idea that French society must face up to its own past if integration is to be achieved, not only of immigrants but also of their descendants (Stora 1992: 441). Didier Lapeyronnie has described this situation in terms of a 'passé qui ne passe pas' (a past which does not pass), evoking the persistence of colonial ideology in the discrimination and segregation experienced by communities arising from immigration (2005: 210). It is this haunting persistence, exacerbated by collective denial, that is depicted in Michael Haneke's film *Caché* (*Hidden*, 2005). As the title suggests, the film's focus is not on representing past events but rather on the destabilising effects of the return of the repressed. Georges Laurent, a television presenter leading a comfortable, bourgeois life, starts receiving mysterious videotapes of his house and street, accompanied by violent, child-like drawings. As he begins to suspect that childhood acquaintance Majid is responsible, Georges becomes increasingly paranoid and confrontational, resisting the memory of his boyhood mistreatment of the orphaned Majid. This personal guilt intersects with the horrific spectre of the massacre, on 17 October 1961, of peaceful Algerian demonstrators by French police, in which Majid's parents are supposed to have been killed, an event barely mentioned in the film, yet which none the less acts as its 'hidden' central vortex. As Guy Austin has argued, 'Georges incarnates postcolonial France: guilty, in denial, fearful, yet also powerful and violently assertive' (2007: 530).

Significantly, this absent historical centre allows the film to spiral out to encompass broader concerns about collective memory and guilt. Many critics have observed that the choice of the October 1961 massacre as the defining moment of repressed guilt suggests connections with France's implication in the Holocaust, through the figure of Maurice Papon, who was in charge of the French police in 1961 as well as having been an official in the Vichy regime (see for example Rothberg 2006, Saxton 2007b, Khanna 2007). For Michael

Rothberg, the film exemplifies what he has termed 'multidirectional memory', which he defines as 'the interface, overlap, and mutual constitution of seemingly distinct collective memories' (2006: 162). Taking as a starting point *Les belles lettres* (1961), a collection of letters about the Algerian war by Charlotte Delbo, now best known for her Holocaust memoirs, Rothberg conceives of 'the emergence of Holocaust memory and the unfolding of decolonisation as overlapping and not separate processes' (2006: 160). This multidirectional flow of memory is apparent not only in literature and film but also in historical analysis: Stora makes the connection explicit, seeing 'Vichy' and 'Algeria' as haunting reminders of France's tendency to drift insidiously towards xenophobia (2007: 50). The troubled and troubling return of the repressed that has produced a 'colonial fracture' in collective memory not only mirrors the Vichy syndrome as described by Rousso but also intersects with it, tapping into collective anxieties about what it means to be French. It is this 'circulatory system of cross-references' (Rothberg 2006: 182), weaving across the folds of collective memory and forgetting in France, that forms the context of all the moving image texts discussed in this book.

Forms of Filmic Memory

In focusing on a French context I do not wish to reify national categories. Indeed, Rothberg's concept of multidirectional memory reminds us that histories inevitably cross national boundaries. In *Caché*, for example, Rothberg (2006: 182) notes how television footage in the Laurents' home introduces the Iraq war and Israel–Palestine conflict into the circulation of violent histories in the film. One might also think of the concatenation of cataclysmic events that Godard cites in order to evoke cinema's failed witnessing, in the sequence from *Histoire(s) du cinéma* with which this introduction began. Most of the works I have chosen to study go beyond national borders in some way. Godard is Swiss, and his histories of cinema have a global scope, while Chris Marker's explorations of technology and memory in *Level Five* (1997) centre on the tragic events in Okinawa, Japan, during the Second World War. Natacha Samuel's film *Pola à 27 ans* (2003) documents her German-Polish grandmother's return to Poland for the first time since her detainment in Auschwitz. Benguigui's documentary focuses on a French context, but the memories recounted take us to Algeria, Morocco and Tunisia. Claire Simon's *Mimi* (2003) documents the life of a woman who has grown up in Nice, and in so doing reveals the multiplicity of nationalities and ethnicities that constitute the city. As part of a global preoccupation with the ruptures of the twentieth century, each of these works could be said to intersect with the concerns about violent episodes in French history and their connection with collective identity in the present. What is certain is that they were produced in a cultural context where memory, both as a concept and as a process, was a source of fascination for intellectuals and the general public alike.

The objects of my study are unlikely to be classified as 'popular'. With 509,787 admissions on its theatrical release in France and wide distribution on the arthouse circuit abroad, *Caché* is perhaps the most mainstream of the works discussed: hardly a Hollywood-style blockbuster. However, in order to examine the intertwining of memory and the moving image, I have been more interested in works that set out to investigate memory, or self-consciously examine the relationship between past and present, rather than testing how popular cinema might unconsciously reflect national preoccupations. In this sense, these works testify to the way collective anxieties about and tensions in French history have led to a preoccupation with memory itself. As the analyses in this book will further demonstrate, films do not have to reach massive audiences in order to participate in the workings of cultural memory. In his discussion of *Le Chagrin et la pitié*, Rousso asks how a film seen by a relatively small minority of the public (in 1971–2 it was seen by about 600,000 spectators) could send shock waves through the collective consciousness. Part of his conclusion is that the film's powerful impact is attributable to the way its intention of demythification coalesced with the perverse effect of state censorship, revealing the fragility of official myths. Significantly, however, Rousso also deems the originality of its form a vital factor in its influence, because of the way it actively engaged with the personal experiences of the spectators:

> Le rôle prépondérant des témoignages, leur démenti immédiat rapprochent *le Chagrin* du récit de famille, qui parle au quotidien, et accepte la contradiction. D'où les rapports passionnels que les Français ont entretenus avec l'œuvre. En ce sens, *le Chagrin* est sans doute le premier film sur la mémoire de l'Occupation, plus que sur son histoire. (Rousso 1987: 174)

> (The prominent role of testimony, which is immediately contradicted, brings *The Sorrow and the Pity* close to a family narrative, speaking in everyday language and accepting contradiction. This explains the passion with which the French people related to the film. In this sense, *The Sorrow and the Pity* is doubtless the first film of the memory of the Occupation, rather than its history.)

This is an important point, for it emphasises the power of film to shape its content and frame its images in ways that resonate with cultural conventions and deconstruct (or reconstruct) cultural mythologies. A fundamental aim of this book will be to explore these relations between film form and cultural memory. In order to do this I have selected films and other works that in some way engage with the problem of understanding memory and its relation to the moving image. They therefore foreground the workings of memory in a particularly 'filmic' way, drawing on audiovisual signs, the illusion of space, the expression of time and the rich scope for multi-layered juxtaposition. My exploration will move through three key figures of memory in film: objects, faces and city space. Each of these will be seen to act as a conduit of memory, situated at the intersection between individual and collective memory. I will examine how the films' formal aspects frame and shape these figures, engaging with the spectator's own subjective representations of the past as well as mirroring and revealing the workings of memory in themselves. It is this dual function of both mould and mirror that I will term the 'mnemonic role' of moving image texts.

Documentary and Fiction

If we accept that the way a film presents its content is crucial for its mnemonic role we must in turn confront the question of genre. The debate over the relations between memory and history is reflected in the problem of fiction versus documentary in film. My analysis will span a range of different genres, from films clearly marked as documentaries, such as *Mémoires d'immigrés*, *Les Glaneurs et la glaneuse* (Agnès Varda, 2000), *Pola à 27 ans* and *Mimi*, through texts that self-consciously challenge the fiction/documentary boundary such as Marker's *Level Five* and *Immemory* to fiction features such as *Se souvenir des belles choses* (Zabou Breitman, 2002) and Haneke's *Caché*. While the category of documentary implies a factual mode that might seem to present a more useful and authentic repository for cultural memory, it is now widely recognised that films made under the sign of documentary are just as subject to the ideological biases, subjective framings, factual lacunae and persuasive rhetoric as fiction films. As documentary theorist Bill Nichols puts it:

> 'Documentary' suggests fullness and completion, knowledge and fact, explanations of the social world and its motivating mechanisms. More recently though, documentary has come to suggest incompleteness and uncertainty, recollection and impression, images of personal worlds and their subjective construction. Documentary has its troubles and opportunities, which these changes reflect. (Nichols 1993: 174)

Each of the moving image texts discussed in this book could be taken as an illustration of the 'troubles and opportunities' of documentary, whether one takes Mimi Chiola's wonderful storytelling as she relates memories of her life in *Mimi* or filmmaker Agnès Varda's physical and vocal presence in her journey through France in search of stories and histories of gleaning in *Les Glaneurs et la glaneuse*. Chris Marker approaches the matter more rhetorically, using a fictional framework to tackle a violent moment in history: the battle of Okinawa in 1945. Even a film firmly classed as fiction, *Se souvenir des belles choses*, has a documentary impulse at its heart. A sincere attempt to portray disturbances of memory by focusing on a young woman suffering from early-onset Alzheimer's disease, Zabou Breitman's film presents us with a fictional narrative but is inspired by the non-judgemental, 'objective' collection of words and images attempted by certain schools of documentary. Breitman cites documentary filmmaker and photographer Raymond Depardon as a key influence when making this, her first feature film:

> J'ai une passion pour les documentaires, leur manière d'accueillir, de recueillir les mots, les regards, sans juger. J'ai beaucoup pensé à Raymond Depardon en travaillant sur ce film, notamment à certaines séquences d'*Urgences*, où il suivait le quotidien des urgences psychiatriques de l'Hôtel-Dieu à Paris.[6]

> (I have a passion for documentaries, their way of receiving and gathering words and viewpoints, without judging. I often thought of Raymond Depardon while working on this film, especially certain sequences in *Urgences* where he followed the psychiatric emergency room at the Hôtel-Dieu hospital in Paris.)

Ultimately I would argue that all films are 'documents' in some sense, as Daney and Ramonet (Ferro 1993: 63) suggest with their notion of the accumulated body of film as a gigantic, dispersed archive. A similar notion underpins Godard's *Histoire(s) du cinéma*, which conceives of the history of cinema *as* history. Most cultural products capture or embody something of their time, and moving image texts are no exception. However, their capacity to preserve representations of sounds and images in time and motion marks them out as a very particular kind of relic. They allow us the illusion of experiencing the past 'as now'. It is an illusion that brings with it challenges for any filmmaker or spectator turning to film as an evocation of a past moment, for, as Nichols remarks: 'to present a realistic likeness of something is to efface the agency of representation so that the likeness comes to the fore' (1993: 175). As the analyses in this book will show, 'likeness' in film, whether of things, beings or places, is an important part of its power to transmit and disseminate cultural memory. However, the strategies for framing and making use of 'likenesses' in the evocation of past(s) make all the difference, for film's inherent (so-called) realism may just as easily be a tool used for concealment, propaganda and cultural amnesia. If all films are 'documents' so too are all documentaries 'movies', inevitably constructed, fashioned and selected, the product of agencies in a social framework. As will be discussed in detail in Chapter 1, these are also precisely the characteristics of memory itself, for forgetting is always the counterpoint to the forming and recalling of memories.

OBJECTS, FACES, CITIES

It has been my aim in this introduction to provide a historical and cultural context for the moving image texts that form case studies for this exploration of memory and the moving image. However, when dealing with the notoriously intangible topic of memory it is important to explore in more depth ways of understanding memory, particularly the relation of individual to cultural memory, a fundamental preoccupation throughout the book. This is why Chapter 1, concerned with theories of memory and theories of the moving image, forms a vital framework for the more detailed analyses of the works themselves in the subsequent chapters. The elaboration of my argument in this book is driven by a dual process of film analysis and theoretical reflection through a range of different films. When undertaking preliminary research it quickly became clear that, although 'memory studies' has taken off as a thriving field in the arts and humanities, there remains a need for studies that take current thinking about memory seriously in a moving image context and that draw from a broad range of disciplines (such as philosophy, sociology, science, history) in an attempt to make them speak to each other in a productive way. So this book is guided not by a single philosophy (or brand of philosophy) but rather by the belief that the moving image and current Western ideas about memory both arise from the same tradition of Western thought and science and must be understood in that framework.

The second chapter examines the role of filmic, or 'screened', objects in memory. Objects have a memory too; they carry our memories. Shown on screen, juxtaposed with other images, words and sounds, they become charged with real and imagined possible pasts, as they draw on the cultural and personal memory of the viewer. Exploring the virtual museums of Varda, Marker and Godard, I will look specifically at how objects, both on and off screen, relate to cultural memory. Objects can act as the Proustian Madeleine (a trope that is key to the oeuvre of Chris Marker), triggering highly personal memories. There is a constant relay from the personal to the collective and each object is imbued with the potential to trigger the processes of memory. I will argue that Godard, Marker and Varda make use of a museal accumulation of objects in order to evoke the past as a pure virtuality. The filmmaker's subjectivity is made present on screen through the accumulation of objects of personal (as well as shared) significance and through the mingling of their own image with the other memory objects on screen. As subject becomes object, film is seen as a point of intersection for subjectivity and objectivity, public and private, allowing the filmmaker's memories to meet those of the viewers in the sphere of cultural memory.

Chapter 3 explores the mnemonic power of the filmed testimony or interview. It focuses on films that employ interviews and people speaking to the camera about the past as a mnemonic device. In developing an understanding of the face as a figure of memory on screen, my argument here moves away from the common-sense view of the face of the witness as guarantor of testimony and instead conceives it as a conduit of memory, an intersubjective interface, framed and shaped by the operations of film. In two of these films two women face each other through the camera and filmmaking process, evoking the past via this connection: Samuel with her grandmother, Simon with her friend Mimi. Benguigui, for her part, confronts the inscrutable past of her parents' generation in her filming of their testimonies in *Mémoires d'immigrés*. Occluded memories of North African immigration to France are given voice through a film that is a personal quest as well as a public intervention. These intimate memory interfaces insistently remind us of the triadic formulation of cultural memory in film. Memory takes shape between filmmaker, film and viewer, as we face the past through the faces of others. For Godard and Marker, women's faces are a privileged cinematic object, bound up with personal (im)memories of cinema. Here I will suggest that the face as screen object has emotive rather than veridical significance for memory, functioning as a memory object that elicits a subjective participation in the evocation of the past.

The final chapter discusses urban architecture and space and its relation to memory and film's mnemonic role. Just as objects can act as conduits of memory, so places may house or contain memories, as the city of Nice does for Mimi Chiola in *Mimi*. I will argue that by revealing multiple temporal layers, the moving image can map for spectators an embodied, moving experience of place. This can be intensely painful when disjunctions emerge between the shifts in our memories and the flux of space, as will be discussed with reference to *Pola à 27 ans* and *Se souvenir des belles choses*. Conflict between memory and place can also be the symptom of an uncanny return of the past. In *Caché*, for example, the segregation of space in the city is perturbed through the transgressions of moving images, reminding both protagonists and viewers that something has been hidden in the city. This chapter will continue to explore the moving image as a locus of intersubjective remembering, as individual memories intersect with the broader, collective sphere of the city. Although situated within a broader geography, the city, as a mobile and inhabited landscape, a place of transit and a site of intersubjective communication, is conceived as a privileged space of memory. As protagonists move through the city on film, their trajectories taking them through explorations of the past as well as of urban space, we are reminded that memory, like the city, is a continual process of construction and demolition.

Over the course of the book I intend to develop three key theoretical tenets. First, although our experience of it may be intensely private, I will argue that memory is fundamentally an intersubjective process, mediated through cultural objects, such as film. Secondly, since memory can no longer be seen as something that resides purely in the individual, instead of conceiving memory in terms of storage and recall, we should be thinking of it in terms of a radical virtuality, potentially actualised in the form of memories but also in the course of perception. Finally, as detailed analyses of the works under discussion will show, film (as well as the hybrid varieties of moving image media that make use of filmic form) is a privileged and powerful means of conceptualising the processes of memory, because of its potential to represent space and time, to juxtapose sonic and visual images and to mirror the associational movements of memory itself.

NOTES

1. Translations of quotations from the French are my own throughout, except where a published translation is cited. I have tried to refer to published translations of fundamental theoretical texts where possible to enable those who do not read French to refer to those key works. Very occasionally I have modified published translations where I believe that the published version does not fully reflect the force or emphasis of the original sentence. I have indicated where this is the case.
2. A note on terminology: throughout the book I will follow common parlance in using the term 'film' even when referring to digitally produced/formatted works, though I turn to the broader designation of 'moving image texts' when needing specifically to encompass CD-ROM or installations within my frame of reference. The use of the appellation 'moving image' in the title of the book reflects this need for a more open terminology, though I recognise its insufficiency to convey the importance of sound. I have on the whole avoided the term 'movie' because of its association within the UK and Europe with mass-market Hollywood products.
3. 'Cinema: Dead or Alive?' was a symposium convened by Professor Laura Mulvey (Birkbeck College, London) and Professor David Rodowick (King's College, London), 14 February 2003.
4. Signalled in a special edition of *Label France*, the magazine of the Ministère des Affaires Etrangères, March 1995, vol. 19.
5. See Chapter 1 for a more detailed elaboration of these ideas.
6. Zabou Breitman, interview with the author, 18 March 2009.

1. MEMORY AND THE MOVING IMAGE

What are the connections between memory and motion pictures? In order to set in motion an investigation into this question, I will need to begin at the beginning, with an inquiry into the nature of memory. How can it be defined? And what are the implications of those definitions for thinking about cinema? The first section of this chapter draws on a range of modes of thinking about memory, from the philosophical to the psycho-sociological to the scientific. However, in pursuing this subject such disciplinary demarcations become unclear. Memory, that elusive topic, seems to pervade and trouble the boundaries not only between academic disciplines, but also between the individual and the collective, self and other, mind and body, inside and outside. In response to these tendencies it seems appropriate to weave together theories from different disciplines, drawing out the points that will form a productive framework for thinking about memory in contemporary French cinema. It is not my intention for this framework to impose a rigid lens through which to read films, however. Rather, my aim in this chapter is to raise the ideas, questions and problems that will remain at stake throughout the book. I therefore intend to leave them open to further exploration as both theorisation of film as medium and analyses of individual films are drawn in to the argument in subsequent chapters.

THEORIES OF MEMORY

One way of beginning a definition of memory would be in terms of its myriad functions. It is necessary for learning, for reading, writing and speaking, for constructing and maintaining a sense of identity, for interacting in a social group and forging a collective sense of identity. Indeed, it seems impossible to see it as anything less than a crucial part of being human, and even perhaps (as certain scientists might argue) of being a living creature. But 'memory' is a slippery term, recognised since ancient times as naming something absolutely vital, yet applied to many seemingly different activities and experiences. To name but a few, learning, training and habit-formation, recognition, nostalgic reverie and even storytelling and monument-building within families, subcultures and societies have all been placed in the category of memory. What is the connection between these seemingly disparate functions and activities? One might begin to question whether it is useful to call them by the same name.

They do, however, have one key characteristic in common, for each involves a temporal relationship between past and present. In his extensive study of memory, history and forgetting, philosopher Paul Ricœur emphasises the connection of memory with the past as a crucial starting point for any investigation of memory, designating Aristotle's proposition that 'la mémoire est du passé' (memory is of the past) as 'la phrase clé qui accompagne toute ma recherche' (the key phrase that accompanies my entire investigation) (Ricœur 2000: 19, Ricœur 2004: 15). For Ricœur, whatever form memory may take, 'c'est le contraste avec le futur de la conjecture et de l'attente et avec le présent de la sensation (ou perception) qui impose cette caractérisation majeure' (it is the contrast with the future of conjecture and expectation and with the present of sensation (or perception) that imposes this major characterisation) (Ricœur 2000: 19, Ricœur 2004: 15). I follow Ricœur in a conviction that memory is fundamentally 'about the past', though the details of that relationship remain in need of exploration. This means, however, that a conception of time becomes vitally significant for how one conceives of memory, taking us from one notoriously slippery theoretical inquiry to another. Reinhart Koselleck has pointed out that the modern tripartite and linear notion of time (past–present–future in which the future is asynchronous with the past) implicit in Ricœur's delineation is itself only one, relatively recent way of understanding time (Kosselleck 1985). Drawing on Koselleck's insights leads Andreas Huyssen to assert that our current understanding of time is particularly 'modern':

> The way our culture thinks about time is far from natural even though we may experience it as such. In comparison with earlier Christian ages that cherished tradition and thought of the future primarily and rather statically, even spatially, as the time of the Last Judgement, modern societies have put ever more weight on thinking the secular future as dynamic and superior to the past. [. . .] the move from the past to the future has been linked to notions of progress and perfectibility. (Huyssen 1995: 8)

This serves as a reminder that any conception of time and memory is itself culturally and historically influenced, whether by the philosophical givens of the time, a particular cultural world-view or even scientific discoveries. As Huyssen puts it: 'Human memory may well be an anthropological given, but closely tied as it is to the ways a culture constructs and lives its temporality, the forms memory will take are invariably contingent and subject to change' (p. 2). This is why, as I indicated in the introduction, my discussion of contemporary French film will be underpinned by the notion that the forms of memory at issue in this particular domain and period are culturally and historically contingent, that they have grown out of a particular combination of traditions, thought and circumstances. Conceiving of memory as 'du passé' will therefore entail an interrogation of temporal structures that will both arise out of and feed back into my analyses of films. In the second part of this chapter, my examination of the implications of digital technologies will lead me to question linear conceptions of time through Gilles Deleuze's concept of the time-image, which draws on cinematic images to posit the coexistence of non-chronological layers in perception, suggesting time in terms of a perpetual becoming rather than a linear sequence.

Whatever the temporal and historical nuances that inform a conception of memory, what does seem clear is that for the human subject, whether individually or in a group, the material and intellectual world can only take shape in terms of an accumulation of experience. At the turn of the twentieth century, films such as *Memento* (Christopher Nolan, 2000) and *Novo* (Jean-Pierre Limosin, 2002) showed the extent to which not only the more complex intricacies of human identity, but also practical, day-to-day needs, require elements of past experience to be conserved. Both films depict men who have suffered injuries to the brain and whose memories fade after about 20 minutes, meaning that they constantly have to re-establish their identity and that of the people, places and situations around them. They have no sense of the past and thus live in the perpetual threat of confusion and blankness. In both films the characters attempt to overcome this problem by frantically noting everything down, even, in the case of *Memento*'s protagonist, going as far as to tattoo information onto his skin. In this way these films dramatise the fear of forgetting (or being forgotten) that leads most individuals and cultures to supplement their memories with material traces, be they cave paintings, monuments, holiday photos, manuscripts or films, a process I will be examining in detail further on. On the other hand, Jorge Luis Borges' tale 'Funes, his memory' reveals the function of forgetting to be equally indispensable, by imagining a man unable to discard even a moment of his past perceptions from his conscious memory (Borges 1998). We need our memories to be selective, picking out the salient parts of experience and evoking them at relevant moments in order to make life intelligible.

It seems then that memory is vital for any kind of consciousness, for how can one be aware of the present moment, which is itself always already becoming 'past', without any sense of continuity created by a feeling of accumulated experience? The protagonists of *Novo* and *Memento* at least have a short-term memory that allows them to be conscious of the flow of their perception for small sections of time. On the other hand, opinions are divided over whether consciousness is a condition of memory. Clearly some of the operations of memory mentioned so far can occur without consciousness. Learning, training and habit-formation are all possible in animals with only the simplest of neural networks, from sea-slugs to fruit flies, and even human beings do not have to be aware that they are remembering how to write as they form groups of letters on a page. Yet, in the case of learning and training at least, these activities require a mental preservation of past experience which is subsequently reproduced in a present movement. Neurobiologists such as Stephen Rose, who sees memory as the potential 'Rosetta Stone' for translating between the languages of mind and brain, would most probably call this memory (Rose 1993). For the philosopher André Lalande, however, memory was primarily defined as the 'fonction psychique consistant dans la reproduction d'un état de conscience passé avec ce caractère qu'il est reconnu pour tel par le sujet' (the psychical function consisting in the reproduction of a past state of consciousness, with the distinguishing feature of being recognised as such by the subject) (Lalande 1932: 451). In other words memory is not memory unless the subject is conscious of re-experiencing a state of consciousness from the past and distinguishes it from present experience. Seen in these terms the relationship formed by memory between past and present would be one that both bridges and divides. But this definition glosses over just what such a 'reproduction d'un état de conscience passé' might be. When we recognise a friend, we would usually describe that as 'remembering', but are we really reproducing a prior state of consciousness (and simultaneously experiencing the present moment) when we see a familiar face? It seems that for Lalande memory is manifested in those Proustian moments when we are flung back, by the feel of stepping on a certain uneven paving stone perhaps, to a sensation or impression from our past, or when, in a reverie on past experience, images come into one's mind's eye. Even in these situations, we might question whether past and present really are so perfectly distinct for the subject (is there not, as Proust's own reflections on the subject suggest, a moment of confusion, of dizziness?). We might also probe the notion of 'reproduction' in these conscious operations of memory. How can we ever be sure that the 'state of past consciousness' has not been transformed, distorted or even imagined? Even brushing such questions aside (for we will return to them later), surely this purified, isolated and highly subjective experience of memory is only the tip of the iceberg?

In response to its elusive character, there have been many attempts to create a taxonomy of memory, dividing it up into different areas and functions. Procedural memory (doing things) has been distinguished from declarative memory (recall and recognition of names, images etc.), which has in turn been divided into episodic (one's own life history) and semantic (other facts and information). Of course in Lalande's terms, procedural 'memory' does not count as memory at all. The categories of episodic and semantic, on the other hand, seem rather artificial and difficult to differentiate, since memories of one's own life are, as I shall argue over the course of this chapter, reinforced by, narrativised by and intertwined with stories friends and family have told, photographs, films and books with which one has come into contact. Two other attempts to divide up the vast and hazy domain of 'memory' seem pertinent here: those of Ricœur, to whose work I alluded above, and Henri Bergson, whose work was so influential for French conceptions of memory, as

I indicated in the introduction. Though Ricœur works painstakingly through a detailed phenomenological taxonomy of memory, drawing on an immensely wide range of discourse on the subject, the principal distinction underpinning his investigation is the distinction between memory as *affection* (affection) and memory as *rappel* (recollection) (Ricœur 2000: 18). This is derived from Aristotle's division between *mnēmē* and *anamnesis*, the former a kind of feeling (pathos), the latter an effort to recollect, a *recherche* (search). The categories also recall Proust's concepts of involuntary (*affection*) and voluntary (*rappel*) memory. Bergson's 'two forms' of memory are along the lines of the proce-dural/declarative system, dividing 'spontaneous', representational memory from habitual, motor-oriented memory: 'l'une *imagine* et [. . .] l'autre *répète*' (Bergson 1939: 87) ('the one *imagines* and the other *repeats*' [Bergson 1988: 82]). For Bergson, spontaneous recollection actualises memory-images from the representational layer of pure memory formed constantly as we perceive, a notion that will inform Deleuze's philosophy of the time-image and will be significant for the arguments about memory and film developed in this book.

Bergson's use of the verb *imaginer* points to a problem that lies at the heart of much discussion of memory. This is the problem hinted at when I wondered, above, to what extent memory could be seen as a reproduction of the past. How can memory be relied upon if it is a function of the imagination and therefore located in the realm of fantasy and fiction? Ricœur finds in Bergson's analysis a useful approach to the problem of differentiating imagination from memory. Habitual memory, in repeating movements and responses made in the past, can be said to reproduce. Spontaneous memory, on the other hand, visualises and recreates. However, Bergson is careful to distinguish between memory and imagination. The key, once again, lies in the notion of 'past':

> *Imaginer* n'est pas *se souvenir*. Sans doute un souvenir, à mesure qu'il s'actualise, tend à vivre dans une image; mais la réciproque n'est pas vraie, et l'image pure et simple ne me reportera au passé que si c'est en effet dans le passé que je suis allé la chercher, suivant ainsi le progrès continu qui l'a amenée de l'obscurité à la lumière. (Bergson 1939: 150)

> (To *picture* is not to *remember*. No doubt a recollection, as it becomes actual, tends to live in an image; however, the converse is not true, and the image, pure and simple, will not refer me to the past unless, indeed, it was in the past that I sought it, thus following the continuous progress which brought it from darkness to light. [Bergson 1988: 135–6, transla-tion modified])

Ricœur sees Bergson as negotiating a path that both links and separates memory and imagination, thus providing a new angle on a problem haunting discussions of memory since the ancient Greek philosophers. The role of imagi-nation in Bergson's theory of memory is to visualise rather than invent.

À l'inverse de la fonction irréalisante qui culmine dans la fiction exilée dans le hors texte de la réalité tout entière, c'est sa fonction visualisante, sa manière de donner à voir, qui est ici exaltée. (Ricœur 2000: 63)

(In contrast to the function of derealization, culminating in a fiction exiled to the margins of reality considered in its totality, what is celebrated here is instead the visualizing function of imagination, its manner of giving something to be seen. [Ricœur 2004: 52])

For Bergson, nothing is *lost*, that is to say nothing is really forgotten, for the *souvenir pur* (pure memory) 'enregistrerait, sous forme d'images-souvenirs, tous les événements de notre vie quotidienne à mesure qu'ils se déroulent' (Bergson 1939: 86) ('records, in the form of memory-images, all the events of our daily life as they occur in time' [Bergson 1988: 81]). Thus anything that really is memory will actualise these images from the flux of *souvenir pur*. On the other hand, however, only the repetitive, habitual kind of memory can be recalled with near-certainty and, 'conquise par l'effort, reste sous la dépendance de notre volonté' (1939: 94) ('conquered by effort, remains dependent upon our will' [1988: 88]). Representational memory, by contrast, 'toute spontanée, met autant de caprice à reproduire que de fidélité à conserver' (1939: 94) ('entirely spontaneous, is as capricious in reproducing as it is faithful in preserving' [1988: 88]).

Much of Bergson's *Matière et mémoire*, first published in 1896, argues against the possibility of mental representation arising in the brain itself, and aims to elaborate a dualist conception that, in opposition to traditional dualism, sees mind and body working together to translate perception into movement. However, I do not think it inappropriate to bring certain recent developments in neuroscience into juxtaposition with Bergson's arguments at this stage. For one thing appears to be certain: when memories are formed and recalled, biochemical changes take place in the brain, leaving physical traces. This does not necessarily contradict Bergson's theory, for it has not been proven that these cerebral traces engender mental representation. Indeed, it is generally recognised that the connection between memory traces and representation remains mysterious. These traces, however, according to a paper by Karim Nader, have shown something highly significant for the way we think about memory and its relation to the truth of the past: memory traces become highly labile each time they are recalled (Nader 2003). In other words, the act of remembering is liable to alter the memory itself. The standard picture of memory in scientific circles had, until these relatively recent discoveries, been a far more static one. In the short term, memory patterns are stored in specialist memory organs such as the hippocampus, but over days, weeks and years they move to more general areas of the brain, fixed by protein changes and eventually lodged in the cortex (McCrone 2003). 'The dogma was that once a memory trace has been consolidated, it is permanent,' said Nader after experiments with rats, 'but here it was labile – subject to interference in exactly the same way as a brand-new experience' (cited in McCrone 2003: 28). At last the metaphor of memory as a storage and retrieval warehouse that had long dogged neuroscience had been exploded. At a cerebral level, memory is revealed to be fundamentally dynamic and plastic, continually reconstituted. This makes sense when translated empirically to the memory of mind.[1] After all, we have all had the experience of discovering that certain memories have become altered or confused. But now science suggests that such experiences are just the most extreme and/or noticeable instances of alteration. Though a memory may be 'of the past', it is constantly being reformulated through present experience. This is not to say that memory is purely fictional, for this process may lead to reinforcement of the memory, or to a subtle reinterpretation or recontextualisation of a past situation in the light of present events, not only to deformation in the negative sense. When we remember that a key function of memory is to make sense of the world, as I discussed with relation to the Borges tale above, the necessity of its being dynamic and adaptable becomes apparent.

The idea of memory as dynamic reconstitution, rather than preservation and reproduction, is central to much recent thinking about the subject in the area of cultural studies. Huyssen affirms that 'the past is not simply there in memory, but it must be articulated to become memory' (1995: 3). Though he recognises that 'all memory in some ineradicable sense is dependent on some past event or experience', Huyssen sees memory as constituted by a 'tenuous fissure between past and present', which for him makes it 'powerfully alive and distinct from the archive' (ibid.). The idea of memory as 'alive', requiring articulation in the present and subject to external influences upon recall, supports the idea, which I have already suggested above and which will be discussed further with regard to cinematic technologies in particular, that the visual images and narratives in our environment, in eliciting memories, leave them open to interference and mutation. This also suggests the crucial role that other people may have in the individual's experience of memory, leading to the question of collective or cultural memory.

Until now, I have been describing what might be considered a somewhat solipsistic notion of memory, taking place entirely in terms of the individual human subject. In opposition to this, Maurice Halbwachs argued as long ago as 1925 that collectivity is a condition of memory. Memory, for Halbwachs, is a dynamic and interactive process of reconstitution, rather than a system of preservation and reproduction: 'le passé, en réalité, ne reparaît pas tel quel, [. . .] tout semble indiquer qu'il ne se conserve pas, mais qu'on le reconstruit en partant du présent' (the past, in reality, does not reappear just as it was, [. . .] all indications suggest that it is not conserved but is a reconstruction based on the present), a proposition that fits broadly with the arguments outlined above (Halbwachs 1925: x–xi). But Halbwachs takes the argument a stage further, arguing that 'il n'y a pas de mémoire possible en dehors des cadres dont les hommes vivant en société se servent pour fixer et retrouver leurs souvenirs' (memory is not possible outside the frameworks used by men living in society to fix and recall their memories) (p. 107). Individual memory is seen to be *constituted* by a framework of intersubjectivity. In this case, the 'stories friends and family have told, photographs, films and books one has come into contact with' mentioned above as reinforcing, narrativising and intertwining with personal memories would not be seen as simply interiorised, forming a part of the individual's declarative memory, but as constitutive (along with all the other social structures) of memory itself. As we begin to bring together the different approaches discussed so far, we move towards an understanding of memory as situated neither purely inside nor outside the individual human subject, but in between, in a liminal space between self and other, subject and object. The relationship between past and present also becomes more complicated in this dynamic, interactive view of memory, with the former constantly being re-formed and reformulated in the active and intersubjective process of remembering.

But can this liminal, intersubjective view of memory account for the notion of a collective memory? In what sense can communities, generations or societies be said to remember? Following Halbwachs we can speak of a subjective recollective stance, constituted by the social framework, but can we speak of collective memory as something more objective and observable? And what is the role of the material objects, such as films, which record and preserve the past in the structuring of collective memories? In her discussion of the artist Ken Aptekar's work, Mieke Bal argues that in cultural memory, private memories and history are inextricably linked:

> What is at stake here is cultural memory as an alternative to traditional history on the one hand, and as an alternative to private subjectivism and uncontrollable self-indulgence on the other. Memory is a function of subjectivity. Cultural memory is collective, yet, by definition, subjective. [. . .] it counters the conflation of subjectivity and individualism. (Bal 1999: 180)

For Bal, Aptekar draws on shared experiences in his work, thus bringing into play the social frameworks of memory, whilst recognising that each individual's experience is nevertheless unique. Through shared spaces, experiences and cultural reference points, communities and societies can be said to share memories. This is the basis of the idea of a collective memory. Bal's point that Aptekar's work draws on such memories reminds us of the crucial role of cultural objects (e.g. films, museum displays, books) for collective memory, for not only, as I have indicated above, can they interact with individuals' memories (and to the extent that cultural objects are public, they have the possibility of a broad sphere of influence), but they can also be seen as a kind of repository for the memories of collective groups, in terms of records and supplements. The idea that cultural memory depends on imaginative investment, and by extension that memory is indeed transmissible via mediation, recalls

Marianne Hirsch's conception of 'postmemory', a term she uses to describe second-generation remembering of the preceding generation's traumatic collective experience of the Holocaust:

> Postmemory is a powerful and very particular form of memory because its connection to its object or source is mediated not through recollection but through an imaginative investment and creation. This is not to say that memory itself is un-mediated, but that it is more directly connected to the past. (Hirsch 1997: 22)

The role of cultural objects in the memory of groups and individuals is something I will discuss at length in Chapter 2, and I will return to the concept of postmemory at that point. In particular this notion of 'imaginative investment' will be central to thinking about these interactions. I will examine in particular the ways in which films, which are cultural objects in themselves, make use of other objects, such as photographs, paintings, books and postcards, to evoke the past and to probe the workings of its remembrance. However, it is first necessary to investigate further the relationship between human memory and material traces.

COLLECTIVE MEMORY AND THE SUPPLEMENT

The French historian Pierre Nora perceives a clear distinction between traditional, oral, collective memory and the 'historicised' memory of supplementary forms of preservation, such as writing, video- or audiotape, archives and photographs:

> Dès qu'il y a trace, distance, méditation, on n'est plus dans la mémoire vraie, mais dans l'histoire. [. . .] La mémoire est la vie, toujours portée par des groupes vivants et à ce titre, elle est en évolution permanente, ouverte à la dialectique du souvenir et de l'amnésie, inconsciente de ses déformations successives, vulnérable à toutes les utilisations et manipulations, susceptible de longues latences et de soudaines revitalisations. (Nora 1984: xix)

> (As soon as there is a trace, distance, or mediation, we are no longer in true memory but in history. [. . .] Memory is life, always carried by living groups, and as such it is permanently evolving, open to the dialectics of memory and amnesia, unconscious of its successive deformations, vulnerable to all kinds of use and manipulation, susceptible to long periods of latency and sudden revitalisation.)

Like Halbwachs, Nora sees memory, or at least *la mémoire vraie*, true memory, as dynamic, collective and in constant reconstitution. Indeed, he implies that memory, as a living process, is fundamentally fictional, a characteristic inherent in its very flexibility and dynamism. For him, the external supplements of memory used by individuals and society serve to fix and stabilise the past, making the relationship of present to past one of perfectly preserved loss, rather than of constant renewal: 'Notre perception du passé, c'est l'appropriation véhémente de ce que nous savons n'être plus à nous' (our perception of the past is the vehement appropriation of that which we know no longer belongs to us) (p. xxxii).

Nora is not the first to view such 'prosthetic' memory as potentially detrimental. It has been viewed with suspicion since ancient times and seen as ultimately fatal to Memory herself. In Plato's characterisation, the sophists saw writing as both seductive and nefarious for this very reason. In the *Phaedrus* Plato cites, in the voice of Socrates, the ancient Egyptian myth of Theuth, the Greek name for the god Thoth, god of the occult sciences, of astrology, of incantations for calming the seas, of dice and draughts, of numbers and medicine and, of course, of writing. Thoth, as Socrates relates it, presented each of these arts to the king of Egypt, Thamus, indicating the benefits and advantages of each one. The god claimed that writing was a cure or drug (*pharmakon* in the original Greek, an ambiguous word meaning both poison and cure) for both memory and wisdom, but the king objected that those who use it will no longer need their memories and so lose them, relying on external marks rather than internal mental powers. Jacques Derrida, in his deconstructive reading of Plato's text, notes that the 'drug' of writing, that ambivalent *pharmakon*, aids *hypomnesis*, which is to say 're-mémoration, recollection, consignation' ('re-memoration, recollection, consignation') and damages the *mnēmē*, 'mémoire vivante et connaissante' ('living, knowing memory') (Derrida 1972a: 113, Derrida 1981: 95). Writing is seen as an artificial supplement to memory, a poison-cure which both defies death by enduring and signifies it by persisting shamelessly in spite of the death of the human subject:

> Sachant qu'il peut confier ou abandonner ses pensées au dehors, à la consigne, aux marques physiques, spatiales et superficielles qu'on met à plat sur une tablette, celui qui disposera de la *teknè* de l'écriture se reposera sur elle. [. . .] Ils le représenteront même s'il les oublie, ils porteront sa parole même s'il n'est plus là pour les animer. Même s'il est mort, et seul un *pharmakon* peut détenir un tel pouvoir, sur la mort sans doute mais aussi en collusion avec elle. Le *pharmakon* et l'écriture, c'est donc bien toujours une question de vie et de mort. (1972a: 129–30)

> (Knowing that he can always leave his thoughts outside or check them with an external agency, with the physical, spatial, superficial marks that one lays flat on a tablet, he who has the *tekhnē* of writing at his disposal will come to rely on it. [. . .] They will represent him even if he forgets them; they will transmit his word even if he is not there to animate them.

Even if he is dead, and only a *pharmakon* can be the wielder of such power, *over* death but also in cahoots with it. So with the *pharmakon* and writing, it is always a question of life and death. [1981: 107])

This conception of the memory supplement as taking the place of the human subject and signifying death rather than life has its resonance in Nora's account: 'Plus tout à fait la vie, pas tout à fait la mort, comme ces coquilles sur le rivage quand se retire la mer de la mémoire vivante' (not quite a part of life any longer but not yet consigned to death, like shells on the shore when the sea tide of living memory retreats) (1984: xxiv). Nora situates himself in the tradition of the sophists by positing writing as the beginning of such petrification, almost as if their warnings were being realised in modern technology: 'le mouvement qui a commencé avec l'écriture s'achève dans la haute fidélité et la bande magnétique' (the shift that began with writing culminates in high fidelity and magnetic tape) (p. xxvi). Of course, since 1984 much has changed and we now have digital recording, for both sound and image, still and moving, something I will discuss later in the chapter. We also have the vast reserves of information diffused across the no man's land of the internet. However, although he situates technologies of preservation in a genealogy beginning with writing, Nora's standpoint can be seen to diverge considerably from the one characterised in Plato's text. For one thing, Nora conceives of living memory, along Halbwachsian lines, as collective and social and so, implicitly and perhaps unwittingly, has already blurred the inside/outside distinction so vital to the condemnation of writing of the sophists, Socrates or Thamus. Secondly, as can be seen in the quotation above, Nora associates living memory with amnesia, vulnerability, deformation and fiction rather than seeing it as an embodiment of knowledge and truth, as the *mnēmē* is presented by Plato.

This difference also points, however, to something Nora's and Plato's texts clearly have in common: a fundamental and irresolvable ambivalence towards the memory supplement. As Derrida shows in his intricate unfurling of the lexical and conceptual patterns of Plato's texts, the *pharmakon* as ambiguous concept, both poison and remedy, inscribes Plato's ambivalence and acts as a kind of textual philtre, undoing the rigid binary oppositions in Plato's text from within. In Nora's case, he is introducing, as a historian bemoaning the historicisation of memory, the project of a vast *written* work on sites of memory: a search for living memory in places which often must be accessed via documents and records, the very objects which he claims supplement and supplant the memory of the living human subject. His project can be seen, in certain ways, to run counter to elements of nostalgia manifested by him for oral, dynamic and fluid memory. Moreover, his project itself is an attempt to capture something which by definition cannot be captured. However, as the *Lieux de mémoire* project developed, Nora became aware of another interesting paradox brought about by a widespread recuperation of the work undertaken by him and his collaborators. In his essay 'L'ère de la commémoration' (the era of commemoration), the closing bracket of the project, published in 1992 (six years after the introductory essay on memory and history cited above), Nora reflects on the impact of the work, commenting on the culture of commemoration that had developed in France. He observes that a project that had intended to revivify history, introducing a critical dynamism to an approach to the study of the cultural heritage of France, had unwittingly contributed to another kind of petrification of the past, in the form of the repetitive re-enactment of commemorative rituals. He notes a proliferation of regional and diverse commemorations, eclipsing the importance of national celebrations and fixing the idea of commemoration as an essential tool for the promotion and constitution of the identities of small or marginalised groups. Almost everything, he argues, has become doubled by a reclaimed past: 'La nation mémorielle [. . .] a investi l'espace tout entière du soupçon de son identité virtuelle, doublé toutes les choses présentes d'une dimension de l'antérieur' (the nation of memory [. . .] has invested every corner of space with the suspicion of its virtual identity, has doubled all present things with an anterior dimension) (Nora 1992: 1011). Instead of a means of revivifying history, Nora sees memory, in its mode of commemoration, as tyrannical, constantly recuperated without adequate critique. Ricœur's conception of the work of memory as opposed to repetition, which derives from the Freudian notions of acting out and working through, provides a productive approach to Nora's critique of the commemorative era.[2] For Ricœur, an obsession with commemoration corresponds to the repetition compulsion of the traumatised patient, not far removed from amnesia, and must be undone by a careful *travail de mémoire* (work of memory), which implies a critical stance ethically necessary for societies to forgive, forget and repair: 'que de violences par le monde qui valent comme *acting out* "au lieu" du souvenir!' (Ricœur 2000: 96) ('how much violence in the world stands as acting out "in place of" remembering!' [Ricœur 2004: 79]). But while Nora and Ricœur account for the potential that memory itself, as repetition, can be seen as stuck, or fixing even as it is recuperating and transforming the past, the question of the supplement, those material inscriptions of memory such as writing or films, continues to be troubling, and there remains a lingering suspicion that they might be the poison rather than the remedy.

Stephen Rose, the neurobiologist briefly mentioned above, sees technology as somehow fixing what is inherently fluid in memory, but makes explicit the bivalent effect of this, which is that it preserves and protects as well as constraining:

> A video or audiotape, a written record, do more than just reinforce memory; they freeze it, and in imposing a fixed, linear sequence upon it, they simultaneously preserve it and prevent it evolving and transforming itself with time, just as much as the rigid exoskeleton of an insect or crustacean at the same time defends and constrains its owner. (Rose 1993: 61)

His metaphor hints at a life somehow contained within the frozen past. Unlike Nora's empty shells, the 'coquilles sur le rivage' cited above, Rose's wash-ups from the sea of living memory have living crabs inside them, albeit unable to evolve into larger creatures. For, as he later points out:

> For all the ingenuity of fishermen, breeders and genetic engineers [. . .] a lobster the size of even a small dog isn't on; it would implode under its own weight [. . .] Such a design also strictly limits the size of ganglia and brains. (Rose 1993: 173)

It should be pointed out that throughout his book, Rose is making a compelling attempt to integrate a justification for studying memory in terms of the networks and pathways of neurons in the brain with a wider, more nuanced conception of what memory is. He refers frequently to collective memory and especially to what he calls 'artificial memory', which is crucial to social memory in the modern world. In terms of artificial memory, the example he uses most often is that of video and film images, which he sees as 'peculiarly powerful as a way of providing social coherence. They have become part of our shared history. But equally we can no longer make and re-make them in our own minds [. . .] because they are for ever fixed by the video' (p. 98). In line with Halbwachs, one might question Rose's assumption of a clear and fixed distinction between 'our own minds', which, like Plato, he sees as determinedly internal, and the social (again, for Rose this is explicitly external). But what I find interesting to draw out of Rose's argument is the emphasis on video and film in the context of a less negative view of memory's supplements in general. Could it be possible that the life in the shell of artificial memory is the movement and depth of the filmic image? This speculation leads me into my next section, where I want to explore the possibility of just such a 'life'. Without wishing to take a Platonic stance on writing, in that, following Derrida, I would deny the primacy and privilege of the *parole* whilst recognising its differences, I want to explore the possibility of film as a different kind of supplement to writing. In so doing I hope to examine from a different angle the relationship between such material objects and memory.

For Bergson, talking about the operations of perception, compared to 'presence', 'representation' would be 'la croûte extérieur, la pellicule superficielle' ('its external crust, its superficial skin'), something formed by and attached to presence, yet nevertheless distinct from it (Bergson 1939: 23, Bergson 1988: 36). Could film, by analogy, be seen as a kind of skin formed on the surface of real experience, a surface, produced via contact with real presences, that marks a liminal point between the real and material representation? It is hard to resist the analogy of film or screen in this phrase, but of course a film is much more than that: it is the combination of projected light, chemicals, film, reel and screen. In the case of digital images there is no longer a *pellicule* and information is stored in the form of numerical code. However, filmic representation could none the less be seen in terms of surfaces: the moving images on a television monitor or cinema screen are in some ways inherently 'superficial': they move over a surface. One might say the same thing for written text; marked in the early days on animal-skin parchment, it is imbued with a history of surfaces which link back to the body and evoke Plato's distinction between external supplement and internal thought. That which is written on the skin is strongly felt to be outside me; in fact it marks the very limits of the self. But whilst words on parchment remain two-dimensional signs, images recorded on film give the illusion of three-dimensionality. Indeed, any sense of the screen surface might be said to be overpowered by the sense of depth conveyed. It is this, and the impression of movement, which make film stand out as a very different kind of record of the past. Like writing, filmic images do, as Rose points out, fix the past. But they fix it in the illusion of motion and in space, conjoining sound with image. Some, following André Bazin's seminal arguments, would argue for the importance of film's indexical nature, drawing its specificity from the connection to the photographic image. The indexical sign differs from the written sign in that is bears a physical imprint of the real. Add movement to these spatial qualities, and what you have, according to Bazin, is time embalmed in movement, or a 'momie du changement' (Bazin 1958: 16) ('change mummified' [Bazin 1967: 15]). Film, like writing, can persist after all those who produced it are dead. Like writing, it is a matter of life and death, but it persists in the form of a haunting. As Derrida points out in an interview with Bernard Stiegler, cinema is a 'fantomachie', a struggle with ghosts (Derrida and Stiegler 1996: 129). Like a ghost, a filmic image is a moment from the past given form and movement. The life in the shell, then, could perhaps more accurately be termed the ghost in the machine.

In discussing film in terms of a supplement to memory, which is to say a material object which supplements the psycho-social operations of memory, a further distinction needs to be proposed: between film as a manifestation of a collective notion of the past and film as a constitutive element of that collective memory. This distinction leads to a two-pronged question: how does cinema shape memory and how does memory shape cinema? We have already seen that there are convincing grounds for arguing that cinema, and indeed any cultural object that elicits memory, can interact and intertwine with shared and individual memories, forming an essential part of the process of individual and collective remembering, an issue I will return to in this chapter and throughout the book. To answer the second part of the question will entail a detailed analysis of the manifestations of memory within the films themselves, a process that will underpin subsequent chapters. Another approach to relating film to memory is to see film as a kind of analogy for the workings of memory, as has been suggested by Jacques Aumont with relation to Jean-Luc Godard's *Histoire(s) du cinéma* (1989–98) (Aumont 1999: 105). Seeing film as an analogy for memory suggests another way in which film may act as a constitutive element of collective memory: filmic images may shape the form of our memories as well as the content. If we are to situate memory as interactive and dynamic, and if we agree that, as I have argued here, experiences of memory are shaped by cultural forms of representation, then the ghostly *pharmakon* of film may not so much be teaching us how to forget as changing the way we remember.

MEDIA, MEMORY AND TIME

Cinematic images, it would thus seem from Bazin's argument, inevitably bear a trace of a past event, acting like an externalised memory-in-movement to signify both the existence of a lived past and its inevitable loss. To what extent, however, does this remain the case when the 'film' bears no photochemical trace of the past, when the camera has simply converted the profilmic image into pulses of electronic code, as is the case in digitally recorded images? I now want to examine further the relationship of cinematic media to memory and also to time: for if filmic images preserve the past in space and in motion as I suggested above, they also unfold in time and duration. I will be exploring the extent to which the ontology of the moving image inflects the status of cinema's relationship to memory and its role as bridge between past event and present spectator. Does the ontological divide between digital and photographic imaging (if indeed it is as significant as theorists would have us believe) mean that cinema's mnemonic role is changing, or even ending? Or can a revisiting of the ontology of the digital image reveal in a new light the relationship of all moving image media to memory and time? Having explored these issues, I then want to refer to Gilles Deleuze's concept of the time-image in order to re-examine questions of time, movement and the image, with the aim of folding these back onto the debates surrounding digital technology. In this way I hope to augment the scope of theories of digitality and to contribute to a re-reading of Deleuze's theories for the digital age, in order to consider the implications for the relation of memory to the moving image.[3]

One of the difficulties in thinking and writing about cinema and digital technology lies in defining terms across an increasingly eclectic and hybrid range of production, distribution and exhibition possibilities. To speak of 'digital film', for example, becomes confusing, sounding almost like a contradiction in terms. 'Film' has traditionally referred to the acetate or celluloid support used to create motion pictures, which have then become known as 'films' (in the UK) with reference to these supports. Digital technology dispenses with the need for film (which I shall refer to as 'photographic film' where the potential for ambiguity arises) in the creation of images. However, to complicate matters, 35mm photographic film has until recent times continued to be used almost exclusively for theatre exhibition even in the case of digitally produced motion pictures. D. N. Rodowick proposes a distinction between *medium* and *support*, where medium would encompass the production techniques (e.g. digital or 35mm or both) and support would refer to the physical means of distribution (e.g. 35mm, VHS/DVD, internet) (2007: 32). This distinction also creates certain broad parameters for locating the viewing experience (for example, 35mm usually in cinema theatres, DVD usually at home etc.). However, it has been argued that the digital cannot really be considered a medium at all, in that whilst it may have dominant characteristics as a technology, it has the capacity to simulate any other medium, making it more of a hybrid technique than a self-contained medium of its own (Le Grice 2001: 310). Though we may be able to identify the support of contemporary motion pictures, the idea of a medium is becoming increasingly difficult to sustain. At the same time, with developments in both medium and support, the very concept of cinema, as a global term that encompasses the industrial processes as well as individual motion picture products, is now difficult to define.

When Chris Marker made *La Jetée* (1962) almost entirely out of photographic stills, thereby drawing into question the idea of the 'motion picture', the concepts of 'film' and 'cinema' were still considered to be relatively stable: it may not have been a conventional 'movie', but it would still have been viewed on 35mm film in a darkened cinema theatre. Indeed the power of the fleeting moment of movement in *La Jetée*, when the longed-for woman of the past opens her eyes, comes in part from the expectations of a traditional movie experience: by denying the viewer the illusion of movement for all but a moment, that moment takes on a strange new magic, as if the motion picture were being invented before the spectator's eyes. By 1998, when Marker released the multimedia CD-ROM project *Immemory*, the widespread, quasi-universal presence of television, the growth of video sales (and the beginnings of DVD's popularity) and the expansion of the internet had transformed the possibilities of the movie-watching experience, reducing theatrical exhibition to a small corner of the industry, a throwback from an earlier age when there were no alternatives to this form of consumption. It has even been suggested that theatrical exhibition only lingers on as a form of advertising for video and merchandising sales, which provide by far the greatest revenue for mainstream production companies: 'theatrical screening of films is a marketing device to enhance video/DVD sales and to promote and sustain franchises in toys, games, and related sources of revenue' (Rodowick 2007: 27, see also Arnoldy 2005: 28). Even arthouse movies, by virtue of their relatively small-scale theatrical distribution, rely on video sales for increased dissemination. Marker's decision to move away from making feature films and towards hybrid multimedia projects reflects the dramatic changes in the parameters of cinema. Conventional film theory has been racing to catch up. Filmmakers like Godard who have chosen to work directly with video, as in the video work *Histoire(s) du cinéma*, have further demonstrated that the 'movies' can no longer be seen in terms of an experience defined by the big screen, the darkened room, the proximity of other viewers and the linear projection from start to finish of 35mm film. Such an experience still exists, but any theory of time and memory in cinema will need to take into account the changes in both medium and support, which have transformed what we call cinema into something far more heterogeneous. It is now a term with unstable borders and perhaps can only be defined in terms of a grouping of social and artistic discourses.

It can of course be argued that what we call cinema was never a stable, unified experience, whether in terms of an industry, a category of products or a viewing experience. Our heightened awareness of contemporary change may make way for new approaches to past objects of study. For example, Giuliana Bruno's meditations on the structuring role of the architectural space of the cinema in the spectator's reception of a film remind us that the traditional cinematic experience was far from stable and monolithic:

> One can never see the same film twice. The reception is changed by the space of the cinema and by the type of physical inhabitation the site yearns for, craves, projects, and fabricates, both inside and outside the theatre. [. . .] different models of spectatorship are figured in the architecture of the theatre itself. (2002: 45)

Studies of the so-called 'new media' often take us back to 'old media' and force us to confront the lack of satisfactory theoretical and ontological accounts of those media. As Rodowick puts it, 'one consistent lesson from the history of film theory is that there has never been a general consensus concerning the answer to the question "What is cinema?"' (2007: 11). None the less, if both the past and future of cinema appear to unravel it before our eyes as an object of study, the attempts of theorists such as Rodowick to define it persist, partly because the analysis of change exhorts us to an understanding of what went before: 'as film disappears into the electronic and virtual realm of numerical manipulation we are suddenly aware that something *was* cinema' (p. 31). As the twentieth century dissolved into the twenty-first, the sense that digital media were bringing radical changes to the moving image fuelled debates that have sought to capture the ontological shift that new technologies might imply: what was cinema, and what will it be in the future? Malcolm Le Grice's distinction between photographic film and the hybrid 'medium' constituted by digital technology points to common themes at the heart of the debate over cinema's relationship to the digital.

> While cinema, based on the optics, wheels and cogs, the physical base of acetate film and chemistry, can be treated as physical substance and manipulated in a way continuous with the 'tactile' traditions of art, the computer has no graspable substance – or what graspable substance it has, the boxes in which the components are housed and the micro-chips themselves, have a completely arbitrary relationship between their visual form and their function. Where we can see, however small, the picture on a film strip, and grasp the relationship between projected image, camera shutter, mechanics, physics and chemistry, the 'image' in the computer

is no more than an invisible sequence of electronic impulses combining together at the speed of light. [. . .] the physicality of the computer function is beyond reach. (2001: 302–3)

Where photographic film chemically registers light reflected by profilmic objects, digital images convert those light emissions into pure code. Thus, as mentioned above, claims are made for the indexical nature of photographic film: it retains an indexical trace of the real. Like the biochemical memory traces in the brain, it is in a very concrete way *du passé* (of/from the past). Rodowick uses the categories of 'transcription' and 'conversion' (or 'calculation') to account for the two types of technique (2007: 116). Photographic film transcribes analogically: it has direct contact with the image or its referent through a physiochemical contact with the profilmic event. On the other hand the digital converts, by means of an abstraction that exists independently of (or pre-exists) the profilmic event. It is in the realm of virtuality in the mathematical sense, which is to say that it belongs to the category of that which is computable, having a numerical basis: *'digital acquisition quantifies the world as a manipulable series of numbers'* (ibid.). The indexical photographic image, then, requires a space or event to have existed, whereas the digital image's only referent is numbers and codes. This distinction refers back to Bazin's ontology of the cine-photographic image mentioned above, in which the latter is described as embalming a trace of the past in motion (Bazin 1958: 16, Bazin 1967: 15). I want to reconsider these issues through a reading of Walter Benjamin's seminal essay 'The Work of Art in the Age of Mechanical Reproduction'. Focusing on the indexical quality of the photographic image evokes a nostalgia for an age when the presence of the master was inscribed in the masterpiece, giving the work of art a unique aura. Of course Benjamin's argument is rather that the shift from human artist to mechanical camera marks a departure from the art of auras: 'that which withers in the age of mechanical reproduction is the aura of the work of art' (Benjamin 1999a: 215). Indeed the emphasis has shifted. The aura in the Benjaminian sense arises from the notion of the authority of an original artwork created, and therefore physically 'touched', by a master, of which all copies will be imperfect forgeries. The cinematic aura as I am defining it here, on the other hand, evoked by an emphasis on the indexical quality of photographic film, arises from the notion of the authority of an authentic image of a profilmic event, an event that has 'touched' or even moulded the acetate of the film. This is why Le Grice describes photographic film as being 'continuous with the "tactile" traditions of art' (see above). Though the touch of the master artist has been replaced by the touch of the past event, a metaphysics of presence manifested by a tactile trace (rather like the laying on of hands in the rituals of Christian clergy, where each clergyman is part of a chain leading back to Christ himself) links the Benjaminian conception of the aura to a nostalgia for the indexical referentiality of the photographic image. It is not irrelevant, however, that the past event should have taken the place of the revered author whose touch gives the image its aura. The physical trace of a real past might be understood as film theory's replacement cult value, embodying a desire for referentiality, preservation and an anchoring in space and time. Digital technologies would thus represent a Benjaminian ideal of perfect and limitless (and therefore antifascist) reproducibility,[4] but for the nostalgic filmmaker, theorist or spectator the idea of the digital as pure abstract virtuality represents a stark loss of contact with the referent, as if the anchor in time were being hauled up and the ship of memory set adrift in a sea of code.

While I would agree that an ontological distinction can be made between the digital and the photographic image, I would argue that one should be wary of fetishising the indexical character of the photographic image. To situate the digital on the side of artifice and the photographic on the side of truth would be to fall into a trap. Not only is it possible (and common) to manipulate the photographic image, it is also highly constructed into juxtapositions, contexts and narratives through the use of editing. With the cut, pure referentiality is already to some extent cut loose. Stuart Minnis reminds us that 'it is no secret that the physical alteration of photographic images is as old as the medium itself' (1998: 54). Furthermore the context of the process of production of the images should be taken into account and, as I have hinted above, in contemporary movie production it is often not a case of using one or the other. Lauren Rabinovitz points out the mixture of production techniques involved not only in the images seen on screen but also in the shooting process itself:

> The world's dominant film industries fully and freely utilize computer technologies in the production of films, in everything from the more obvious special effects spectacles displayed onscreen – spectacles that are only possible as digital images – to the integral role of video cameras and video playback in the profilmic event. (1998: 4)

In other words the medium itself (as opposed to support) is already in some sense hybrid, even when 35mm film is being used.

A further, important element of the debate is that digital images need translation into analogue form in order to be comprehensible to the viewer. Rodowick points out that we are not able, as Cipher is in the Wachowski brothers' *The Matrix* (1999), to read lines of code as visual images: 'humans have not yet developed the cognitive capacity to translate binary code into a perception. This is because digital encoding is not analogical: it does not produce an isomorphic impression of its subject' (2007: 112). This is why, according to Rodowick, digital technology's ultimate goal has always been to provide photorealistic images (pp. 11, 110). However, interesting use has been made of digital images that precisely do not resemble 35mm photographic film images, the desired effect being images that look altered, distorted or enhanced. Thus many Dogme projects, such as *Festen* (Thomas Vinterberg, 1998), were shot with low-tech equipment, giving a grainy texture to the image.[5] The sense is that though less photorealistic, these images provide a different kind of realism by drawing attention to the presence of the recording equipment itself, thereby signposting the real process of filming that created the images. It is also noteworthy that, by suggesting a lack of high-cost, high-technology production technique, such Dogme works imply a lack of manipulation in the recording process, despite the fact that manipulation is precisely what digital technology makes so easy. An important element of the debate on ontology is whether the use of digital has changed the cinematic (and particularly documentary) relationship to authenticity. Rodowick suggests that it has made us sceptical towards images, but it could be argued that it is precisely a sense of scepticism towards the glossy, smoothly edited and contrived quality of the images in traditional Hollywood movies that led the Dogme movement to turn towards hand-held digital cameras in quest of a more 'authentic' image. The problem of authenticity is pertinent to a discussion of memory in cinema, for, as we have seen, part of this study relates to the idea of film as potential cultural memory supplement, a place where shared memories can be preserved and transmitted. However, since, like memory itself, film will always be a representation, distinct from though connected to the past event itself, it can never return to its origins in the past. As well as preserving and protecting shared memories, film always has the potential to manipulate and alter them. Indeed, if we are to speak of authenticity at all, I propose that it can only be in terms of the inevitable interaction between spectator and images. Since we cannot return to the past, and film cannot provide some kind of pure representation of past events (there will always be the camera's point of view if nothing else), authenticity can only be arrived at through a recognition of this, and an unceasing awareness of memory's fundamental instability.

Catherine Lupton puts forward the idea that when images declare themselves as images rather than as a compact preservation of an already inaccessible reality, they better reflect the distorting and transformative nature of memory itself, forcing the viewer to reflect upon memory rather than be lulled into the illusion that he or she is really experiencing a kind of mechanised, perfect form of memory. Lupton's argument relates to Marker's film *Level Five* (1997), which incorporates a computer game, a video diary and archival footage, as well as to his 1983 film *Sans soleil*, where photographic images are interspersed with altered, computerised versions. Lupton is working in opposition to Huyssen's argument in *Twilight Memories* (1995) that new technologies have led to a temporal acceleration, for which memory represents a kind of antidote:

> *Twilight Memories* seeks to account for our contemporary cultural obsession with memory, by suggesting that memorial activities are operating as what Huyssen calls a 'reaction formation', against a crisis of temporality brought about by the ever-accelerating pace of technological change, and by what he believes is the insidious tendency of new media

to make all the information they process functionally equivalent. (Lupton 2003: 4)

Indeed, Huyssen sees the contemporary obsession with memory as a desire for temporal anchoring in the face of technologies that accelerate time and obliterate duration, suggesting a sense of threat from technologies such as digital imaging. For Lupton, though Marker's work offers 'a dizzying and intricate display of digital image processing', it none the less 'maintains a powerful sense of the temporal relation of past to present, but suggests that in the contemporary world it is impossible to represent that relationship without recourse to the medium of the digital and the virtual' (ibid.). The digitised images in *Sans soleil*, realised by video-artist Hayao Yamaneko, have a defamiliarising effect, transforming mimetic images into barely recognisable moving shapes. The presence of these abstracted images serves to remind the viewer of the distorting power of the photographic images and narrated letters that stand in for protagonist Sandor Krasna's memory. The letters are narrated by their recipient (the voice of Florence Delay in the French version), and the images are edited in a montage whose geographical leaps are connected through Krasna's musings, recollections and conceptual bridges. Breaking down the images in a synthesiser highlights the artificiality of these mimetic images, given their selection and juxtaposition, and by implication the artificiality of any fixed memory map. With respect to this last notion, Lupton comments that *Sans soleil*, unlike the CD-ROM *Immemory*, is still limited by the chronological viewing process. However, I would argue that Yamaneko's computerised images already add volume to the viewing process, sending our thoughts beyond the (already fragmented) narrative line and layering Krasna's mnemonic offerings with a visual meta-commentary on the manipulability of all images, including those in human memory. The release of *Sans soleil* on DVD (in 2003) stands as a reminder of the potential reproducibility of the viewing experience, allowing the viewer to take different paths through the film's rapid flow of images on different occasions, as well as through use of rewind, fast forward, division into chapters, zoom and a high quality freeze-frame image.

Not only can combinations of moving image media represent by analogy the vicissitudes of human memory, but these same media can also embody those vicissitudes by coming to replace or alter human memories of events, a process I have examined above with relation to the science and theory of memory. Chris Marker highlights this in *Sans soleil* with Krasna's remark that filmic images have replaced his memories of Tokyo: 'I remember that month of January in Tokyo, or rather I remember the images I filmed in that month of January in Tokyo. They have substituted themselves for my memory; they are my memory.' In *The Remembered Film* Victor Burgin draws attention to an important sociological study conducted from 1977 to 1987 at the University of Provence. More than 400 interviews were carried out with residents of the

Marseille/Aix-en-Provence area and in each the subjects were asked to describe their memories of the years 1930 to 1945. As Burgin observes, 'they found an almost universal tendency for personal history to be mixed with recollections of scenes from films and other media productions. "I saw at the cinema" would become simply "I saw"' (Burgin 2004: 68, see also Taranger 1991). It is not simply a question, however, of filmic images replacing mental memory representations. Rather it seems a more complex intertwining may be at work. In *The Queen of America Goes to Washington*, Lauren Berlant describes how her nephew Zak can remember images of himself before his own birth, thanks to a home video of his sonogram, combined with his identification with the TV images that people his existence.

> When I watched this [nephew Zak receiving videotapes on his first birthday], I felt how totally appropriate it was that Zak received videotapes on his first birthday. He was constituted in Valerie's memory as a sonogram, in his own and mine as a sonogram on a videotape. [. . .] He identifies totally with the stars he watches on the VCR and takes on their identities in play. The ease with which video can be made, purchased, copied, and circulated brings the quotidian into our collective memory of him in such a way that the accident of the cartoon videos he received seemed also an accidental truth about him, and the future of this history. (1997: 142)

The family's shared memories of Zak are thus shaped by screen images, which in turn inform Zak's own memories and the way his sense of identity is forming. In addition, Zak's mother Valerie finds, as does Berlant herself, that the narratives of Zak's childhood have in turn been influenced by home videos and photographs of Valerie's own childhood, and Berlant wonders whether 'the home movies and pictures from Valerie's birthday have become so iconic in the rituals of our family memory that she arranged his scene as a repetition of her own' (p. 141). However, the surprise in this story is that Valerie's and Berlant's 'memories', constituted by home movies and pictures, are in themselves false or altered memories, as we see in a footnote:

> After writing this, I called Valerie and asked her about the birthday scene on Zak's video, and she acknowledged that those images and repeated narratives of her childhood did indeed influence her construction of her son's birthday. My mother called shortly after to say that, contrary to both of our recollections, the memorialized event was Valerie's six-month birthday and that only one picture of it, taken by a neighbour, ever existed. (p. 275)

Here the capacity of human memory for displacement and transformation is also revealed, in a palimpsest where imagined and what one might term 'technological' memories layer and overwrite each other. In other words the cinematic object cannot be isolated in its relationship with the past event, but is inextricable from human and social perception and memory. It seems that if one thinks of time as linear and sequential, and memory as a relatively stable and individual process of conservation, then not only digital images but *all* kinds of reproducible imaging may seem a threat to the integrity of the past, given their potential for the alteration, manipulation and substitution of human memories. However, if, as I have argued, we are to view memory as something constantly being reconstituted in a present that is always already becoming past, then we can instead look to filmic representation in general and digital images in particular as a means of reflecting and revealing the complexities of our experience of memory and time.

In examining the issues at stake in the debates around the ontology of the digital image, I have not yet interrogated the linear, tripartite conception of time that underpins the notion of film as a real trace of the past. This is the simple view of cinematic time wherein past events are recorded, the representation is viewed in the present and survives into the future. The cinematic image itself, however, can lead us to rethink the temporal, and in particular its relationship to memory. In *Cinéma 2: l'image-temps*, Deleuze, using readings of Bergson and Nietzsche in a complex analysis of cinematic signs and images, challenges entrenched conceptions of time (1985, 2005). Cinematic images, for Deleuze, can reveal time in all its intricacy. He traces the progression, over the course of the history of cinema in the twentieth century, from the dominance of the movement-image to a tendency to produce the time-image. As Deleuze describes it, the movement-image of pre-war cinema subordinates time to movement. In edited sequences where movement is motivated by continuity of action, time is shown indirectly, as spatial duration suggested by movement. The interval between images is 'rational' in the mathematical sense; it is the end of one movement and the beginning of the next. The time-image instead presents a direct image of time. In the time-image, perception no longer extends into action: characters are lost or immobile, spaces empty. There is simply vision, instead of chains of action and reaction. Duration is emptied of its kinetic quality and shown as pure optical or sonic signs. As Rodowick, in his book on Deleuze, succinctly puts it:

> There is now only linking through 'irrational' divisions. According to the mathematical definition, the interval dividing segmentations of space is now autonomous and irreducible; it no longer forms a part of any segment as the ending of one and the beginning of another. Image and soundtrack are also relatively autonomous. While referring to each other, they none the less resist being made into an organic whole. As a result, there is no totalization of space in an organic image of the whole and no subordination of time to movement. Inside and outside, mental and physical, imaginary and real are no longer decidable qualities. (1997: 5)

In elaborating the concept of the time-image, Deleuze can be seen to move away from traditional conceptions of the temporal, and he draws on particular filmic techniques in order to do this. Bearing in mind my intention to examine memory through cinema, I want to focus on one form of the time-image as discussed by Deleuze, which I find particularly relevant to the relationship between digital media and memory: the crystal-image. The crystal-image is a virtual image that disrupts a linear, tripartite conception of time. It is a concept that draws on Bergson's theory of the *souvenir pur* (pure recollection), in other words the layer of representation that is formed continuously throughout perception and becomes particular memory-images when reactualised in relation to the present. Deleuze describes the virtual as a *passé-en-général* (past in general), which coexists with the present: 'le passé ne succède pas au présent qu'il n'est plus, il coexiste avec le présent qu'il a été. Le présent, c'est l'image actuelle, et *son* passé contemporain, c'est l'image virtuelle, l'image en miroir' (1985: 106) ('The past does not follow the present that it is no longer, it coexists with the present it was. The present is the actual image, and *its* contemporaneous past is the virtual image, the image in a mirror' [2005: 76–7]). This causes a forking and doubling of time:

Puisque le passé ne se constitue pas après le présent qu'il a été, mais en même temps, il faut que le temps se dédouble à chaque instant en présent et passé, qui diffèrent l'un de l'autre en nature, ou, ce qui revient au même, dédouble le présent en deux directions hétérogènes, dont l'une s'élance vers l'avenir et l'autre tombe dans le passé. (1985: 108–9)

(Since the past is constituted not after the present that it was but at the same time, time has to split itself in two at each moment as present and past, which differ from each other in nature, or, what amounts to the same thing, it has to split the present in two heterogeneous directions, one of which is launched towards the future while the other falls into the past. [2005: 78–9])

Deleuze thus replaces traditional conceptions of time with the idea of a perpetual becoming, exemplified in the crystal-image with its coexisting non-chronological layers, with its constant flow of exchange between actual and virtual, clear and opaque, seed and environment. He was of course writing before digital technology had fully taken root in cinema, though in his conclusion to his volumes on cinema he shows an awareness of the burgeoning of a new computerised culture, in which the traditional automata of movement are being replaced by 'une nouvelle race, informatique et cybernétique, automates de calcul et de pensée, automates à régulation et feed-back' (1985: 346) ('a new computer and cybernetic race, automata of computation and thought, automata with controls and feedback' [2005: 254]). He suggests that information technologies have so far seeped into and been absorbed by cinema, leading to a 'mutation' of form:

Mais de nouveaux automates n'envahissent pas le contenu sans qu'un nouvel automatisme n'assure une mutation de la forme. [. . .] L'image électronique, c'est-à-dire l'image télé ou vidéo, l'image numérique naissante, devait ou bien transformer le cinéma, ou bien le remplacer, en marquer la mort. (1985: 346)

(But new automata did not invade content without a new automatism bringing about a mutation of form. The electronic image, that is, the tele and video image, the numerical image coming into being, had either to transform cinema or to replace it, to mark its death. [2005: 254])

Seeing the transition from photographic to electronic (and to digital) in terms of a mutation reconfigures the ontological divide in terms of a continual evolving of the cinema, a 'becoming' where future variables (transformation, substitution, death) coexist with its present in terms of a potential. The seed of future developments was already, at the time of Deleuze's writing, contained in the work of Chris Marker, amongst others, whose use of computerised images seems to reinterpret the idea of the crystalline image. The digitally altered images in *Sans soleil* mentioned above appear crystalline in the non-Deleuzian sense: their internal numeric pattern gives a geometrical quality to the surface image. But the link goes deeper than that. When a digital image foregrounds its own 'crystals' it is at once an image of something (its forms and movements trigger a search for mimesis on the part of the viewer) and an image of that imaging process. This doubling of actual and virtual creates a time-image even when the content of the shot would be defined as a movement-image. For example, one sequence of images, which only become recognisable as human forms when seen as a moving flow of images, shows soldiers in attack, their rushing movements motivated by action. Yet the digital alteration, undertaken by the fictional Krasna's real friend Yamaneko, reveals multiple temporal layers within the image (event, filming, remembering, altering, rewatching) as the viewer struggles to make sense of the abstract shapes. A more recent and mimetic example can be found in the second part of Godard's film *Éloge de l'amour* (2001). Shot using a digital camera, there are fleeting moments of pixelation, which are at their most emphasised when a blue wave momentarily crystallises before cascading back into its flow. As with the images in *Sans soleil*, the digital section of *Éloge* is presented in terms of memory, for these are images of the past: the second half of the film is chronologically anterior in the diegesis to the first. These 'memory-images', rather than being ontologically troubled in their authenticity by the digital technology's codified non-indexical quality, are already called into question in the fragmentation and splitting within the narrative and in the crystalline image of time, which, in its bifurcation into indiscernible layers of past and actuality, is always, in perception, an ongoing process of memory.

Rodowick comments astutely on the way the time-image refigures memory in Deleuze's theory. In the time-image, he suggests:

Memory is no longer habitual or attentive as a faculty for recollecting or for regathering images from the past. In positing the coexistence of nonchronological layers and incommensurable points, the orders of time figure memory as a membrane joining two sides, a recto and a verso divided by the pure and empty form of time. Here, sheets of past emanate from a pure virtuality (an unreachable interiority where the I divides from the ego), while the actual or perception recedes from us as an absolute horizon (an outside yet to come – an indeterminate future or a world, people or thought who are not yet). (1997: 200)

Thus through a reading of Deleuze in the context of the current possibilities of digital imaging, it can be seen that the ontological differences between isolated photographic and digital images are less crucial for the issues of memory and time than the way such technologies are used to conceal or display the 'orders of time'. Images whose forms and movements reveal to the human eye a visualisation of its own perceptual processes constitute the cinematic as a domain of what Deleuze would call the noosign – an aesthetic embodiment of thought. At the same time, such images have the potential to highlight the interplay between human and technological memories, revealing a point of mutual exchange and ongoing transformation. This may frustrate the desires of those for whom cinema exists to connect us physically with a (fantasised) stable past, but it will excite those who, like Deleuze, see cinema as a scene for visualising thought.

I have aimed to use the crystal-image as a means for rethinking the potential of cinema to mirror forms of memory; however, it is of course just one potential mode of the digital amongst a myriad of possibilities. The use of digital technologies by contemporary French filmmakers is extremely varied. I will be discussing other examples in the work of Marker and Godard later in the book. There are, however, many other French filmmakers and video-artists who are making use of different capacities of the digital, from the potential for imaginative special effects in post-production – for example in the 2001 hit film *Le Fabuleux Destin d'Amélie Poulain* (Jean-Pierre Jeunet), where the female protagonist's vision of the world is exuberantly rendered in digital effects – to the liberating portability of lightweight digital cameras. The latter has opened up the potential for a host of personal quests, amongst which is Natacha Samuel's intimate documentary *Pola à 27 ans* (2003) which I will discuss in Chapters 3 and 4. Varda's *Les Glaneurs et la glaneuse* (2000), discussed in Chapter 2, privileges the novelty of the tiny digital camera with a scene devoted to the various creative effects it makes possible. However, it is in the possibility of filming one hand with the other, and thereby mirroring the process of gleaning in a double gesture, that the digital camera makes its aesthetic and conceptual mark on the film. The current expansion of the use of digital technologies in all aspects of cinema is providing filmmakers with new opportunities for changing both how we think about memory and how we remember. The virtuality of our memory, making our perception double, is becoming ever more layered with other virtual images, presenting new challenges and avenues for filmmakers who want to interrogate the contemporary mnemonic relationship to the past, and to time itself. But before exploring in detail various responses by filmmakers to this situation, I want to examine further how the constructed nature of film, whether digital or photographic, can be seen to work intertextually and intersubjectively to interact with spectators' memories and double the mnemonic process.

THE MEMORY OF THE TEXT

Famously, Bazin ends his essay on the ontology of the photographic image with the single-paragraph sentence: 'D'autre part le cinéma est un langage' (1958: 19) ('On the other hand, of course, cinema is also a language' [1967: 16]). In the context of the linguistics-inspired structuralist and poststructuralist movements in theory, the emphasis in film theory moved away from questions of pure ontology and on to questions of language. In the late 1960s and early 1970s theorists such as Christian Metz were interrogating the problems of signs and meaning in the cinema, and exploring the possibility of a uniquely filmic or cinematic language. While Metz retained Bazin's idea of the 'impression of reality', in other words the idea that cinematic representations correspond to reality in ways other than the purely symbolic, his main concern seemed to be picking up where Bazin left off with that provocative final sentence of the ontology essay. Metz argued that though cinema is not a language system (*langue*) like French or Chinese, it is nevertheless a language (*langage*), because of the inherent narrativity of its signifying process. In the essay 'Le cinéma: langue ou langage?', Metz examines filmic images in terms of linguistic enunciations (irreducible to words) and the concept of paradigmatic and syntagmatic axes, privileging the syntagmatic, or sequential, aspect of film over the paradigmatic or selective aspect. 'Passer d'un image à deux images,' he famously stated, 'c'est passer de l'image au langage' (to move from one image to two images is to move from image to language) (Metz 1971: 53).

Deleuze objects that the filmic images cannot be likened to linguistic enunciations, because this leaves out film's defining features, movement and time. For Deleuze, film is neither language system nor language: 'c'est une masse plastique, une matière a-signifiante et a-syntaxique, une matière non linguistiquement formée' (1985: 44) ('it is a plastic mass, an a-signifying and a-syntaxic material, a material not formed linguistically' [2005: 28]). Though Deleuze's arguments against the notion of film as *language* are convincing, I believe that the notion of film as Text can be retained.[6] Deleuze himself affirms that, though the filmic image is a supple mass, it is also 'formée sémiotiquement, esthétiquement, pragmatiquement' ('formed semiotically, aesthetically and pragmatically') (ibid.). Drawing on the work of C. S. Peirce, he distinguishes between semiology, which derives from linguistics, and semiotics, a theory of the sign taking the image, rather than the word, as its starting point. I would argue that the analogy between the cinematic and written text stands because both are fundamentally constructions of signs, whose origins are absent in the present. At the same time, a specificity of the moving image can also be proposed, because it has a different type of power and expression, involving signs that work differently to written enunciations. The idea of film as Text, however, goes beyond a simple analogy with the written text and into a broader concept of Text I want to draw from the work of Roland Barthes.

Barthes argued that all texts are inherently based on quotation, for comprehension always requires recognition. Furthermore, he suggested that texts are necessarily multidimensional, with a multi-referential power beyond the scope of the author's original intentions or message:

> Nous savons maintenant qu'un texte n'est pas fait d'une ligne de mots, dégageant un sens unique, en quelque sorte théologique (qui serait le 'message' le l'Auteur-Dieu), mais un espace à dimensions multiples, où se marient et se contestent des écritures variées, dont aucune n'est originelle: le texte est un tissu de citations, issues des mille foyers de la culture. (1984a: 67)

> (We know now that a text is not a line of words releasing a single 'theological' meaning (the 'message' of the Author-God), but a multi-dimensional space in which a variety of writings, none of them original, blend and clash. The text is a tissue of quotations drawn from the innumerable centres of culture. [1977a: 146])

Although Barthes' concern at this point was the literary text, the very notion of Text he is elaborating shifts the focus away from the isolated work and onto a fluid plane of production, reading practice and activity. This change of emphasis both releases the notion of Text from its linguistic confines and at the same time elicits the idea of intertextuality, for the Text's web of citation and signification may weave across many works. Barthes makes explicit this distinction between the individual work and the Text in the 1971 essay 'De l'œuvre au texte':

> *Le Texte ne s'éprouve que dans un travail, une production.* Il s'ensuit que le Texte ne peut s'arrêter (par exemple, à un rayon de bibliothèque); son mouvement constitutive est la *traversée* (il peut notamment traverser l'œuvre, plusieurs œuvres). (1984b: 73)

> (*The Text is experienced only in an activity of production.* It follows that the Text cannot stop (for example on a library shelf); its constitutive movement is that of cutting across (in particular it can cut across the work, several works). [1977b: 157])

The question remains: can this transversal movement operate across media, allowing us to conceive intertextuality operating through cinema, as well as in written texts? If we agree that it can, then this may also be a useful conceptual tool with which to approach the current hybridity inhabiting cinema. Though a caution must be placed against flattening out the different modes of expression and signification that operate in writing on the one hand and the moving image on the other, I would argue that the concept of the Text seen in terms of an active encounter with a web of citation, where cultural and personal connotation mingle, is just as applicable to films as it is to books. Certainly I am making Barthes' term overflow from its original conception, in suggesting that the same textual operations may be seen to activate across media boundaries, through the intertextual references, connotations and citations that pervade all cultural production. I do so because it seems vital to me, in addition to the ontological mnemonic operations of film I have elaborated so far in this chapter, to posit a textual one. In other words, as well as mirroring human memory's temporal complexities in the time-image, and intermingling with human memory's personal and collective representations, film also draws on the spectator's memory in order to function. This is of course the case, as with writing and music, at the most basic level of comprehension, but also in an ongoing encounter between personal and cultural memory that comes to bear upon the weavings of formal elements, patterns, spoken words, music, colours and objects that weave through a film. Each film can be seen to have a horizontal, linear progression, requiring a certain kind of accumulative perceptual memory for comprehension (assuming it is watched in the traditional manner, straight through from start to finish, a viewing practice that is still dominant, though no longer essential thanks to digital viewing technologies). However, on the one hand the time-image may create vertical and crystalline layers, and on the other, a textual web of connections bursts the boundaries of the individual film, traversing both media and works. With multi-layered audiovisual composition, film is, even more so than writing, what Barthes calls an 'espace à dimensions multiples' (a multidimensional space). This runs counter to Metz's argument that film is, because of 'certaines structures de l'esprit humaine, ce diachroniste impénitent' (certain structures of the human mind, that shameless diachronist), inherently linear in its reception process (Metz 1971: 54). According to Metz, as soon as two images are juxtaposed (and not solely as an effect of montage but within a given shot) a longitudinal narrativity is born that suppresses any 'transversal' reading:

> Le film, que l'on croirait susceptible de donner lieu à une lecture transversale, par l'exploration à loisir du contenu visuel de chaque 'plan', est presque à tout coup l'objet d'une lecture longitudinale, précipitée, déphasée vers l'avant et anxieuse de la 'suite'. (pp. 52–3)

> (Film, which one would think susceptible to giving rise to a transversal reading, through the leisurely exploration of the visual content of each

shot, almost immediately became the object of a longitudinal reading, disconnected and precipitated forwards, anxious about what happens next.)

Metz here ignores not only the possibility that certain kinds of film may elicit the very 'lecture transversale' he describes, but also the myriad criss-crossings of personal and collective memory that traverse all texts, making narrativity itself multidimensional.

It is true that this is not operative in the same way or to the same extent in all films. At one extreme of the spectrum films may foreground and exaggerate an operation already at work in reception, making the spectator aware of his or her role. At the other extreme the process of recognition may be all but disguised, encouraging the reception to be almost 'unthinking'. I turn once again to Barthes' writing on literature to examine this way in which the Textual may be made to function differently in different works. In declaring that 'the text is a tissue of quotations' Barthes can be understood as giving new breadth to the concept of quotation, which expands to encompass connotation and cultural references, rather than simply the intentional quoting of one author by another. In S/Z, in Barthes' discussion of the *lisible* (readerly) or classically readable text, we find him adding yet another layer to our understanding of the verb 'citer':

> 'cité'; on voudrait donner à ce mot son sens tauromachique: *citar*, c'est ce coup de talon, cette cambrure du torero, qui appellent la bête aux banderilles. De la même façon, on cite le signifié (la richesse) à comparaître, tout en l'esquivant au fil du discours. (1970: 29)

> ('cited'; we would like to give this word its tauromachian meaning: the *citar* is the stamp of the heel, the torero's arched stance which summons the bull to the banderilleros. Similarly, one cites the signified (wealth) to make it come forth, while avoiding it in discourse. [1990: 22])

This vivid description of the functioning, in the classical text, of quotation in its broadest sense shows how the signified is aggressively 'cited' or 'incited' to appear without ever having to be connected to one particular signifier. In this case Barthes is discussing Balzac's novella *Sarrasine*, where references to a party being given in a certain kind of house, in a certain quarter of Paris, all evoke wealth without the signifier 'wealth' ever being mentioned. The performance of this naturalisation of the connection between signification and meaning depends of a near-invisibility of the citing: 'Il faut que le trait passe légèrement, comme si son oubli était indifférent et que cependant, surgi plus loin sous une autre forme, il constitue déjà un souvenir' (1970: 30) ('the touch must be light, as though it weren't worth remembering, and yet, appearing again later in another guise, it must already be a memory' [1990: 22–3]).

To the *lisible* (readerly) text, functioning via an unconscious acceptance of the supposedly natural operations of syntax and connotation, Barthes opposes the *scriptible* (writerly), a process of inscription in certain modern texts that situates the reader not as consumer but as *producer* of the text, replacing the notion of reading as intransitive with that of reading as thought. It is a term that, if we bring Barthes' writings to bear upon one another, can be said to be applicable to the Text rather than to the work, but is none the less foregrounded, or activated by certain kinds of writing practice in specific works. As with the concept of Text, a transposition of the notions of the *lisible* and the *scriptible* to film is both possible and useful. Like Barthes, I would want to avoid the use of these terms simply to describe specific works, and see them instead as Textual processes that traverse various films and even stumble across each other within a single film. It also is important to see them at two extremes on a continuum rather than simply as two opposing terms. The concept of *scriptible* is, however, important for the conceptual framework of my study, since it shows up the mnemonic function of quotation, recuperation and recontextualisation in film. For while the *lisible*, as Barthes says, acts *as if* 'l'oubli était indifférent', as if details, fragments, traces, might just as well be forgotten, whilst almost invisibly reiterating themselves in the narrative memory of the film, in the *scriptible*, the touch or mark does not pass lightly. Fragments, debris, quotations: these markers of the past stick out, foregrounding the mnemonic Textual operations of film, which is to say the constant intertextual referencing and triggering of the spectator's memory. At the same time they reveal the ways in which images (visual and sonic) carry memory, bearing a trace of former contexts when they are repositioned in a new environment, a trace which constantly oscillates between potential and actualised. For the idea of the Text as a multidimensional web of citation supposes not only intertextuality, but also a constant recontextualisation and recuperation. Whether he knew it or not, Barthes' notion of the Text seems implicitly bound up in the function of memory, for the past is always jostling with the present in the Text, as well as being 'incited' or called up in the mind of the reader-viewer. In this way, Barthes' literary understanding of intertextuality meets a Deleuzian concept of the image-crystal, that cinematic incitation to perceive multiple temporal layers.

To reflect upon memory and the moving image is in some sense to reflect upon encounters, not only between various theories but also between the spheres of memory, media and time themselves, as they combine to produce cultural memory. Arising in that virtual space where our interior worlds encounter external objects, cultural memory is always profoundly fluid and contingent, subject to chance encounters, loss and forgetting. In the 'era of commemoration', however, in the context of a nation obsessed with remembering the past, a diverse range of filmmakers have attempted to experiment with the ways moving images might be able to incite memory with their particular aesthetic and technical resources. It is to the fruits of such exploration that I will turn in the next three chapters.

NOTES

1. Nader's findings fit with a chance but hitherto unsubstantiated discovery made in the 1970s by psychiatrist Richard Rubin, who found that asking patients to focus on their traumatic memories just before electric shock therapy (which acts on the hippocampus) weakened or erased memories of the trauma. This suggests that the effect is at work in declarative memory as well as the procedural memory of the rat experiments (McCrone 2003: 28).
2. This is linked to Ricœur's primary distinction between memory as affection and memory as recollection, discussed earlier in this chapter.
3. For an alternative, complementary approach to re-reading Deleuze's theories of cinema in the age of new media, see Tim Murray's essay 'Time @ cinema's future' (in Murray 2008: 238–60).
4. This is particularly pertinent since the home copying of DVDs has become an accessible activity, thanks to the proliferation of affordable and widely available technology.
5. Although the 'Ten Commandments' in the manifesto of the Dogme 1995 group stipulate the use of Academy 35mm film, the rule was repeatedly broken, often in favour of 'low-fi' stock such as 16mm, or using digital, as in the case of *Festen* and Harmony Korine's *Julien Donkey-Boy* (2000) amongst others (see Ezra 2004: 312).
6. Here I am using 'Text' as opposed to 'text' to refer to a specific understanding of the word that arises from the work of Roland Barthes.

2. VIRTUAL MUSEUMS AND MEMORY OBJECTS

In the previous chapter I suggested that certain films actively elicit a 'transversal' viewing, contrary to Metz's suggestion that as soon as two images are juxtaposed a longitudinal narrativity is born, suppressing any such lateral movement. In this chapter I want to look at recent French films and moving image material that can be seen to summon transversal readings by drawing on an intertextual deployment of objects that resonate with personal and collective memory. To a certain extent all films can be seen to activate cultural memory in this way, especially in the age of DVD and other viewing technologies, where it is easy for the viewer to pause and meditate on any single frame. However, the films and artworks I shall be discussing incorporate these intertextual operations into their very structure, thereby foregrounding the mnemonic possibilities of film and moving image texts. They make use of objects and references to evoke the past, creating a space where the memories of filmmaker and viewer meet in the context of a broader cultural sphere. All of these works in one way or another take memory and history as their subject, engaging with the possibilities and limits of a filmic evocation of the past.

Jean-Luc Godard's *Histoire(s) du cinéma* (1989–98) is a series of eight films that explore his personal approach to and theorisation of the history of cinema through a montage of film clips, paintings, photographs, music, soundtrack excerpts and specially filmed/recorded pieces. Chris Marker's *Level Five* (1997) looks back at the tragic 1945 battle of Okinawa through the device of a computer strategy game being played by a woman whose lover, the creator of the program, has died. Bereavement is also central to Agnès Varda's exhibition at the Fondation Cartier in Paris, *L'Île et elle* (2006), which was made up of installations connecting thematically to the Île de Noirmoutier (Noirmoutier Island), an island off the Atlantic coast of France that Varda came to know through her late husband, filmmaker Jacques Demy, and where she still owns a house. Shrines, snapshots and souvenirs came together in a hybrid spatial configuration that took the moving image beyond the screen's two dimensions, while retaining a powerful sense of the cinematic. After all, as Varda's recent autobiographical film, *Les Plages d'Agnès* (2008), highlights, film and cinema are inseparable from her memories, not just of herself as an individual but also of those she has encountered throughout her life, including the much-mourned Demy. Like *L'Île et elle*, Marker's CD-ROM *Immemory* (1998) moves beyond a conventional moving image format. The work is presented as a *musée imaginaire* (museum of the imagination) of key motifs, moments and images that have particular resonance in his life and in recent history. Here too cinematic memories remain central, while the web-like format reconfigures the workings of film for the digital era. Varda's *Les Glaneurs et la glaneuse* (2000) and its sequel *Deux ans après* (2002) are less evidently films about remembering and evoking the past. However, they combine a quest to discover the ways in which gleaning as an activity has survived into the present day with meditations on, amongst other things, recuperation and the passing of time. Like all the films that provide focal points for this book, Varda's gleaning documentaries constitute an audiovisual catalyst for thinking about memory and the moving image. In particular, they foreground a resonance between filmed objects and gleaned or recuperated objects that also gestures to the virtual realm of cultural memory, in which diverse memories may intersect.

In their different ways, all of these works focus visually and conceptually on material objects as traces of the past, bringing to mind the concept of the museum. The museum, a space in which objects of perceived historical, educational or artistic value are kept, studied and displayed, can be seen to have certain elements in common with the documentary film or artwork. In both cases the problems of selection and preservation, narrativity, historiography and transmission are crucial issues. How does one choose what to film or collect? How does one make history into a story and what kind of narrative(s) does one create or evoke? Finally, how does one transmit or convey this and what kinds of slippage and connections are at stake in transmission? Similar difficulties face curators and documentary filmmakers. But the parallel becomes even more striking in films where material things (and I shall discuss in detail below the notion of the thing, in terms of object, image, monument, gesture) are given prominence through the use of close-ups, momentary stillness, collage and commentary, as if in an accumulation or collection. Varda's metaphor of the filmmaker as gleaner comes to join that of the filmmaker as curator, albeit of a rather curious type of museum. Indeed, in many ways the works of Godard, Marker and Varda depart from traditional museum exhibitions, in which the curators' subjective input tends to be concealed within a conventionally didactic framework and chronological ordering. As Joan Gibbons points out in her discussion of contemporary art and memory, there is already a counter-institutional practice dating back to the 1960s, in which artists have made use of alternative methods of collection, preservation and display precisely in order to critique curatorial practice in museums and galleries (Gibbons 2007: 122–4). The three filmmakers whose works are discussed in this chapter participate in this counter-tradition, in work that reflects critically both on film and on museums.

In recent years Marker, Godard and Varda have all moved beyond the space of the screen to experiment with interventions in galleries and museums. Exhibitions such as Marker's *Silent Movie* at the Wexner Centre, Ohio, in 1995, Godard's *Voyages en Utopie* at the Centre Pompidou, Paris, 11 May to 14 August 2006, and Varda's *L'Île et elle* at the Fondation Cartier in Paris in the same year, 18 June to 8 October, demonstrate a blurring of the roles of artist, filmmaker and curator. In each case the filmmakers' museum exhibitions manifest a concern for filmic operations such as editing, projection and the unfolding of sound and image in time, thereby extending the self-reflexive explorations of their filmmaking into architectural space. Such exhibitions remind us that contemporary films that engage with objects of the past do so in the context of an art scene where audiovisual technologies have facilitated the transition of the moving image from cinema theatre to gallery or museum, a scene in which filmmakers themselves are active participants. Godard's *Voyages en Utopie* exhibition at the Pompidou Centre was notorious thanks to his much-publicised rift with the curator Dominique Païni and the museum's administration, resulting in a delayed, apparently unfinished, deliberately sabotaged installation. Emphasising the connections, crossovers and parallels between the moving image and contemporary fine art, *Voyages en utopie* ran alongside a vast exhibition called *Le Mouvement des images* (5 April 2006 to 29 January 2007, Centre Pompidou). This exhibition presented the museum's permanent collection of modern art alongside key pieces from international collections, displaying the works according to a thematic structure based on four key components of cinema: frame roll ('défilement'), projection, story and editing. This concept encouraged spectators to examine both the differences and the common threads between film and the plastic arts. It brought to the fore, for example, the cinematic montage effect created in works such as Moï Ver's *Paris: 80 photographies* (1931), a book of photographs that played with overlapping, juxtaposed contrasts of textures and angles, or the documentary sense of temporal succession in On Kawara's date paintings, such as *Today Series 1966 . . .* (1975), monochrome canvases stencilled with dates and accompanied by binders filled with newspaper clippings. The exhibition's point that contemporary art has long been permeated by cinematic influences, while cinema in turn has resonated with the impact of artistic movements from Dada to the New Realists, is hardly revolutionary. However, coming in the same year as both Godard's and Varda's major exhibitions in Parisian contemporary art institutions, *Le Mouvement des Images* serves as a helpful reminder of the way filmic form can reappear, albeit transfigured, in different contexts and spaces – a crucial point in a digital era of diversification and hybridity.

In attempting to understand the way moving images mobilise the memory of objects, I have chosen as examples an installation exhibition (*L'Île et elle*) and a CD-ROM (*Immemory*) alongside the analysis of films. Through this approach I want to suggest that these alternative formats not only incorporate the moving image, but continue to dwell on the memory of film as part of a formative cultural sphere. This is in line with Tim Murray's speculation that the emergent digital aesthetic is haunted by the memory of cinema, especially where questions of memory and mourning are thematic concerns: 'the cinematic code might be understood to linger in digitality as something of a crypt or a carrier of the discourse of loss, mourning and melancholia so familiar to cinema studies' (1999: 9). The media and approaches of the works I will discuss may vary, but certain key concepts none the less emerge. Ultimately I hope to show how screen museums, like their architectural counterparts, create a space where personal and collective memory meet and overlap, a space of cultural memory.

AUDIOVISUAL OBJECTS AND MEMORY

The notion of object I shall be dealing with poses certain difficulties simply because the word can of course mean any*thing*. It is useful to start by distinguishing a material object (something that can be seen or touched) from an object in the wider sense of the focus of someone's attention or emotion. A material object can be the focus of someone's attention or emotion, but an object of attention is not always a concrete thing; it might also be a thought or idea. However, this definition of material object does not account for sound objects, so important in cinema since the advent of the sound film. I want to incorporate aural objects into the notion of material object with the justification that, in the recording process, such objects become distinct and external, and also because recorded aural materials are often included in museum collections. This moves towards a definition of the object as something external, physical and discrete that can be apprehended by the senses. I therefore question the assumption that the object is inanimate (in the sense of motionless, still), as has often been assumed by theorists of objects (see for example Csikszentmihalyi 1993, Kavanagh 2000). Recorded speech or moving images may require mechanical operations in order to manifest movement, but that movement is none the less part of them as objects, just as the sound and music are part of the piano as object. Thus screen objects, both aural and visual, are as much objects as a stone that one can touch. This concept may sound counter-intuitive, departing as it does from the notion of a clear boundary between object and representation, but I would contend that it is suggested by the films by Godard, Varda and Marker that I discuss in this chapter, especially when approached from a Deleuzian–Bergsonian perspective. It will also be vital for my analysis to distinguish at a basic level this concept of object from that of the sign, which is an element of signification embedded in a signifying context, whereas the object is prior to signification and only becomes a sign by means of certain operations of framing, contextualisation and juxtaposition. This is of course precisely what film does, meaning that screen objects are always both objects *and* signs. As signs they continually strive to evoke meaning; as objects they, like memories, bear the trace of a past time whilst being experienced only in the present. In this sense, as I shall argue, objects can become part of the operations of intertextuality in film and other visual media that I outlined in Chapter 1. Though they are altered as signs, objects that are transplanted into new contexts still hold a ghostly memory of their previous existences. A book, a painting, a piece of music incorporated into the visual and sonic fabric of a film take on significance as part of that text but none the less have their own past and context. It may require recognition or research to tease out the possibilities of such past meanings, but the potential to trigger involuntary memory (via recognition) or a willed delving into the past (via research) is inherent in the objects themselves. The films in this chapter show an awareness of this potential and have various ways of deploying it, from Godard's rhythmic amassing of objects in *Histoire(s) du cinéma* to Varda's integration of them into the associative structure of her quest in *Les Glaneurs et la glaneuse*. Their common thread is that they all use the potential memory of objects to add temporal depth and interpretative richness to their work.

It would seem commonsensical to assert that objects cannot in themselves remember. Gaynor Kavanagh, in arguing against museums as mere accumulations of objects and for a more 'archival' (in the sense of interconnecting, contextualised, humanised) organisation of the museum space, rightly asserts that objects are defined by their lack of agency: they are not subjects.

> Objects are inanimate, and unless animated in some way by us or through us, cannot be the subject of an active verb. So an object cannot embrace, determine, decide, although we may embrace, determine or decide something in reference or with reference to it. (2000: 101)

The implication of this is that objects are inherently mute, motionless and in the present, unless a human subject makes them speak, move or connect with the past in some way. This is an assumption with which Laura U. Marks takes issue in her work on intercultural cinema. As she says in a chapter on the memory of things, 'objects are not inert and mute [. . .] they tell stories and describe trajectories' (2000: 80). Marks' primary focus is on those particular objects that have travelled across different cultures, but the wider implications of her insightful study are pertinent to my aims here. Moreover, that she draws many of her central tenets from Deleuze's writings on cinema, as well as Walter Benjamin's readings of Baudelaire and Proust, reinforces the idea that the French cultural heritage provides a useful set of conceptual resources for thinking about the relation of screen objects to cultural memory, even when the films and objects in question traverse cultures and profoundly undermine Western ideological assumptions along the way. What I find particularly interesting in Marks' approach is the delicate line her argument treads between the memory of subjects and objects. She uses a dialogical understanding of the fetish as the product of contact between two cultures (for example in colonial ethnography – the contact is always invested with the question of power) to conceive of the transnational memory object as a fetish glowing with a Benjaminian aura, or alternatively, picking up on an image used casually by Deleuze, an incandescent, 'radioactive' fossil (Marks 2000: 84–92). In both of these analogies, Marks moves away from the assumption made by theorists of museum space that objects have no memory and must be assigned it, literally given signification by texts, labelled with context. Instead, she argues, both fetish and fossil bear physical, indexical traces of the past and bear sensorial witness (tactile, as well as visual) to that contact.

I take a slightly different stance on the question of real, physical contact and the index, as the previous chapter will have indicated in relation to the ontology of film and digital media. While I agree with Marks that the idea of the contact of film with its referent and the memory of touch can be powerfully intertwined catalysts of cultural memory, I am wary of the implication that the touch must have been physically real for contact to occur, which would undermine the power of digital media to screen memory objects. Marks herself acknowledges the limitations of such an implication, stressing in a footnote that she wants to talk about 'indexical and nonindexical *practices*' rather than 'indexical and nonindexical *media*' (2000: 253). However, she is keen to emphasise the materiality of the fetish, which is powerful because 'it is constituted from a physical rather than mental contact between objects, it is not a metaphor' (p. 92). In fact, as the subsequent chapters of her book illustrate, touch that is sensed, imagined, reconstructed from other sensory information need not be less powerful; indeed this is one of the extraordinary qualities of the audiovisual moving image. It returns me to the ontological debate about digital media discussed in Chapter 1 and to my suggestion that the indexicality of film (as opposed to digital media) might itself become fetishised in media studies, in spite of its manipulability. My view is that it is through imaginative investment, or what Vivian Sobchack calls an 'experienced difference in our mode of consciousness' (2004: 261), that the power of the index touches us, and this can happen whether or not reflected light once made contact with film. This is an argument for a concept of cultural memory that, like film watching, is constituted through affective as much as physical contact. In this context, what is perhaps most significant for me in Marks' analysis is the idea of the object as a point of intersection between individual and shared memories:

> To be dependent upon an object affirms not only the materiality of one's body but also the incompleteness of one's self: it suggests that meaning inheres in the communication between self, objects, and others, rather than in a communication mediated by the mind alone. (Marks 2000: 120)

This idea of meaning arising in between the self, objects and others is precisely what I want to develop in this chapter in relation to memory. The significance of objects may arise from their interaction with humans, yet we are just as dependent on them for the transmission of our memories as they are on us.

The recuperation artists in Varda's gleaning films would most probably agree. In *Les Glaneurs et la glaneuse* and the film revisiting its people and themes two years later, *Deux ans après*, Varda's associational explorations of gleaning show that the practices of recuperation and recycling reveal the dynamic potential inherent in found objects. Like Benjaminian bricoleurs, gleaning artists patch together the debris of a past time and create of it something new.[1] Hervé, an artist from *Les Glaneurs*, explains that for him, 'ce qui est bien avec les objets de la récupération, c'est qu'ils ont une existence déjà, ils ont déjà vécu' (what's good about reclaimed objects is that they already have an existence, they've already lived). More radically, in *Deux ans après*, theatre director and installation artist Macha Makeïeff feels that 'les objets nous contiennent' (objects contain us). She goes on to explain that the shabby, forgotten, found objects she collects for her artworks form part of a circulation that connects people. If objects contain us, they also contain in some way all those who have come into contact with them: 'c'est une trace magnifique, c'est une trace de . . . Je m'imagine, je m'imagine le rapport que chacun a eu avec ces objets' (it's a wonderful trace, a trace of . . . I can imagine, I imagine the relation that each person has had with these objects). This notion of a trace which evokes imagined past lives is a key element of cultural memory, as we shall see below, since any sense of collective identity or shared experience depends upon the intersubjective transmission of memory. This is a form of memory that is not confined to the body of an individual but is instead mediated through cultural artefacts and imaginative investment. As we saw in Chapter 1, the memories of individuals are physiologically open to mediation in a similar way. Marianne Hirsch's conception of 'postmemory' mentioned in Chapter 1, the memory of events experienced by previous generations, fits with this line of argument. However, Hirsch retains a clear sense of distinction between 'memory itself', with its more 'direct' connection to the past, and 'postmemory' (1997: 22), whereas I argue that these forms of memory are always interlocked and part of the same processes. If we bear this in mind, we can start to consider the idea that objects do indeed 'contain us', in that our cultural memory is mediated through them, giving them a role in the way our identities are constituted as individuals in a given society or community.

Film, as I shall demonstrate throughout this chapter, can deploy formal strategies that foreground objects and reveal them as objects both of the present and of the past. The filmed objects become screen objects, operating both as signs in the text of the film and as traces of something prior – not just of the profilmic object in itself but of virtual past existences. Even as Macha is explaining her ideas about the traces of past lives in found objects, Varda's filming and editing exemplify the way in which the most insignificant of objects can function in film as a screen object, serving as a point of connection between different subjectivities and temporalities. Varda cuts between shots of Macha

Figure 2.1 Macha Makeïeff's memory object in *Deux ans après* (2002).
(Source: © CinéTamaris.)

speaking and of her hand holding a doily she has found. The close-up creates
a striking pattern of circles on the screen: the doily, the hand, the coat-sleeve
(Figure 2.1). It serves to draw the viewer's eye to the object itself, and, as
Macha flips it lightly in her hand, to the object in movement. Throughout the
sequence, the shots oscillate between Macha speaking and close-ups of her
hands touching the odd little objects she has found, taking them out of boxes,
placing them on her desk. The tactile materiality of the scene reinforces the
idea of these objects as links between different people at different moments in
time, as we imagine other hands touching them for quite other purposes. In
response to Varda asking her whether she means that objects tell our story or
really 'contain' us, Macha is quite clear: they contain us. Her remarks suggest
that although, like Kavanagh, she feels that it is an interaction between objects
and humans that gives objects significance and temporal depth, she does not
see humans as in some way primary, subjects who 'animate' otherwise mute,
empty and lifeless objects. It is as if for her, objects are a virtual realm of
human meaning and experience *in themselves*, and the act of (de)contextu-
alisation and imagination is the actualisation of some part of that virtuality.
Varda's decision to include a sequence on Macha in the second of her gleaning
films indicates that Macha's art of recuperating lost objects and her feelings
about the way objects relate to the past is something Varda would like to add

to her own collection of testimonies and anecdotes about different forms of gleaning. Certainly the implications of this sequence on Macha strike a chord with Varda's own relationship to objects and film as depicted in *Les Glaneurs et la glaneuse*. For Varda too, as we shall see in more detail below, sees objects as containers of memory, and film as a means of activating that memory and glimpsing the past in the present.

In my reading of them, Macha Makeïeff's comments resonate with Deleuze's reading of Bergson. It is to this revisiting of Bergson through cinematic concepts that I now want to turn in order to look deeper into the relation of objects and screen objects to memory. In Bergson's theory of matter and perception, that which he calls *images vivantes* (conscious beings) and other images are all part of one universal plane of immanence, with the difference that the *images vivantes* are *centres d'intérêt* (centres of interest) that single out particular images from the immanent whole and react to them. As Paola Marrati puts it, 'notre conscience de fait, c'est seulement une opacité qui permet à la lumière d'être révélée' (our consciousness is in fact only an opacity which allows light to be revealed) (Marratti 2003: 45). Perception is already 'in things', revealing them thanks to an interest that picks out elements from the flux of the whole, as opposed to being a kind of contemplative ray of light emanating onto the world from human subjects. This supports my earlier suggestion that objects and screen objects are but two orders of a single plane of existence. But can memory also be said to be 'in things'? If we think in terms of Bergson's concept of a *passé en général*, outlined in the first chapter, then we discover just such a conception. As Deleuze sees it:

> De même qu'on perçoit les choses là où elles sont, et qu'il faut s'installer dans les choses pour percevoir, de même nous allons chercher le souvenir là où il est, nous devons nous installer d'un saut dans le passé en général, dans ces images purement virtuelles qui n'ont pas cessé de se conserver le long du temps. (Deleuze 1985: 107)

> (Just as we perceive things in the place where they are, and have to place ourselves among things in order to perceive them, we go to look for a recollection in the place where it is, we have to place ourselves with a leap into the past in general, into these purely virtual images which have been constantly preserved through time. [Deleuze 2005: 78])

Rather like Macha, I would argue that objects contain this infinitely vast, virtual past, which can be actualised in the form of either a memory-image ('I remember that yellow doily, it was on my desk in my childhood bedroom') or a dream-image ('that yellow doily once sat gathering dust on top of a child-size desk'). But memory-images and dream-images are not perfectly distinct from one another in this case, for the object connects us, albeit virtually, to a *passé en général* that exists in its own right and does not reside in one particular human subject. This brings us back to Kavanagh's analysis of memory and the museum. For whilst her justifiable argument against a coldly object-based collecting policy in museums leads her to ignore the object's inherent dynamism and temporality, she is at the same time arguing in favour of the museum as a 'dream space' where personal and collective memory can meet, a compelling approach that actually reinforces the points I am making here. She takes her lead from Sheldon Annis' theory of the museum as an expressive medium, where visitors move between the overlapping symbolic spaces of the cognitive, the pragmatic or social and the dream (Annis 1987: 168–71). The 'dream space', writes Kavanagh, 'energizes both our imaginations and our memories':

> Anarchic and unpredictable, through the dream space we can arrive at all sorts of possibilities not considered by those who make museum exhibitions. In dream space, many things might tumble through our minds: bits of songs, half-written shopping lists, things left unsaid. The shape or shadow of something, its texture or colour, the operation of space and the people moving through it can be triggers to an endless range of personal associations. (2000: 3)

Though Kavanagh's analysis remains in the tradition of a dualist conception that prioritises the perception of a human subject over matter, her characterisation of the concept of a dream space none the less allows for reinterpretation via Bergson and Deleuze. It is a space where, rather in the way of the Proustian Madeleine, objects can call forth spontaneous actualisations of the virtual layers of past that they contain. As a passage from the CD-ROM *Immemory* suggests, one might even call such objects 'Madeleines': 'On en vient ainsi à nommer Madeleines tous les objets, tous les instants qui peuvent servir de déclencheurs à cet étrange mécanisme du souvenir' (so we come to call Madeleines all objects, all instants which can function as triggers for this strange mechanism of memory). Viewed in this way, even a little yellow doily can be a Madeleine, even if it does come from someone else's past.

This notion has consequences for the formulation of a conception of collective memory and the role that objects can play as points of connection both through time and between people. Mieke Bal draws on a similar idea in her discussion of the work of artist Ken Aptecar, who in his exhibition 'Talking to Pictures' drew on images from the Corcoran Gallery of Art in Washington, changing the framing or detail, and covering them with a layer of glass imprinted with text. For Bal, the paintings, as cultural images, bring with them their past, in terms of both their official history and personal associations, into the new context, where they are transformed and new associations created:

> Any visual or textual expression is a patchwork of fragments taken from different sources. The fragments have a memory: the word does not

forget where it has been, nor does the image. At the same time, every reuse of pre-existing material changes and exceeds it. (1999: 176)

Clearly for Bal the virtuality of the past resides in things in themselves, independently of subjective actualisation, but always carrying the potential for it. Her statement takes us back to the theory of intertextuality I elaborated in the first chapter. Film is, as Barthes said of writing, 'un espace à dimensions multiples' ('a multi-dimensional space') (Barthes 1984b: 69, Barthes 1977a: 146), woven with traces of the past. However, Bal's remark is in the context of an argument about cultural memory, which is to say a memory that is at once collective and personal, at once public and private.[2] It is a memory that operates through objects of common cultural knowledge, such as photographs, paintings, music, film and television, but still depends on the chance of either knowledge and recognition or research. She contends that such cultural objects have the potential to connect with shared traditions and histories. They are public objects, both on display and circulated as representations and reproductions, and therefore more likely than other objects to be familiar. To return to Macha Makeïeff's yellow doily, it is clear that most, perhaps all, objects have cultural associations of some sort. Nevertheless certain cultural objects stand out at one end of the spectrum because of their more obvious public visibility, while others might have accumulated less public knowledge or collective recognition. Yet this does not mean that such public cultural objects are not also quite private, even intimate, at the same time: they too may elicit the highly personal and unpredictable reactions and memories of the dream space.

It is perhaps this idea of a point of intersection, mobile and fluid though it may be, between public and private that is particularly attractive to filmmakers who want to find a means of representing the past in a way that recognises the blurred boundaries between the subjective and the objective. It could be one reason why Varda chooses to focus on Millet's famous painting Les Glaneurs (1857, Musée d'Orsay, Paris) as a catalyst for her films about gleaning. The painting is well known to the point where, as she points out with a close-up shot of the page at the start of Les Glaneurs et la glaneuse, it features in the illustrated Larousse dictionary. It is therefore a particularly suitable object both to evoke spectators' memories and to situate her own film in the history of representations of gleaning. By the second film, Deux ans après, the extent of the public familiarity of and private affection for Millet's painting has become an explicit theme. In what becomes a repeated gesture or pattern in the film, we are shown close-up shots of Varda's hands piling up postcards and images of the painting sent to her by friends and fans: 'Des glaneuses à gogo' (gleaners galore), as she says in her commentary, and, one is tempted to say, The Gleaners gleaned (Figure 2.2).

In her layering of these images one on top of the other, Varda mirrors the way one cultural object, in this case Millet's painting in the Musée d'Orsay, has been overwritten in cultural memory by layers of representation, rather like

Figure 2.2 *The Gleaners* gleaned in *Deux ans après* (2002).
(Source: © CinéTamaris.)

a palimpsest. Each individual object among the postcards or reproductions, in varying colours and textures, connects virtually not only to the original painting but also to the history of souvenirs and to the individual owners who cherished or disliked them. At the same time, through her use of 'je' in the commentary ('on m'en montre, j'en reçois, j'en vois partout' [people show them to me, I get sent them and I see them everywhere]) and through the filming of her hands, Varda inscribes herself into that history and those memories, a move I shall explore below in a discussion of the autofictions present in these filmic museums. In its visual and conceptual layering of memory objects, this scene of postcards of *The Gleaners* is another example of a crystalline time-image, where actual and virtual are coexistent and indistinguishable, and both past and present are rendered visible.

Such an image, a direct image of time, can form the basis of a historiography that recognises the fundamental strangeness of time, its distance from the common-sense linearity of clock-time that enables us to go about our daily business. Recent critical approaches to Godard's *Histoire(s) du cinéma* have attempted to theorise the kind of historiography at work in the films (for examples see Temple et al. 2004). In doing so, Walter Benjamin's theories have been called upon, his concept of the 'monad' in particular, to try to describe the way images function within the complex texture of the films. Youssef Ishaghpour's interviews with Godard have revealed how many of Benjamin's writings resonate with the conceptions behind Godard's own work since the mid-1990s (Godard and Ishaghpour 2005), but more specifically I find this discussion of historiography important as it provides another way of understanding how screen objects can function as time-images. In her essay on the Benjaminian character of *Histoire(s)*, Monica Dall'Asta sees the video works as constituting an approach to history that eschews the overarching narratives of conventional historians, by using découpage to convey what she calls 'the inexhaustible temporal density of the monad' (Dall'Asta 2004: 356). She draws the term 'monad' from Benjamin's 'Theses on the philosophy of history', in particular 'Thesis XVII' where Benjamin continues his opposition between two methods of history: 'scientific' universalising historicism and constructive materialistic historiography:

> Materialistic historiography [. . .] is based on a constructive principle. Thinking involves not only the flow of thoughts, but their arrest as well. Where thinking suddenly stops in a configuration pregnant with tensions, it gives that configuration a shock, by which it crystallizes into a monad. (Benjamin 1999b: 254)

Dall'Asta focuses on the film stills that Godard incorporates into the collage-like texture of *Histoire(s)*, seeing this stillness in terms of the 'sudden stopping' of thought, 'a sort of ideal filmic translation of Benjamin's "Messianic cessation of happening"' (p. 356).

In fact the concept of the monad can be aligned with a much broader consideration of memory objects in *Histoire(s)* and film more generally, if we revisit it via Deleuze's time-image and my reading of the latter in relation to the screen object. While the objects cannot in themselves be said to be monads, when they become direct images of time through their insertion into the filmic flow each one becomes a miniature shock or arrest, as the virtuality of the past constantly threatens to interrupt the forward motion of the film, and may actually succeed in doing so should the viewer pause to reflect on the historical or mnemonic evocations of the object. In this sense films that encourage 'transversal' readings, like those I am discussing here, have the potential to make historical materialists of us all, as we 'take cognizance of [the monad] in order to blast a specific era out of the homogeneous course of history' (Benjamin 1999b: 254). My primary concern here, however, is how these 'monadic' qualities of screen objects impact upon film as a space of cultural memory. In order to elaborate this I will need to examine in more detail the operation of the virtual and the actual in relation to movement and stillness in works by Godard, Marker and Varda.

Real and Virtual Museums

In some ways Godard's *Histoire(s) du cinéma* and Marker's *Immemory* could not be more different. The former is a video project, the latter a CD-ROM.

Histoire(s) is an exploration of the history of cinema and *Immemory* is a fictionalised autobiography, or what has come to be known as an *autofiction*. Godard's video films seem to mourn the end of cinema, while Marker's CD-ROM revels in the possibilities of new multimedia technologies. In addition, the styles of commentary differ somewhat between the two works, with Godard's spoken words forming a part of the collage on equal terms with the other images, and Marker's accompanying and unfurling words tending more towards a kind of meta-text, usually referring quite clearly to the images and objects in question. Despite these differences, however, there are areas in common between the two projects. For one thing both arise from long-term experimental projects on the part of their makers. Godard, commissioned to make a television series on the history of cinema by Canal Plus, began piecing together his extraordinary video montage in 1989, only completing the current four-volume version in 1998. *Immemory* grew out of Marker's 1985 *Zapping Zone* project, a multimedia interactive installation composed of fourteen video monitors, seven computers, thirteen PAL video disks, 80 colour slides, 28 photographs in black and white and colour, and seven computer programs on disk (Pourvali 2003: 89). The CD-ROM idea was launched in 1993, the same year that the definitive version of *Level Five* was begun, and was finally released in 1998, after another installation exhibition in the Georges Pompidou Centre in 1997, entitled *Immemory One*. *Histoire(s)* and *Immemory* could therefore be seen as two roughly contemporaneous, quasi-epic journeys into the past.

What is more, both works, in spite of the mournful tone of Godard's project, are explorations of the creative possibilities of rendering the past using the techniques and technologies of the present. Godard's use of the video editing suite allows him to exaggerate the operations of montage to an extreme extent, the juxtaposition of images becoming a rapid succession, or, more often, a high-speed flickering back and forth until they almost merge. At other times photographs, paintings or film stills dissolve slowly into one another, allowing the images to permeate and transform each other. Marker's experimental use of the CD-ROM format also offers new imaging possibilities. Of course such a format prevents any *Histoire(s)*-style speed of movement from appearing in *Immemory*, for the inclusion of a large quantity of filmic images would require more disk space than the humble CD-ROM could provide. In the book accompanying the original exhibition, Raymond Bellour explains that the installation title, *Immemory One*, anticipates not only the release of the CD-ROM but also a potential DVD-ROM, which would allow the work to take advantage of the ever-evolving possibilities of information technology. The vastly increased memory space of DVD-ROM would enable the incorporation of longer and more numerous film clips, which are the elements that require the most amount of disk space (Bellour and Roth 1999: 82). The clips, currently viewed in relatively small 'windows', might also be shown in a larger format. For the moment one can only dream of the use Marker might make of such increased capacity. The moving image itself would perhaps become a far more prominent memory object amongst the texts, paintings and photographs. In its current form the moving image remains a delightful discovery among relative stillness, akin to the precious moment of lifelike movement in Marker's 1962 film *La Jetée*, whose fleeting quality endows it with a particular poignancy.

Immemory none the less incorporates movement even in its current CD-ROM format, most obviously in the form of the few small film clips, but also in the movement between screens, the speed of which is dictated by the viewer. Something akin to the cut takes place at the click of the viewer's mouse, except that the cut, as in *La Jetée*, occurs almost always between still images. However, the click that takes you from one screen to the next often creates a movement between images in the form of a 'wipe', in particular one that involves the second image scrolling in from both left and right, seeming to squeeze out the first image in the middle. One final form of movement occurs in *Immemory*, and that is the movement of animation: words unfold across the screen, images peel away to reveal words underneath, and marks appear on the image. The movement of animation acts as a marker on *Immemory*'s screen objects, a move of appropriation that signals their place in a new context. Starting with one such moment of animated marking on the screen, I now want to focus on particular moments in *Immemory* and *Histoire(s) du cinéma* in order to explore the operation of appropriation of objects of cultural memory into the moving textures of film and CD-ROM. I will show how the alteration and juxtaposition of objects in Godard's and Marker's works affect their role as memory objects, ultimately suggesting that as *musées imaginaires* they create a dynamic, virtual zone of cultural memory, a dream space where the private intersects with the collective.

In an early screen of the *Voyages* zone of *Immemory*, a thick orange line draws itself around a particular sentence on a page of *La Famille Fenouillard*, picking out the words: 'ouvrage destiné à donner aux jeunes français le goût du voyage' (a work intended to give French youths a taste for travel). A shimmering sound accompanies this act of highlighting, reinforcing the effect of a kind of *invitation au voyage* (an invitation to travel, as in the Baudelaire poem with that title, see Baudelaire 1972: 83). The image is of an old edition of the book *La Famille Fenouillard*, open at the first page, perhaps the very copy that our 'imaginary' author cherished as a child. By the use of a childhood object the proposed journey is designated as being through time as well as space. It is a cultural object, an early precursor of the comic strip, first published at the end of the nineteenth century and reissued throughout the first part of the twentieth century, thus forming a childhood memory for several generations of French men and women. Even for those of us who were born in another time and country, however, it provides a connection with the past, a transmitted memory or postmemory.

In his article on the role of things as 'objectified identity', psychologist Mihaly Csikszentmihalyi proposes that objects 'reveal the continuity of the self through time, by providing foci of involvement in the present, mementos and souvenirs of the past, and signposts to future goals' (1993: 23). What is particularly striking about his study, which examined the meanings that household objects had for a representative sample of American families, is his conclusion that objects can hold memories of times that pre-date the lifespan of the remembering subject:

> It is not only the immediate family whose presence shines forth from special objects. [. . .] This is the quilt sewn by Aunt Elly, the bed in which Grandmother was born, porcelain cups from Great-grandmother's family, and the Bible inscribed by even more distant memories. (p. 27)

The idea of an object that bears a kind of memory that links us to a past we have not known seems quite normal in this everyday, familial context. Yet it is the same virtuality that connects Macha to the unknown owner of a tawdry yellow doily found on the streets of Paris, or the viewer of *Immemory* to the children who read a cartoon travel book, beautifully bound in red leather. In *Immemory* the complex unfolding of this opening part of the *Voyages* zone reflects a key theme in the work, that of the *musée imaginaire* that provides a virtual memory space conceived in terms of geography, a conception that, as we shall see, is also pertinent to the conceptual structure of *Histoire(s)*.

Godard too offers the viewer a double *invitation au voyage*, which like Marker's is through both time and space. In *Histoire(s) du cinéma: 2A seul le cinéma*, we see images of a young Julie Delpy in a domestic setting, reading out loud and reciting Baudelaire's poem *Le Voyage*. It seems to be the ideal image of the present, embodied by youth, connecting with the past through the nineteenth-century text. But the words of the poem also speak of memory, as well as the young person's relationship with the past and the future.

> Pour l'enfant, amoureux de cartes et d'estampes,
> L'univers est égal à son vaste appétit.
> Ah! Que le monde est grand à la clarté des lampes!
> Aux yeux du souvenir que le monde est petit!
>
> (Baudelaire 1972: 66)

> (For the child, in love with maps and prints, the universe is equal to his vast appetite. Ah, how wide the world is by the bright lamplight; how small it is in memory's eye!)

Here the child is figured as an avid collector of beautiful images, rather like Godard, Marker and Varda in their different ways. Postcards and prints are cultural objects that are recontextualised as screen objects in *Histoire(s)*, *Immemory* and Varda's gleaning films. It seems the perfect analogy for the cinema, whose history Godard sees arising out of the modernism of the nineteenth century, as he states in an earlier section of *2A seul le cinéma*, in an interview with Serge Daney: 'le cinéma, c'est l'affaire du vingtième siècle, c'est l'affaire du dix-neuvième siècle, mais qui s'est résolue au vingtième siècle' (cinema is the business of the twentieth century, it's the business of the nine-teenth century, but which was resolved in the twentieth century). Cinema, like a child in love with images, dreams of conquering the world. But in the place of a real journey through the world, travel is accomplished by fantasising about images seen in the 'clarté des lampes'. Godard has on more than one occasion used 'lamplight' as a metaphor for the cinema itself. One such occasion is in his *King Lear* (1986), where William Shakespeare Jnr V, on the hunt for the art of his ancestor after world culture has been destroyed in the Chernobyl disaster, is invited by the Fool (played by Godard) to see his new invention. This 'inven-tion' turns out to be a bulb, projecting onto a screen through a cardboard box where some plastic dinosaurs have been placed. As one French journalist has wittily pointed out, 'dans sa boîte à chaussures lumineuse, Godard dispose des dinosaures en plastique. Prophétie réussie, *Jurassic Park* sera tourné cinq ans plus tard' (in his luminous shoebox, Godard sets out some plastic dinosaurs. It is a successful prophesy: *Jurassic Park* will be made five years later) (Sotinel 2002: 31). In other words, a dark room, a lamp, a screen and a few scattered objects can symbolise a whole industry, with the emphasis on light reinforced by the coincidental name of those siblings most famously associated with the invention of the cinematograph, the Lumière brothers (*lumière* meaning light).

In the context of *Histoire(s)*, then, the start of Baudelaire's poem seems to offer an invitation to journey into the history of cinema, back past the moment of its invention to the nineteenth-century poetry and painting that seemed to dream it up. As Delpy recites, her youthful face dissolves into the image of a J. M. W. Turner painting, *Peace – Burial at Sea* (1842, Tate Britain, London), whose colours have been altered from dreamy greys to burning reds, yellows and greens, at once suggesting 'la clarté des lampes' and the distorted colours of postcards and print reproductions also made visible in the accumulated images of *The Gleaners* in Varda's film. As with the copy of *La Famille Fenouillard* in *Immemory*, the object is altered in becoming a screen object. Of course, all objects are altered in their incorporation into other artistic texts, by the operations of framing and juxtaposition that situate them in a new signifying context. But this is an alteration at the level of the object-image itself, which serves to defamiliarise it even as the potential for shared cultural memory it holds is being deployed. Altering the object as well as bringing it into a new context foregrounds the appropriation of the object by its collector-curator, setting up a series of virtual resonances within the screen object itself, which will then interact with the new signifying context.

This is rather like the Aptecar artworks discussed by Bal in her theorisation of the idea of cultural memory (see above). Aptecar not only covers his copies of the Corcoran Gallery paintings with a layer of glass sandblasted with text, but also changes them subtly, for example adding a faint telephone wire with birds on it to a landscape by seventeenth-century Dutch painter Meindert Hobbema (*A Wooded Landscape*, 1663, Corcoran Gallery, Washington, DC). Bal remarks how the incongruous addition oscillates in her vision with the familiarity of the landscape painting, the text overlay stimulating childhood memories of her own, at the same time as the painting draws on her memories of the Hobbema:

> I have an eerie sense of being surrounded by two temporalities simultaneously. [. . .] Wait a minute. A telephone wire, in a Hobbema? [. . .] The old masterpiece is wrested from its then-and-there to be planted in the here-and-now. (Bal 1999: 171–2)

Alterations, it seems, are a means of opening up museum objects to the dream space, as if giving the viewer permission to let personal memories mingle with shared, cultural ones. Thus the Turner painting becomes a burning ship rather than a burial in its new, glowing colours, the peaceful scene seemingly transformed by the explosion of the child's imagination, as well as by cinema's projection lamp. 'Aux yeux du souvenir que le monde est petit' (how small the world is in memory's eye), proclaims the Baudelaire poem, but the appropriation and transformation of objects from the past in Godard's cinematic history suggest that the world of the past is as limitless in its potential as the child's imaginary voyages, especially when seen in the bright lights of film itself. Read alone, the poem suggests that the dreams of youth enlarge the world, which shrinks with age and experience until, in old age, one has 'nothing but' memories. However, in the context of *Histoire(s)*, this stanza can be re-read in terms of the importance of traces of the past for the creative imagination. For, like the child's postcards of evocative images, cultural objects enrich our memories with images that extend back before the time of our birth, just as Godard extends his history of cinema back to before its invention.

I have been discussing just a few moments of *Histoire(s)*, but though the films are stocked like a museum with a wealth of cinematic, literary, photographic and artistic objects, these are all edited into a rhythmic flow that seems to resemble music rather than the stability of a museum. Indeed one might claim that it actively resists the museal in this sense. This impression is enhanced by the rhythmic clattering of the electric typewriter, on which Godard is seen to tap out slowly the words he is speaking, before setting off the typing mechanism. The click-clacking noise seems to beat the rhythm of the flickering images on the screen, emphasising their pulsing speed and continual changes. Antoine de Baecque has explored the paradoxical attitude to museums in Godard's work, picking out two models of museum that appear in Godard's oeuvre: the stultifying, conservative space of authoritative preservation on the one hand and a space of dynamic juxtaposition on the other. Drawing on a scene from Godard's 1964 film *Bande à part*, in which the characters Franz, Arthur and Odile race through the Louvre's Great Gallery in a less-than-ten-minute dash condensed into twenty-four seconds of screen time, De Baecque argues that 'from the outset, Godard has always entertained an initial polemical relationship with museums; to him they are derisory sites of great learning, which is inherited, defunct and conservative' (De Baecque 2004: 118). De Baecque points out, however, that the concept of the *musée imaginaire*, coined in André Malraux's *Le Musée imaginaire de la sculpture mondiale* (1952–4), allows Godard to reconceive the museum in filmic form, becoming what De Baecque terms a practitioner of museum-montage. In this way, De Baecque argues, Godard 'creates a work of art using the imaginary form of the museum: his ideal museum, following in the footsteps of Malraux, and later Langlois, is where artworks are brought together' (De Baecque 2004: 119–20). Marker also takes up the concept of *le musée imaginaire*, in his case quite explicitly. In the 'Musées' zone of *Immemory* a playful series of sequences explores the interplay of imagination and museums, culminating, according to the text that precedes it, in 'le vrai Musée Imaginaire, où les personnages vont au bal, échangent leurs vêtements et s'invitent l'une chez l'autre. Ici toute rencontre est bienvenue, nul étranger n'est mal venu' (the true Imaginary Museum, where the characters go to the ball, exchange their clothes and invite one another in. Here every encounter is welcome and no stranger is ill-received). There follows a series of screens in which Marker has wittily altered well-known paintings, adorning the slender back of Jean-August-Dominique Ingres' *Odalisque* (1814, Musée du Louvre, Paris) with a vast tattoo in the style of a Japanese samurai and having the two lustful men from Édouard Manet's *Le Déjeuner sur l'Herbe* (1863, Musée d'Orsay, Paris) gawp at the female nude on the internet, as pre-Impressionist cyber-porn. Here Marker takes the possibilities of montage suggested by the *musée imaginaire* to their digital extreme, allowing images to go beyond superimposition and to fuse together so that the virtual and actual jostle within a single frame. The CD-ROM format, seemingly more easily aligned with the fixed architecture of real museum buildings, in fact creates a space for virtual explorations, whilst allowing the movement and stillness between images or frames to remain in the control of the viewer.

It is important in this respect to note that the *Histoire(s)* films, seen on video or on the Gaumont (2007) and Artificial Eye (2008) DVDs, are made in a medium that allows the viewer to pause and rewind, pondering the connections between images. There is therefore a play-off between movement and stillness, between the forward-flowing pulsing of images and sounds and the vertical and even diagonal readings that come from breaking down this movement, following up the quotations and finding links between recurrent motifs. Even when watching the films without pausing, the frequent use of a flashing alternation between images or unfolding sequences prevents the viewing from being simply linear; a circularity is already present within the flow, a monadic crystallisation that continually flashes up and fades. Moreover, whether a Turner painting, a photograph of Rita Hayworth or an excerpt from an Ingmar Bergman film, the objects viewed are constantly drawing on the cultural and personal memory of the viewer, eliciting a transversal reading even as they interact with each other and are replaced by the next image.

In this respect the process of viewing the CD-ROM *Immemory* is less different than it might at first seem. For, as I have suggested, there too is a play between the linear sequence on the one hand and on the other a non-linear movement that both operates within the space of the work (the option of bifurcations and links) and extends beyond it into the past, via objects that contain the virtual layers of cultural memory. As we have seen in the *Musées* zone of the programme, Marker uses the formal possibilities of the digital format to elaborate the creative, dynamic possibilities of the museum. The *musée imaginaire* as an explicit theme extends beyond the *Musées* zone and into the overall structure of the work. Once you have chosen the option 'Entrée dans la mémoire' (Entry into memory), *Immemory* begins with a home menu screen offering seven zones, each represented by an image: *Cinéma, Voyages, Musées, Mémoire, Poésies, Photos* and *x-plugs* (Cinema, Journeys, Museums, Memory, Poetry, Photos and x-plugs). Each zone offers 'points de bifurcation' (bifurcation points) that appear during the sequence, either by clicking on a gold button that appears in the lower left-hand corner of the screen or via the appearance of Marker's 'mascot' cartoon cat and screen alter ego, Guillaume-en-Eygpte, whose speech bubble hints at the connection being made or the new direction being taken. The viewer can return to this point after a short detour by clicking on a red arrow in the lower part of the screen, or can make new turnings and end up in a completely different zone. Besides this, there is always the option to return to the beginning of a sequence or to the opening menu screen. It is an attempt to offer a new, more spatial approach to a screen media art form, perhaps inspired by the internet and its associated concepts of browsing and surfing through a web of linked information. As we have seen, however, elements of this spatial structure are already present in the collage form of *Histoire(s)*, and the structure is not the only means of creating depth from the screen's surface and temporal depth from the 'linear' movement. There are also the accumulated fragments, in the form of sounds and images, that bring memory with them into their new context.

BEAUTIFUL ACCIDENTS: CINEMATIC DEBRIS, POSTCARDS AND THE MEMENTO MORI

Varda's multi-installation exhibition *L'Île et elle* also offered the viewer a series of interconnected encounters with objects of cultural memory. Like *Histoire(s)* and *Immemory*, the exhibition, consisting of ten installation pieces disposed across two floors in the Fondation Cartier in Paris, created a play between movement and stillness, as well as between linear sequences and non-linear associations. Unlike the viewer of the works by Godard and Marker discussed above, however, the viewer of *L'Île et elle* had to move through real space rather than screen space, meaning that one particular location became integral to the experience of the work. Moreover, the exhibition was site-specific, conceived in response to the structure and ambience of the Fondation Cartier pour l'Art Contemporain, which since 1994 has occupied a magnificent glass-and-steel edifice designed by the acclaimed architect Jean Nouvel. Since the role of the Fondation Cartier is to host temporary exhibitions, this connection with a specific location meant that, unlike with videos or a CD-ROM, it was only possible to experience the exhibition during a finite period of time. It is of course possible that parts of the exhibition could be recreated in other locations at other times. Indeed, the three-screen video piece, *Le Triptyque de Noirmoutier* (2005), was previously commissioned by Martine Aboucaya and shown at the opening of her gallery on rue Sainte-Anastase in Paris (Varda 2006: 64). However the exhibition experienced as a whole existed only between 18 June and 8 October 2006. So while it might seem that this work by Varda moves a step closer to a real museum environment, its objects being displayed in the physical space of a public building, it nevertheless moves away from the kind of museal preservation (albeit dynamic and creative) offered by somewhat more permanent formats such as video and CD-ROM, to which viewers can repeatedly return.

Instead the work remains as a trace in the shared memories of the visitors to the exhibition, as well as in the aide-memoire of the accompanying book published by Actes Sud: a colourful collage of commentary by Varda, cartoon drawings by her friend Christophe Vallaux and photographs of the installations, as well as additions such as piles of old postcards, maps and preparatory sketches (Varda 2006). Thematically, as I will explore further on, the work is acutely concerned with questions of memory and mourning. Yet its temporal finitude means that reflection upon and analysis of the work also depend upon memory, mediated by material traces in the form of publications, photographs and notes. In this way *L'Île et elle* serves as an important reminder of the contingency involved in all engagements with cultural memory objects. Godard too draws attention to this when a series of titles in *Histoire(s) du cinéma: 4B les signes parmi nous* warn us that 'qui veut se souvenir / doit se confier à l'oubli / au risque de l'oubli absolu / et ce beau hasard que devient le souvenir' (those who want to remember / must trust themselves to forgetting / at the risk of absolute forgetting / and the beautiful accident that memory becomes). Objects can be lost, images forgotten, cans of fragile film stock eventually perish. Books, DVDs and videos can fall out of distribution and disappear from view. Already, some owners of the Macintosh version of *Immemory* may find that a recent change in the infrastructure of the Macintosh operating system (from OS9 to OSX in 2002, already ancient history in computing terms) means that their copy is no longer functional on their computer. Despite the seductive notion of digital media as virtual museums that would house the artefacts of shared experience forever, the circulation of cultural objects, even in digital forms, is in reality always at the mercy of accident and chance, in other words more akin to the workings of memory.

This undoes the dichotomy, discussed in Chapter 1, between the unreliability of living memory and the supposed permanence of the supplement. As I have suggested, the two can instead be understood as interdependent, each supplementing the other. It is in the contingency of moments of contact that memory-images are actualised from the virtuality of the past. To write about *L'Île et elle* is to subject myself to the beautiful accident of memory, mediated through the objects and traces that remain at my disposal. This seems particularly apt for a work that is so deeply concerned with that which is, or might be, forgotten or lost. As my analysis will show, Varda's fleeting and mobile virtual museum offered a brief encounter in a shared space of (im)memory.

Varda's gleaning films had already demonstrated her interest in waste, in that which is pushed to the margins of society. In those films, that which is forgotten, unnoticed or rejected by others finds new significance as part of an alternative creative context. This trope can be traced back to earlier films too. The short film *Les Dites caryatides* (1984), for example, is a playful contemplation of the sculpted figures that adorn the columns and archways of the nineteenth-century architecture in Paris. Nobody notices these graceful statue-women and powerful Atlases. They are forgotten in plain sight. Yet Varda's filmmaking brings them to our attention once more and reinserts them into the fabric of the city's cultural history, intertwining their stories with readings of Baudelaire poems and her own idiosyncratic musings. In *Ma cabane de l'échec* (2006), an installation in *L'Île et elle*, one of Varda's own films became the waste material that is seen, quite literally, in a new light. Inspired by the fishing huts and sheds of Noirmoutier, which are often cobbled together from reclaimed materials, Varda envisaged her own reclaimed shed made of unwanted debris. As well as emulating the use of undulating old sheets of corrugated iron, however, the primary material of Varda's 'hut of failure' consisted of strips of ageing 35 mm film stock from distribution copies of her film *Les Créatures* (1966), which was filmed in Noirmoutier. Seen from a distance, the rusty greys, reds and browns of the different materials, iron and film, blurred together anonymously. On closer inspection, however, the translucent walls and roof of the hut revealed themselves to be composed of hundreds of bands of tiny photographic images, each one imperceptibly different from those on either side of it. Placing the construction on its own in a spacious, light-filled section of the Fondation Cartier's ground floor meant that the strips of film were illuminated, no longer by the lamp of a projector in a darkened cinema, but instead by the natural daylight flooding in through the gallery's elevated glass walls. Some strips had deteriorated during the years spent languishing in their cans, and had become tinged with red or pink, like panels of stained glass, giving hints of rosy colour to the structure. In a manner akin to the altered tints of postcard reproductions of *The Gleaners*, or the over-saturated hues of Turner's *Burial at Sea* in Godard's *Histoire(s)*, here it is the film pellicle itself (originally black and white) that has taken on different colours as part of a new artwork. Undoubtedly we see the film with fresh eyes, witnessing the static secret of its photographic frames as well as its existence as a material object, vulnerable to the corrosive effect of the passing of time.

Les Créatures is a curious object of cultural memory, since it was chosen precisely because of its status as waste material, rejected by audiences and forgotten by critics. By definition we are not supposed to remember it. Varda makes a point of stating, both in the exhibition pamphlet and in the published book, that the film was a failure: 'tourné dans l'île bien sûr, ce film fut un échec commercial malgré de beaux et bons acteurs' (filmed on the island of course, this film was a commercial flop in spite of its handsome and talented actors) (2006: 38), a remark reiterated in the title of the work. Yet these images from *Les Créatures* sit nevertheless at the interstices of a shared, cinephile memory, since the actors visible in so many of the frames are easily recognisable, even in miniature. Both Michel Piccoli and Catherine Deneuve are iconic stars of French cinema, having acted in some of the best-known and most influential films in the French canon. Piccoli is eighteen years older than Deneuve but both were a part of the invigorating and transformative years of the *Nouvelle Vague*. Piccoli co-starred with Brigitte Bardot as the flawed and quietly frustrated writer Paul to her contemptuous Camille in one of Godard's most famous films, *Le Mépris* (*Contempt*, 1963). Just one year after *Les Créatures* Piccoli and Deneuve appeared together again in Luis Buñuel's notoriously perverse classic, *Belle de jour* (1967). Most significantly perhaps, the 20-year-old Deneuve acted and sang in Jacques Demy's colourful and poignant musical melodrama *Les Parapluies de Cherbourg* (*The Umbrellas of Cherbourg*, 1964) (later appearing in other films of his), so her appearance in *L'Île et elle* points to a connection with Varda's late husband, who is the central and absent 'Il' (he) of the exhibition's punning title (as in 'il et elle': he and she). Now veterans of the silver screen, both Piccoli and Deneuve continue to star in French and European films; unlike *Les Créatures*, they have not been consigned to the scrap-heap of cinematic history. This means that *Ma cabane de l'échec* not only brought to light a forgotten and marginal film; it also intersected with a broader cultural memory of French cinema, a shared domain with potentially infinite personal configurations for each viewer. There is also, of course, a personal significance for Varda, as the possessive pronoun in the title reminds us. Her life in cinema, her relationship with Demy and memories of happy holidays together in Noirmoutier, were evoked in a virtual 'dream space' of intersecting possible memories: beautiful accidents creating new encounters.

With her move into the gallery, the traditionally static realm of the plastic arts, Varda entered into a game of movement and stillness that is ultimately haunted by a preoccupation with death. Like film, the exhibition had a linear flow. It took us from *Ping-Pong, tong et camping* (2005–6), a playful collage of brightly coloured beach memorabilia incorporating a 6-minute looped film of seaside activities, to the final installation, *Les Veuves de Noirmoutier* (2004–5), a filmic polyptych consisting of fourteen videos of widows telling their stories, positioned around a central panel, a looped, 9-minute film of the widows circling a table on the beach.[3] Yet although the exhibition began with an upbeat evocation of childhood memories and seaside holidays, in fact, as we had no doubt realised by the time we reached the sombre image of widows on the beach, Noirmoutier is overwhelmingly a space of mourning for Varda. This adds to the significance of the attention given to waste and debris: lost objects are found, while found objects evoke the memory of what has been lost. Thus the objects encountered in this particular virtual museum engaged with the relationship between memory and death. In *Ping-Pong, tong et camping*, for example, the stillness of death haunted the rhythmic mobility of summer memories. A 6-minute film, accompanied by abstract music suggestive of underwater movement and the bouncing of ping-pong balls, was projected onto the undulating surface of an inflatable mattress, making wave-like ripples across the surface of the film. The screen itself became a memory object, a holiday souvenir surrounded by other found objects: plastic buckets and spades, beach rackets, and brightly coloured plastic bags. A slide show of photographs of patterned flip-flops (the *tongs* of the title) was projected within the circular frame of a vivid green inflatable ring. Within the overwhelming impression of movement and colour, these static photographs brought the artistic tradition of the 'still life' into the lively depiction of summer by the sea. The flip-flops were arranged with a painterly eye for composition and colour, placed against varying backgrounds such as tulips, peas, wallpaper or gift ribbons. The incongruity made it funny, but within the joke lay the suggestion of a memento mori, akin to the seventeenth-century Dutch canvases of flowers and vegetables, whose inevitable withering and decay reminded the viewer of the end of all living things. The appearance of plastic and plaster feet in some of the photographs reinforced this impression. Immobile and detached from any limb, there was something unnerving about these lifeless body parts. Although unlike flowers and even the silver acetate of film these feet would resist decay, their frozen fixity suggested death rather than life, making the empty flip-flops in other photographs seem curiously bereft of ghostly owners. Just as *Ma cabane de l'échec* reminded us of the still frames hidden within the illusion of cinematic movement, the exuberant dynamism of childhood memories was here subtly infused with the reminder of death. In Varda's Noirmoutier, as it is emblematically figured on the exhibition poster in an image of Varda seated on the beach next to a poignantly empty chair, memory is always a memento mori, reminding us of time's passing and the losses that it entails.

If in *Ping-Pong, tong et camping* an immobile foot hinted at death within the moving images of memory, in *La Grande carte postale ou Souvenirs de Noirmoutier* (2006) it was a moving hand that drew on the accidents of cultural memory in order to evoke the remembrance of the dead. This vast souvenir postcard (1.7m x 2.5m) was also not all it appeared to be. A multi-layered and explicitly interactive installation, it seemed to dramatise the way postcards can circulate as memory objects, as discussed above in relation to *The Gleaners*. But here film appeared within the postcard, rather than the other way around.

Varda's own take on *La Grande carte postale* recalls my argument about the transversal readings elicited by some films: 'il suffit de traverser la surface des images pour voir autre chose ou réveiller des souvenirs' (one need only pass through the surface of images to see something else or awaken memories) (2006: 31). In this case, however, this piercing of the two-dimensional surface was materialised in the physical structure of the work rather than solely taking place in the interaction with the viewer's memory, though the virtual dimension of memory was also simultaneously evoked. The jaunty postcard image of a female nude reclining on a sandy beach beside a shimmering sea (personalised with the face of Varda's daughter Rosalie) incorporated other images, both hidden behind its surface and projected, intermittently, over the top like a palimpsest. By pressing buttons operated from a podium opposite the giant postcard, viewers could open small windows in its surface to reveal four different 40-second videos. Behind the shapely buttocks were naughty schoolboys spying on a woman undressing, then playing a scatological practical joke on a neighbour. The seagull soaring through the sky concealed a bird in a very different plight: covered in black petrol, sticky and flightless, this was a victim of an oil spill. More sinister still, the dappled surface of the sea opened to reveal a drowned sailor drifting lifelessly down to the seabed, his hat floating upwards as the only trace of his presence (recalling the ownerless flip-flops). As for the blonde sunbather's hand, behind it lay another hand, a man's this time, with a fist of sand running between his fingers. Each of these moving image snippets embodies the potential associations called up by the contemplation of a postcard. In fact, the book of the exhibition reveals them to be just that: the filmmaker's associations, called forth metonymically from the forms in the image as they encountered her own memories. In turn they will have entered into circulation, awakening further memories in the exhibition visitor's mind, invoking other, unseen temporal layers.

But it was the hand in particular that offered the viewer a chance encounter in the sphere of cinematic cultural memory. For it was an image that was potentially familiar from another of Varda's films, *Jacquot de Nantes* (1991), the film she made as Jacques Demy was dying, which wove together reconstructions of his childhood with closely filmed and haptic images of his body, as though desperately trying to preserve the details and textures of his skin. Whether we recognised her late husband's presence within this holiday souvenir of Noirmoutier was down to chance, just as the proliferation of cinematic references in *Histoire(s) du cinéma* may or may not intersect with our own cultural knowledge. Beyond this, however, it seems to me that Varda's installation not only participated in the beautiful accident of cultural memory but also acted as a commentary on its functioning, by exposing the ghostly temporal layers that thicken the image from which memory may fleetingly crystallise. As though to emphasise this, the projection of another nude woman, her body glimmering as though underwater, appeared from time to time over the postcard's surface. Only those visitors who lingered long enough or arrived at the right moment were able to see this drowned phantom. Her grey-and-white colouring suggested old photography, while her hairstyle and morphology, so different from the buxom blonde in the postcard, also evoked another era. All objects, this fleeting apparition seemed to suggest, are haunted by the dead whom they survive.

Moving away from both the linear succession of cinema and the repeatability of DVD and CD-ROM, *L'Île et elle* none the less incorporated both these dynamics, while playing with the different layers of the screen that can be generated in three-dimensional viewing spaces. Most significantly, this temporary exhibition offered a critical alternative to the physical permanence of real museums as places devoted to preservation. Instead it created a transitory space that emphasised the double movement of time: its relentless falling into the past and its lingering virtual persistence.

MONUMENTS

Monuments are sites where time has a particular tendency to accumulate and thicken. They not only connote the passing of time through their commemorative function, which specifically suggests the inevitability of forgetting and death (the implication of any willed attempt at commemoration); they also inevitably come to be marked by time: weathered, worn, renovated or even removed. As screen objects they constitute a locus around which constellations of cultural memory may form even while signifying the past as resolutely past, and the continual possibility of amnesia. Chris Marker's film *Level Five*, with its exploration of the mass death and tragedy of war in conjunction with the personal experience of bereavement, provides a striking illustration.

The film weaves its documentary about the collective horror of the battle of Okinawa into the framework of a fictional individual's experience of mourning, in a curious blend of video diary, travelogue and computer game. It is difficult to summarise this complex film, constituted as it is by multiple layers. Its basic outline is as follows: the fictional heroine Laura is trying to reconstruct the battle on a computer program created by her boyfriend, whose recent death she is mourning. Positioned in front of the computer screen, Laura addresses her thoughts and feelings to her dead lover, reflecting on death, memory and, of course, Okinawa. Her video-diary-style monologues are interspersed with a voiceover commentary from a man she refers to as 'Chris', whom we assume to be Chris Marker himself. The second of these interjections deals with monuments, in a complex memorial interplay between public and private, history and fiction, and it is this sequence I want to look at in some detail. As the camera hovers over a series of tombstones, granite or white, broken or intact, the commentary tells us:

> Il était mort peu de temps après leur retour d'Okinawa, dans des circonstances jamais vraiment définies. Pour les amateurs de prémonitoire, ses

dernières images étaient celles du cimetière des étrangers à Naha. Il disait qu'il s'y voyait bien, entre les tombes délabrées des combattants de toutes les guerres inutiles et celle du Commodore Perry. Quatre-vingt-douze ans avant McArthur, le Commodore s'invitait un peu cavalièrement dans ce château de Shuri que les canons de la Deuxième Guerre Mondiale allaient réduire en miette. Et le Japon basculait dans les temps modernes. À croire que tous les siècles se payaient le besoin d'un militaire américain pour rentrer dans une nouvelle époque. C'est devant la tombe de Perry qu'il lui avait expliqué la phrase d'Oshima sur Okinawa sacrifié: le sutaïshi, un terme des jeux de Go, une pièce qu'on abandonne délibérément pour sauver le reste de la partie.

(He died shortly after their return from Okinawa in circumstances that were never really determined. For those who love premonitions, his last images were those of the foreigners' cemetery in Naha. He said he could easily picture himself there, between the dilapidated tombs of those who fought in all the futile wars and that of Commodore Perry. Ninety-two years before McArthur, the commodore had invited himself in a rather cavalier manner to the castle in Shuri, which would end up being reduced to rubble by the cannons of the Second World War. And so Japan toppled into modernity, as though every century had to saddle itself with an American soldier in order to move into a new era. It was in front of Perry's tomb that he'd explained Oshima's phrase about a sacrificed Okinawa: sutaïshi, a term from the game of Go, a piece one abandons deliberately in order to save the rest of the game.)

Here, the cemetery monuments are entered into circuits of meaning that show the way they are caught up in history, or rather, the way history is caught up in them. As screen objects they function as monads, conjuring flashes of history from different eras. The images of dilapidated cemetery monuments to foreign combatants resonate with the image in the commentary of the Shuri fortress reduced to rubble in the Second World War, through the ironic use of the figure of Commodore Perry, the organiser of an expedition to Japan in 1854, which resulted in a peace treaty being made between Japan and the United States. Through the interaction between commentary and image, the gradual corrosion of time and oblivion figured by the ruined monuments is juxtaposed with the explosive devastation of the battle, while McArthur's occupation of Japan in the wake of Okinawa and Hiroshima is underscored by the monument to Commodore Perry's 'cavalier' mission of peace. During the montage of tombs and monuments in the decaying cemetery, we are told that the mysterious (fictional) cameraman 's'y voyait bien' (could easily picture himself there), suggesting not only a curiously retrospective premonition of his imminent death, but also a link between him and the dead of Okinawa, a link that nevertheless keeps him separate, among the outsiders. The fiction of Laura's lover is further entwined with the documentary investigation into Okinawa when it is remembered (Laura's memory, relayed by Chris's voiceover) that it was in front of Commodore Perry's tomb that her lover had explained the Japanese sacrifice of Okinawa in terms of the game of Go. One is here reminded of the game of historical reconstruction Laura rehearses repeatedly, itself a cherished relic of her lost lover, and whose levels structure the film's investigation into Okinawa's past.

The senseless destruction of war is evoked in a series of reflections across the borders of history and fiction, circling around the void created by the absent figure of the lover, in itself a cipher for the pain of death and loss. This subtly woven sequence thus uses the fiction of a personal memory and mourning to reveal a series of circuits of virtual memory in the broken stones of the Naha cemetery, thereby preparing a way, at this early stage of the film, for the progressive anamnesis of the Okinawa catastrophe. Furthermore, as the film continues to accumulate images of statues, museum exhibits, tombs and monuments, we see that every fragment, incorporated into the fabric of the film, becomes a kind of monument. For each screen object, as we have seen, conserves a virtual trace of the past. In this way, even songs become monuments, imbued with multiple memories at the intersection between the private and the collective, the circuits of remembering always expanding to draw in Okinawa. At the level of fiction the song *Laura*, which is sung by Laura with poignant melancholy, the sheet music held up to the screen as though in an attempt to give further substance to the song as relic, acts as a memorial to Laura's relationship (it was 'their song'). But it also sets off a series of resonances: with the 1944 Otto Preminger film of the same name, which features another mysterious Laura who hovers on the boundaries of life and death, image and flesh; with the sad story of the song's composer; with Alain Resnais' film *Hiroshima mon amour* (1959), when Laura searches for a phrase that will express her feeling that her grief is both unique and commonplace, saying 'autant lui donner un nom qui sonne comme une chanson, comme un film: "Okinawa mon amour"' (one might as well give it a name that sounds like a song, or like a film: 'Okinawa mon amour'). The reference to Hiroshima finally leads us back once again to the human tragedy of the battle of Okinawa, through the 'chanson plutôt guillerette' (rather jaunty song), once the favourite song of the nurses. who suffocated in a cave hospital in Okinawa, now sung by the tour guide to coachloads of tourists being taken to visit the cave, which has become a monument to the dead. The song can be seen as a recuperated object that brings the virtuality of its past into a new signifying context. Altered by Laura's mournful voice and incomplete (Laura trails off as she sings it), it is defamiliarised even as it reaches out to the cultural memory of the spectator, ensuring that our attention does not slide off it like water down oilcloth, as the German writer Robert Musil, writing in 1936, complained of monuments.[4]

In Agnès Varda's *Les Glaneurs et la glaneuse*, it is first of all a painting that is presented as a monument: to the activity of gleaning. In the opening sequences of the film, Millet's painting of three female gleaners is portrayed as the material embodiment in cultural memory of this supposedly defunct activity, both as the illustration of the entry on 'Gleaning' in the old Larousse dictionary and as a photo-opportunity in the Musée d'Orsay in Paris. We are shown the comings and goings of tourists in front of the painting as it hangs in the museum, their movements accelerated to give the impression of the canvas as merely one point on a bustling cultural motorway. The film's attention to the multiple cultural significance of gleaning will cause us to wonder exactly what those museum-goers see as they look at the painting, some gazing studiously, many simply glancing at it or clicking the camera shutter before moving on. As a museum piece, does it indeed function as a monument, commemorating the disenfranchised of France's agricultural past, or even marking a crucial moment in the history of art when the ordinary and the poor began to be seen as acceptable subjects in painting? Whatever its position as tourist landmark in the Musée d'Orsay, the film attempts to make us see the painting anew, as part of a filmic monument to past and present gleaners and to the act itself of picking up what others have left behind or ignored. It does this, as only the moving image can, by animating the sculptural figures of Millet's painting into a repeated gesture, cutting from a montage of paintings and photographs of gleaners from the past to a shot of a present-day gleaner in the field, her body forming the same shape as the women in Millet's painting.

The stooping motion of the gleaners is an ambivalent gesture that signifies poverty and resourcefulness, waste and recuperation. Its cultural and political significance are revealed as a virtuality inherent in the repeated gesture, which in the film functions as a mobile monument, recalling the past yet continually reinscribed in a changing context. 'Si le glanage est d'un autre âge, le geste reste inchangé dans notre société qui mange à satiété' (if gleaning is from another era, the gesture remains unchanged in our well-fed society), remarks Varda, over the cut mentioned above, from Millet's gleaners to the mirror image of a modern gleaner in motion (Figure 2.3). In a short essay 'Notes on the Gesture', theorist Giorgio Agamben has described the gesture in terms of 'a crystal of historical memory, the process by which it stiffened and turned into a destiny, as well as the strenuous attempt of artists and philosophers [. . .] to redeem the gesture from its destiny through a dynamic polarization' (Agamben 2000: 53). The gesture of gleaning could indeed be seen in these terms, stiffened and turned into a destiny as an ongoing necessity for the poorest people, even in our age of abundance. Varda's film, in its commemoration of this particular historical memory, attempts to redeem the gesture from its destiny, showing its dynamic polarity. It is a creative, active tradition as well as a sign of destitution. As a gatherer of images and objects, Varda aligns herself with the gleaners, whilst recognising with her use of a politically charged rap song on the soundtrack that the other side of the gesture of gleaning as subversive, pleasurable and creative is the gleaning that is born of grim necessity. This polarity between stiffness and dynamism, that is to say the fixity of repetition versus the dynamism of

Figure 2.3 The gesture of gleaning as monument in *Les Glaneurs et la glaneuse* (2000). (Source: © CinéTamaris.)

change, is mirrored in the oscillations between the motionlessness of the objects we are used to calling monuments and the mobility of film, which as we have seen is inherently dynamic even in its moments of stillness.

These filmic monuments are charged with the virtuality of the past. *Level Five* in particular conveys a sense of this virtuality that emanates from objects by activating a series of commemorative resonances that render the 'could-have-been' (of the unnamed cameraman's 'last images') indistinct from the 'was' (of the cemetery's real dead). This could also be seen in terms of a Benjaminian historiography. As Dall'Asta notes in her gloss of Deleuze's notion of *les puis-sances du faux* (the powers of the false) (Deleuze 1985: 165):

> The power of time is essentially a power of falsification. What the flow of time fatally falsifies are the countless alternative futures that each present contains in the form of virtualities, the multitude of futures that will never become present and that time continually sacrifices in forcing the present to become past. (Dall'Asta 2004: 362)

For those who argue for a scientific historicism in the mode discussed above, the evoking of such virtualities might seem worrying. Indeed one might criticise a film such as *Level Five* for detracting from the real suffering of the events of the war by mingling the historical and the fictional in this way. I would argue, however, that this creates a space within documentary for all that cannot be known, for the pure virtuality of the past that is forever beyond our grasp. Godard seems to suggest something similar in his films, not only generally in his 'truthful' foregrounding of the fictional nature of films through self-reflexivity, but also specifically in a section of *Histoire(s) du cinéma: 3B une vague nouvelle*. In these sequences the titles inscribed on the frame posit an 'Égalité / fraternité / entre le reel / et la fiction' (Equality / fraternity / between [or 'enter'] the real / and fiction), as a series of alternating images flash rhythmically on the screen, mingling scenes from Truffaut's *Les Quatre cents coups* (*The 400 Blows*, 1959) and Hitchcock's *Vertigo* (1958) with a photograph of Godard himself and newsreel-style footage. That Godard should insert a stylised photographic self-portrait into this visual declaration of the interdependence of history and fiction is significant, as we shall see in the next section, for the filmmaker himself is inserted into the flow of objects of cultural memory.

THE FILMMAKER AS MNEMONIC PRISM

Something that the films discussed here, as well as *Immemory* and *l'Île et elle*, have in common is the striking presence of the filmmaker. Godard permeates *Histoire(s)* with the idiosyncratic timbre of his narration, as well as appearing frequently on screen: at a desk typing on a typewriter, standing taking books from his bookshelves (we assume they are his), in an interview with venerable film critic Serge Daney, and in the form of iconic photographs such as the one in the sequence discussed above. Chris Marker is equally present in *Immemory*, as the seemingly autobiographical, though explicitly interrogated, 'I' that leads us through the shifting territories of the past. In *Level Five* too, there is a 'Chris', designated as the filmmaker who has edited together Laura's video diaries and other footage given to him by her or found after her disappearance at the end. We do not see him, but we hear a voice we assume must be his, with the idiosyncratic Chris Marker style of commentary recognisable from his other films. As for Varda, she too is present in the two gleaning films, both in the 'I' of the commentary and visibly on screen. In *L'Île et elle*, she includes herself among the fourteen widows giving their testimony in *Les Veuves de Noirmoutier*, though she remains silent, for the whole exhibition, as we have seen, tells her story of bereavement. If the author is dead, these auteurs none the less haunt their films in body or voice, evoking a personal vision that rejects the totalising view of the traditional 'objective' historian. In *Les Glaneurs et la glaneuse*, Agnès Varda declares 'c'est toujours un autoportrait' (it's always a self-portrait), identifying the sense in which the subjectivity of the filmmaker inevitably shapes any attempt to document, something that revealed itself in the very fabric of *L'Île et elle*, which seemed to be constructed from the debris of her past. In her book *Varda par Agnès*, she also conveys a deep sense of integration between her own interiority, the subject she is documenting and the apparatus of filmmaking. At one point she recounts the making of her film *Daguerréotypes* (1975), describing the realisation, at the editing stage, that her passion for the subject-matter, a documentary about the local shopkeepers, was bound up with the cable she used for the lighting, which only stretched a certain distance through her letterbox, keeping her filming close to home and to her small baby: 'c'était le cordon ombilical, il n'était pas encore vraiment coupé! Mes voisins m'intriguaient depuis longtemps, certes, et ce documentaire me semblait nécessaire. Mais le film, c'était tout autant ce qui se passait en moi' (It was the umbilical cord, it hadn't really been cut yet! It is true that my neighbours had intrigued me for a long time and making this documentary seemed a necessary step. But the film was just as much about what was happening in me) (Varda 1994: 143). This is reinforced in *Les Plages d'Agnès* where Varda reconstructs on film the extension of the cord outwards through the letterbox, transforming visually for the viewer the physical geography of her neighbourhood into a personal, cinematic and affective space.

Les Plages d'Agnès is explicitly an autobiographical film, a cinematic memory journey that inevitably centres on the figure of the filmmaker herself. But as she looks back over her life, an internal movement illustrated by recurrent shots of her walking backwards through space, sometimes alone, sometimes accompanied, Varda brings to the fore the notion expressed above, that although the filmmaker's gaze looks out to the world it is always simultaneously a mirror to the self. Her response to this in the gleaning films is to reveal herself *as* filmmaker, as a subjectivity that acts as a prism through which the socio-cultural realm is refracted. In Varda's works, as in those of Godard and Marker, the subjectivity of the filmmaker becomes a catalyst for the circuits of virtuality that intersect personal and cultural memory. Like the objects they film, the filmmakers are themselves in a liminal position between private and public, between the private self that exists beyond the frame and the public persona of the screen 'I' that we hear or see. At the same time, their personae are partly constructed by the objects that captivate their filming gaze, their (fantasised) subjectivity conjured by the museal accumulation of memory objects and of the personal associations they weave between them in the operations of montage and commentary.

Of the three, Varda conveys the greatest sense of intimacy in her self-portrayal. Her voice relates her encounters in quirky detail, not as a faceless commentator but as an embodied 'I' who is also present on screen and whose body is an image amongst the others she is filming. From the start she casts herself as the eponymous *glaneuse* (female gleaner) of *Les Glaneurs et la glaneuse*, posing alongside Jules Breton's painting of a lone woman gleaner (*La Glaneuse*, 1877) in the art museum of the Ville D'Arras. She explains in the voiceover that 'l'autre glaneuse, celle du titre de ce film, c'est moi' (the other gleaner, the one in the title of this film, is me), before letting fall the sheath of wheat she has held in imitation of Breton's gleaner and putting a small digital camera to her eye. The lightweight, portable digital camera is a crucial factor in the intimacy she creates between the spectator and her body. It allows her, as she says at one point, to undertake 'cet exercice périlleux: filmer d'une main mon autre main qui glanait des pommes de terre' (a perilous activity: filming with one hand my other hand which was gleaning potatoes). Her hand is at once the filmmaker's hand, gleaning images with a camera, and the gleaned image itself. Varda underlines the importance of this by encompassing her whole gleaning project in these terms: 'c'est ça mon projet: filmer d'une main mon autre main' (that's what my project is: to film my hand with the other one). As she says this, we see a shot in which Varda films her own hand in extreme close-up, the wrinkled skin becoming the relief of a strange terra incognita from which the gold band of her wedding ring gleams. 'je trouve ça extraordinaire', she says, 'j'ai l'impression que je suis une bête. C'est pire: je suis une bête que je ne connais pas' (I find it extraordinary, it feels as though I'm a creature. It's worse: I'm a creature that I don't know). It is here that subject becomes object, or rather subject and object have become indistinguishable, yet simultaneously dislocated. The 'I' that speaks, which is the 'I' that films, no longer recognises the filmed 'I', which has become a creature, a thing. This returns to a theme in the film that addresses the passing of time and old age. In an early sequence we see a shot of her hair in close-up as she combs it, the white roots revealing that the rich dark brown, seen in the same long-fringed bob since the sixties, is no longer her natural colour.[5] She does not rail against ageing; instead she describes it as 'vieillesse amie' (my friend, old age). But she nevertheless witnesses the signs of her mortality in the changes in her skin and hair: 'il y a tout de même mes cheveux et mes mains qui me disent que c'est bientôt la fin' (still, there are my hands and hair which tell me that the end is near). Seen in extreme close-up as a filmic object, a gleaned image, her hand is suddenly revealed as old. It engenders the distancing shock of the self laid bare as a body in time, a mortal being. This simultaneous mingling and dislocating of subject and object, self and other, bring to mind a favourite phrase of Godard's, intoned by Anna Karina in *Vivre sa vie* (1962) and reiterated in a much later film, *Notre musique* (2004): 'Je est un autre' (I is an other). Rimbaud's phrase, ahead of its time in its postmodern implications, evokes the 'othering' of the self in writing, the self being implicitly absent from the 'I' speaking in the text, yet constructed there none the less.[6]

In *Immemory*, Chris Marker plays with the distance between the self constructed by the work and the self beyond it by making his cartoon cat, Guillaume-en-Egypte, tell the viewer:

> Si ce CD-ROM joue à simuler le jeu de la mémoire avec ses 'nœuds', comme disait Remizov, il n'est pas une autobiographie déguisée. Le 'Je' qui le commente est largement imaginaire, et l'auteur qui ne s'est évidemment pas privé de puiser dans sa propre mémoire s'est permis toutes sortes de libertés, tandis que moi, le chat intervenant, je ne me gêne pas pour y mettre ma patte.

(If this CD-ROM plays at simulating the game of memory with its 'knots', as Remizov said, it is not a disguised autobiography. The 'I' of its commentary is largely imaginary, and the author, who obviously did not deprive himself of dipping into his own memory, allowed himself to take all kinds of liberties, while as for me, the intervening cat, I have no qualms about sticking my paw in.)

While, as we saw earlier, Godard draws fiction into his *musée du réel* (museum of the real) (a label that repeatedly flashes up as a title), here Marker draws the real into his *musée imaginaire* by letting slip that the author's own memories really do form the raw material for *Immemory*, even as the autobiographical status of the work is being firmly denied. This can be seen in terms of a genre that has come to be called *autofiction* (sometimes referred to as 'faction' in English). This neologism, popularized by the writer Serge Doubrovsky in 1977, designates a text with clear or implied autobiographical elements that is none the less identified as fiction. In the case of Marker, everything we know about him suggests that 'he' is nothing more than autofiction. One might say that Marker (the man) is strikingly 'other to himself', seeming to exist for the viewer only within the realm of his films. He is almost never seen and his voiceover commentary is frequently voiced by someone else. Even outside his films photographs of him are rare: indeed there is only one, on the cover, in Sarah Cooper's book on Marker; only two in the otherwise well-illustrated Cahiers du Cinéma book about his work and life; and one in Catherine Lupton's monograph (Cooper 2008, Pourvali 2003, Lupton 2005). In each case a film camera hides Marker's face or draws attention away from it. It would be difficult to recognise him from this evidence. According to one source, when asked for a photograph, Marker 'mails off a picture of a cat' (Miles 1998). One imagines this could be Guillaume-en-Egypte again. The cat pops up as an alter ego in various of Marker's films including *Chats perchés* (2004), and even makes an appearance as a substitute for the director in Varda's *Les Plages d'Agnès*, with Marker's voice altered as a further layer of disguise. He has only very rarely granted an interview. His authorial name is in fact a pseudonym, his given name being Christian-François Bouche-Villeneuve. A constructed entity, an altered voice embodied only by a cartoon cat, 'Chris Marker' exists primarily in the form of screen objects, which contain the memories that form his identity. His subjectivity has become, in a sense, objective, transferred onto objects and gathered together in a web-like museum that resumes his persona as filmmaker: *Immemory*. It is a realm of virtuality where the dream-image and the memory-image overlap and coincide and where the real and the fictional are 'equals and brothers', to adapt Godard's formulation.

Reminding us of a quite ordinary way in which objects come to remember for us, Varda also suggests an identity constructed through an accumulation of objects: souvenirs. Playing on the double meaning, in French, of *souvenir* (memory/souvenir), Varda tells us in *Les Glaneurs* that for her, with an avowedly poor memory, 'quand on revient d'un voyage, c'est ce qu'on a glané qui résume tout le voyage. Quand je suis revenue du Japon, j'avais glané des souvenirs dans ma valise' (when one returns from a trip, it is what one has gleaned that sums up the voyage. When I came back from Japan I had gleaned memories/souvenirs in my suitcase). She spreads out before the camera her gleaned objects, which, like Krasna's filmed images in Marker's *Sans soleil* (1983), have taken the place of memories and therefore form part of her identity. This makes clear the affinity of Varda's conception of objects with that arising from Macha Makeïeff's art and ideas that I evoked above. The objects are kept and preserved because they have the capacity to carry the past as it is, but revealed on film these souvenirs form a dream space where Varda's 'memories' meet those of the spectator. Taking shape in her gleaning films, this is a concept that will later be elaborated in *L'Île et elle*, in which, as we have seen, moving images themselves become souvenirs, revealing the hidden accretions of memory within the detritus of Noirmoutier holidays. Marker also explores the concept of souvenirs through the association of memory objects and travel in *Immemory*. In the *Voyages* zone he invokes the figure of the Facteur Cheval. Ferdinand Cheval (1836–1924) was a postman from the village of Hauterives in the Drôme regions of southern France who, having experienced strange visions of a fantastic palace, gradually built the edifice of his dreams by accumulating stones picked up (and eventually collected by the kilo in a wheelbarrow) on his 10-kilometre postal route. Marker likens this collection of objects to his own gleaning of photographic images on his travels, describing them as 'de petits cailloux, chacun sans grande valeur, mais dont l'accumulation représenterait une espèce de château rêvé, un monde différent de celui-ci, sans doute meilleur, et pourtant extrait de lui' (little stones, each one without any great value, but the accumulation of which would represent a sort of dream castle, a world different from this one, better no doubt, and yet extracted from it). In a similar way to Varda's, Marker's travel memories are 'resumed', within the domain of *Immemory* at least, by objects: the photographs of distant places, each evoking a story, an impression, a moment in time. As the viewer moves through the different zones of the CD-ROM he or she discovers photographs of scenes from all over the world, often juxtaposed with texts that relate mini-narratives or highlight the particular meaning of the image for 'Marker'. However, the comparison of this accumulation of found objects with the elaborate construction of Ferdinand Cheval's palace emphasises precisely the constructed nature of Marker's material identity in *Immemory*. Here the filmmaker's identity is constructed in the image of a fantasy, a 'dream castle'.

The image of a 'dream castle' of gleaned fragments returns us once again to the idea of a museum as 'dream space', where objects evoke a mingling of imagination and memory, on the threshold of personal and cultural memory. At the start of this chapter I put forward the idea of a filmmaker-curator, but in these films the filmmaker's own identity is very much a part of the museum's holdings. It is through this conjunction of the filmmaker's objectified memories, the fabric of signification in the film, and the memories triggered in the viewer as part of a common sphere of knowledge that the moving image stands as a privileged space for revealing the intersubjective workings of memory. To borrow from and reconfigure Hirsch's formulation of postmemory, it is through 'an imaginative investment and creation' that we access both our own memories and those of others. As Godard suggests by giving the title *Notre musique* (our music) to a film that aims to evoke Sarajevo as a place where the memories of different conflicts can converge, moving image texts can draw on those shared spaces of cultural resonance where personal memories are mediated through a collective flow. Throughout this chapter I have been rejecting a model of memory that depends upon the authenticity of recall and moving towards one which recognises the dynamism of memory as actualisation of the radical virtuality that is the past. The screening of objects in the imaginary museums of moving image texts reveals the ways in which material things form a part of the social frameworks of memory, where film both mirrors the functioning of cultural memory and forms a part of it.

NOTES

1. Marks also seizes upon Benjamin's image of the bricoleur to refer to transnational filmmakers' deployment of objects: 'bricoleurs – people who take the rubble of another time or place, invest it with new significance, and put it to new purposes – create the possibilities of new history' (Marks 2000: 88–9).
2. See discussion of her argument in Chapter 1.
3. In fact, as with a DVD or CD-ROM rather than a film projection in a cinema, the viewer can pause to contemplate an image, return repeatedly to a particular moment, and even disrupt the linearity by ignoring the official 'sens de la visite' (direction of the visit). For further discussion of the emotional role of these simultaneous linear and non-linear possibilities in *L'Île et elle*, see my essay 'Agnès Varda's moving museums' (McNeill 2009).
4. 'There is nothing in the world as invisible as monuments. There is no doubt they are erected in order to be seen, indeed to arouse attention, but at the same time they are somehow impregnated against attention: it runs down them like water on oilcloth, without stopping for an instant' (Musil 1986: 320).
5. Varda's hairstyle is made iconic in her book *Varda par Agnès*, both figuratively – we see it in every photograph of her – and literally, in a mosaic portrait which resembles a Byzantine icon (Varda 1994: 10).
6. The phrase 'je est un autre' appears in both of Rimbaud's so-called *Lettres du 'Voyant'*, declarations of his poetic intent written to Georges Izambard and Paul Demeny in May 1871.

3. FACING THE PAST

In Chapter 2 I explored filmic strategies that offer alternatives to reconstruction in attempting to render the past on screen. Filmed objects were seen to contain potential pasts that generate circuits of virtuality, creating the possibility of both a temporal and spatial overflowing of the filmic text. Varda's postcards and old strips of film, Marker's photographs and monuments, and the myriad melodies and quotations, film clips, photographs and paintings that make up the museal fabric of Godard's *Histoire(s) du cinéma* (1989–98): such memory objects, be they sonic or visual, elicit transversal readings or viewings of films. They offer up intertextual links to the past, thereby acting as a point of intersection between the memories of filmmaker, viewer and the broader collective sphere. In this chapter I want to look at another type of access to filmic remembering. In fictional as well as documentary films, the oral testimony of witnesses has long been employed as a device for figuring the past. It is a strategy that tends to draw our attention to individual subjectivities, focusing on the embodied experience of one person's remembering process. But as a conduit of filmic memory, I shall argue, the faces of testimony, like the filming of objects, offer productive and powerful ways of bridging private and social pasts.

In mainstream fiction films, the tendency has been for the remembering subject's testimony to be consigned mainly to the soundtrack, while the image-track undertakes a simultaneous reconstruction of the events being described, in the form of a flashback. This practice has also appeared in documentary films where either images of archival footage or photographs, or, more unusually, dramatic reconstructions, may accompany the witness's narration of memories. Frequently, however, for a range of different reasons, documentary films that use testimony present us with the remembering witness on screen. In this context a particular importance has come to be attached to the face of the remembering subject or witness (these two designations merge in the testimonial act). As witnesses speak about their memories on camera, responding to questions or other prompting from the filmmaker(s), they are often filmed from the waist or shoulders upwards, creating a particular emphasis on their face. It is as though the camera wishes to capture their words more fully by homing in on the physical body from which they emanate or else to find the truth (or falsity) of their words in the shifting folds and surfaces of the face. Unlike written testimonies, this kind of oral, filmic testimony renders visible the physicality of the witness, showing the movement and stillness of their features as they speak, think, remember, smile or weep, and layering their words with the sonic texture of their voice. I want to begin by exploring the role of the human face in filmed testimony and how filming people's faces as they remember or recount their memories can be seen to inflect the mnemonic operations of films. Taking the discussion through a series of examples from the stark documentary work of Natacha Samuel to the museal, melodic collage of *Histoire(s) du cinéma*, I want ultimately to suggest that filmed faces too become positioned at the intersection between personal and collective memory, figures of a remembering subjectivity yet also part of the sensory framework that structures memory.

Bodies, Time and Authenticity

The emphasis on the visual image of the act of testimony suggests that the body of the witness is seen as a guarantor for the truth of the testimony. We are presented with visible evidence of the two cornerstones of witnessing: 'I saw it' and 'I am here to tell the tale'. Leaving aside the vicissitudes of the fundamentally labile operations of human memory, the idea that what we are seeing is the same body physically present at the remembered events, the same eyes that looked upon those events, the same voice that spoke or was mute in response, suggests a powerful sense of connection between past and present. It is different from written testimony because of this extraordinary sense that the transmission of the testimony comes through a living being whose body has existed in time. The face and body can be markers of time, ruined monuments like the ageing features of Marcel's friends and acquaintances in Proust's *Le Temps retrouvé* (1988b), or of Simone Genevoix, the childhood idol whom Chris Marker's persona in *Immemory* (1998) finally meets as an old woman. The wrinkles and scars of old age in themselves bear witness to the passing of time, and to the continued presence of a physical body in time that is constantly falling away from the present.

However, filming a person in conjunction with a recounting of her or his memories differs from the transient experience of meeting and listening to testimony, for it offers a reproducibility that allows witnesses to be seen long after they are no longer alive to testify in person. Thus when Jacques Aumont writes about the relation of the cinematic face to time, he asserts that 'ce qu'on cherche sur le visage c'est le temps, mais en tant qu'il signifie la mort' (what one seeks in the face is time, but in as much as it signifies death) (Aumont 1992: 192). It was this deathly temporal duality that Roland Barthes discerned in photography. Responding to a photograph in which the subject is both already dead (in the present) and going to die (at the time of the photograph), Barthes evoked in *La Chambre claire* the notion of 'un futur antérieur dont la mort est l'enjeu' ('a future anterior of which death is the stake') (Barthes 1980: 150, Barthes 2000: 96). Photographic images are haunted by the absence of their subject, as their body is frozen into a death-like pose: 'je frémis [. . .] *d'une catastrophe qui a déjà eu lieu. Que le sujet en soit déjà mort ou non, toute photographie est cette catastrophe*' ('I shudder [. . .] *over a catastrophe which has already occurred.* Whether or not the subject is already dead, every photograph is this catastrophe') (ibid.). For Barthes, the cinema lacked this uncanny power. The diegetic temporal movement of narrative and the linear motion of editing smothered the insistence of the photograph's ghostly claim to the real, he claimed, as the spectator was led on from one image to the next:

> Au cinéma, sans doute, il y a toujours référent photographique, mais ce référent glisse, il ne revendique pas en faveur de sa réalité, il ne proteste pas de son ancienne existence; il ne s'accroche pas à moi: ce n'est pas un *spectre*. (1980: 140)

> (In the cinema, no doubt, there is still a photographic referent, but this referent shifts, it does not make a claim in favor of its reality, it does not protest its former existence; it does not cling to me: it is not a *specter*. [2000: 89, translation modified])

However, as Aumont's discussion of the search for time (as death) in the cinematic face implies, the photographic element of film does not slip away as easily as Barthes' distinction would suggest. Laura Mulvey argues that this spectral fixing of 'past-presence' returns in contemporary viewing practices, as pause and delay are introduced into the film via the remote control. In *Death 24x a Second* she explores in detail how the deathly stillness at the heart of the cinematic illusion can be rediscovered in new viewing modes opened up by DVD (Mulvey 2005). However, even in a theatrical viewing situation, the filmed face of a witness can take on the powerful sense of *ça a été* (that has been) and uncanny temporal layering that Barthes ascribes to still photographs, for the reasons mentioned above: the very act of testifying emphasises the witness's body as a marker of temporal duration, the sense that 'they were there and they are here'. The unavoidable implication is that their filmed testimony will survive them into the future. But if the visible presence of the face and body of the witness does signal a former, real presence, what of the inevitable and deathly *absence* of the referent implied by the very fact of reproducible representation? In other words, is filmed testimony in some sense inauthentic by nature: the repetition of the automaton rather than the lived experience of transmission?

To untangle this question we need first to dispel the persistent illusion of the body's power as guarantor of the past. Like the pure, physical referentiality of photochemical traces on film, the pure, physical referentiality of the body (of a being existing at an earlier time) is a myth. Or rather it is a truth elevated to mythical status, marginalising other more significant factors. As we have seen, although an acetate or celluloid film does record traces of real light reflected by real objects, this does not guarantee its referential truth: the image is no less prone to technical manipulation as well as to both formal and contextual framing; reality remains cinematically malleable. At the same time, the lack of a physical, photochemical trace does not preclude referentiality: digital video can just as well signal the presence of real objects at a given moment in time. By the same token, the presence of a recognisable face and body does not guarantee an authentic connection to the past. The problems of deceit and forgetfulness aside, the human body is plastic and malleable, constantly renewing its cells and adapting to its environment. Over a period of seven years every cell in the body will be replaced. Of course we are not in total flux; there is physical continuity in our genetic coding and long-term neurochemical memory traces; but the fundamental paradox of our bodily identity is that, situated in time, we are different as much as we are the same. Moreover, as we shall see below in a discussion of Giorgio Agamben's theory of the face, bodies are inseparable from their socio-symbolic environment, which can be said to construct them as much as they construct it. One should therefore be wary of giving too much theoretical weight to the notion of bodily presence and contact for questions of memory and authenticity, recognising instead the symbolic significance and affective power of the suggestions of presence and absence, visibility and invisibility, that pervade the filming of the act of testimony. The body or face of a witness is no real guarantor of the authenticity of memories or testimony. It does, however, reveal filmed movements and sonorities that have their own language, the language of bodies, and whose interaction with other audiovisual elements can speak volumes both about the past and about our processes of remembering it.

Focus on the Face

There are several reasons why faces appear to hold a privileged position in the visual representation of testimony. Faces, in modern Western traditions of art, have been seen as the most powerfully expressive sites on the body. As John Brophy puts it:

> When we think of the human face we think of it almost always as an instrument of expression, used to convey – to those who are able to understand what they see – an almost infinite variety and gradation of thought and feeling, manifested as decisions and judgements, desires, opinions, moods and instantaneous reactions to external circumstances. We think of the face also as recording the total effect of such transient expressions over a lifetime, so that it provides something like a visible index to the personality of its owner. (Brophy 1963: 16)

While classical and medieval art subordinated the face to the body, giving statues and icons generic, mask-like features, the tradition of inscribing coins, medals and stamps with the head of the monarch has a long history, suggesting that, as our contemporary use of passport photographs shows, it is the face that is our most immediately identifiable body part, our bodily signature.[1] It also seems plausible that, as Brophy argues, the importance of facial representation has grown with the modern conception of the individual self or subject, hence the increasing emphasis on facial likeness in portraiture, which has become increasingly concerned with capturing a unique personality in the features of the sitter and less with signalling the subject's social standing and activities. The face has come to be seen as the surface representation of a subjective interiority. Home of the eyes, which, as the expression has it, are 'the windows of the soul', and the mouth, which is the instrument of verbal communication for all but a small minority, the face also houses two further sensory organs: the nose and the ears. It is therefore one of the key bodily sites for the reception and emission of information about ourselves. By representing what is most individual about us, it seems the face becomes a privileged image of the self, giving rise to the use of photographs in memorials, such as in the museum of Emaioli in Okinawa, the site of the horrific death of a group of schoolgirls, as well as many other civilians, during the battle of Okinawa at the end of the Second World War. In Chris Marker's *Level Five* (1997), as Laura tries to reconstruct the events of Okinawa on the computer game left to her by her deceased lover, Chris's voiceover tells us that 'le jeu n'en avait retenu qu'une chose, les visages. C'était d'ailleurs suffisant' (the game had only retained one thing: their faces. Moreover that sufficed), as Laura's computer screen fills our screen with a sequence of black-and-white portrait photographs of young girls with serious faces. We know that each face we see is that of someone whose life was cut short in terrible circumstances, and the haunting effect of the Barthesian 'future anterior' is emphasised by the rigid immobility of the still photograph. That these images are deemed sufficient to express the tragic loss of such young lives indicates the extent to which faces function as signs of an inner subjectivity, able to counteract the numbing effect of numbers and statistics, or even of images of piles of 'faceless' corpses. But if the face has the ability to engender a sense of subjectivity with such force, it is largely because of its role as an interface between emotions and social interactions, a crucial means of absorbing and responding to the world.

In positing this notion of a focus on the face it is not my intention to divorce the face from the rest of the body. Indeed the hands or other body parts, even clothes or jewellery, may be seen not only as subtexts that frame and interact with spoken or facial language but even as an extension of the face: the face as sur-face, as external locus of subjectivity, as inter-face with the world. The association of sensory organs, such as the eyes and the mouth, with expressivity and communication may account for the significance given in film (and throughout the history of Western art) to the hands – second only to the face in prominence. The hands are powerfully expressive, whether through gestures made while talking or nervous tics and habits, and they are also the focus of our sense of touch. Filmmakers often make use of the expressive possibilities of moving between face and hands in order to send emotional signals to the viewer. The hands are therefore a supplementary means of communication, with their own gestural codes that may either enforce, contradict or form a counterpoint to spoken language and facial expression, as will be seen with relation to *Pola à 27 ans* (Natacha Samuel, 2003). However, the hands are not the only framing element that affects our perception of the face of the witness.

The significance and emotive power of faces move beyond the confines of the body into the surrounding space, social context and other framing elements. In film the editing process in particular allows a whole range of contextual elements to underscore our 'reading' of the minuscule movements of facial muscles, as demonstrated in the famous Kuleshov effect (see Joyce 1999). In 1919 Lev Kuleshov undertook a series of editing experiments which led to a startling discovery. In separate sequences, shots of various objects such as a bowl of soup, a smiling child and a dead woman were juxtaposed with identical archive clips of a famous actor, Ivan Mozhukhin. The audience read a different meaning into Mozhukhin's expression with each combination. This discovery demonstrated the power of editing to alter the perception of emotions and thoughts in a face. Mozhukhin was purportedly praised by the audience for the finesse of his facial expressivity. But while such contextual factors are always crucial in how we read faces, psychological research shows that facial expressions call forth interpretation in and of themselves. The face functions both as the site of involuntary reactions to feelings and thoughts and as an important means of social communication (see Nummenmaa 1992). Indeed, empirical research has demonstrated that not only are we generally able to recognise the facial expression of the so-called 'primary affects' (interest, joy, surprise, fear, anger, distress, disgust-contempt and shame), but recognition of such emotions in the face transcends cultural background (Ekman et al. 1969, Ekman et al. 1992: 63–4). Moving images are the ideal means of recording such expressions, for as John Ligget puts it, 'it is movement which is the essence of expression' (Ligget 1974: 261). Real emotions can be visible in the face, but subjects also use facial expression as an extension of language – coded expression that may or may not relate to the experience of feeling. While these two elements inevitably overlap, they often remain indistinguishable, bar a few recognisable movement-signals that can sometimes allow us to detect deceitfulness in an interlocutor. The filmed face, then, presents us with an image that expresses and communicates, constantly offering up meaning only to withhold any fixed or final truth about the person's inner experience. None the less, seeing an individual's face as her or his testimony unfolds undoubtedly frames the memories just as the act of remembering can be seen to frame our perception of the face.

FRAMING THE FACE OF TESTIMONY

In Claude Lanzmann's seminal nine-and-a-half-hour documentary *Shoah* (1985), the image of the act of testimony replaces any attempt to render visually, through archival footage or fictional reconstruction, the past events that are being remembered and described. Avoiding the potentially sensationalist horror of direct representations of the atrocities of the Shoah, Lanzmann's film is instead structured around interviews in which survivors are asked to remember and talk about deeply traumatic experiences in the death camps of the Second World War, such as Auschwitz. This can be seen as an ethical approach to the difficulty of representing such horrific experiences in a manner that avoids the possibility of easy recuperation on the part of the spectator, an idea embodied in Lanzmann's often polemical statements condemning representation of the Holocaust. Libby Saxton analyses this idea in detail in her book on the ethics of filmic testimony, concluding that in Lanzmann's films, if not in his discourse, representation remains crucial in transmitting the memory of the Holocaust, in particular by highlighting the continuous attempts of the perpetrators to efface the traces of their crimes: 'by juxtaposing oral accounts of the atrocities with the sight of traces under erasure and empty graves, *Shoah* makes disappearance and absence disarmingly present to our eyes and ears' (Saxton 2007a: 32–3). Nevertheless, the rejection of certain kinds of audiovisual representation, such as reconstruction or archival footage, places an emphasis on the otherness of a past we as spectators have not ourselves witnessed. For Lanzmann the spectator must accept a certain blindness to the event in order to recognise the impossibility of a complete understanding of what the witness has experienced.

On the other hand, facing the past through a visual focus on the face is also potentially problematic, as the filmed face of the witness is laid open to an infinite number of unseen gazes. The intimacy of the act of testimony, often experienced in a fairly small group or even as a one-on-one conversation, is revealed to an unknown mass of viewers who do not have to meet the witness face to face in physical proximity. Though this transmission of the message of testimony beyond immediate interlocutors is imperative if personal experiences are to be useful to society, it could also seem like a one-sided encounter, in which the spectator's role resembles that of the interrogator shielded by darkness while the witness sits exposed and blinded by the light. Can showing the face of the witness on film really evoke in the spectator an awareness of her or his blindness to the past experiences of the witness? Or does the face, on the contrary, open up for the spectator an unethical position of judgement and power, a sense of certain knowledge? Drawing on Giorgio Agamben's essay on 'The face' (in Agamben 2000) as well as examples from Natacha Samuel's *Pola à 27 ans* and Chris Marker's *Level Five*, I now want to examine in more detail the shifting operations of framing at work in the documentary use of the face of the remembering subject.

Agamben opens his essay on politics and the face with the following statement:

> All living beings are in the open: they manifest themselves and shine in their appearance. But only human beings want to take possession of this opening, to seize hold of their own appearance and of their own being-manifest. Language is this appropriation, which transforms nature into face. (Agamben 2000: 92)

Agamben is here describing the way that appearance, in itself just an opening onto the world, is framed by social factors and made to symbolise. Filming faces is, in this sense, a double framing, especially where the person is speaking, meaning that two kinds of language – filmic and linguistic – are working to construct the face. Marker's *Level Five* plays on these double framings in an oscillation of proximity and distance. The film draws on the emotive power of the human face (as will be explored in more detail further on), whilst reminding us that just as the face may be seen as a series of masks or projections, so the events of the past are ontologically slippery and always framed in the present.

Level Five suggests at times a televisual aesthetic, this impression being generated in part by the extreme proximity of Laura's face as she talks to the camera in a video-diary-style monologue. Because Laura is frequently positioned closer to the screen than the conventional head-and-shoulders 'talking head' shot, the viewer feels uncomfortable confronted with her vulnerability as she confesses intimate feelings, moving seamlessly between the banal and the profound, as one does in private. In addition, Laura's soliloquy is addressed to her deceased lover, increasing the viewer's perhaps uneasy sensation of glimpsing intimate and private moments. Her 'log-ins' (each dated on the screen, like a precursor of the now-ubiquitous internet 'blog') are interwoven with the sequences of commentators on and witnesses of the battle of Okinawa, whose testimony Laura accesses via the computer 'game' by clicking on the option 'eyewitnesses' on a screen menu. Here we recognise a more familiar mode of face-to-camera testimony, where a combination of witnesses and experts provides commentary and analysis of the battle. Yet when Laura finally discovers that the Kinjo she has read about in her lover's electronic documentation is the eyewitness Shigeaki Kinjo, whom we have seen talking earlier, his words, and face, take on a particular poignancy for the viewer. Suddenly, framed by the intimate quest of a bereaved lover, Kinjo's face becomes marked with the tale of how as a child he, like thousands of others during the battle of Okinawa, killed his mother and younger brothers and sisters rather than let them fall into the hands of the Americans and English. Like the series of virtual masks Laura wears when she logs on to the internet-like virtual-reality world called the Optional World Link (O.W.L), the framing of the testimonial face of the witness is revealed as a series of projections, historical or emotive, through which the filmmaker (whose commentary intersects and interacts with Laura's) and heroine try to construct the past, anticipating and foregrounding the viewer's attempt to do so.

This illuminates Agamben's statement that the revelation of the face does not have any real content, it is, he says, '*only* opening, *only* communicability', vulnerable to co-opting by economic and political structures (2000: 91). Marker's overt foregrounding of technology in *Level Five* serves to draw attention to the face of the witness as participating in the contemporary world of *communication*, a word that in French has come to refer to the consumer world of media and advertising. From the city lights and cyber-network diagrams superimposed on the blank face of a mask or sculpture at the start of the film, to the electronic beeps and tones on the soundtrack, as well as the frequent images of the computer screen itself, the visibility of information technology in the film makes the spectator acutely aware not only of the constructed and produced nature of the image, but also of its situation in a whole network of imaging practices that take hold not only of faces as sites of communication, but also of collective attitudes to remembering.

Tellingly, a sequence of consumer-culture faces follows Chris's commentary on the Japanese amnesia surrounding the Second World War and forms a link to the testimony of the first witness, Kenji Tokitsu.[2] In a phrase that echoes the philosopher Jean Baudrillard's concept of the simulacrum, Chris tells us that 'j'étais devenu tellement japonais que je participais de l'amnésie générale, comme si cette guerre n'avait jamais eu lieu' (I had become so Japanese that I was participating in the common amnesia, as though this war had never taken place) (see Baudrillard 1991). This is followed by a montage sequence that incorporates images from Japanese TV, war footage of aerial bombing, manga anime sequences and footage from the streets of Tokyo. The images are overlaid with the soundtrack of a radio programme called *Tokyo Today*, with a catchphrase – 'Goood Mooorning Tokyo!' – that recalls Barry Levinson's 1987 film *Good Morning Vietnam* (and by extension the original military radio show, hosted by Adrian Cronauer, upon which it was based). Into this dense evocation of war through the circulation of popular culture in Tokyo comes the face of Kenji Tokitsu, slowly forming in thickening pixelated waves until a photographic image is reached. By this time we are already hearing his commentary, in which he states that the Japanese have wanted to bury the Second World War and have tended to avoid confronting this period of their collective past. Tokitsu's face, then, is initially represented as a computerised cipher that must be mouse-clicked in order to view video footage of his testimony. Emerging from a morass of images, his face is where the conceptual threads relating to the memory of war finally converge, with the designation 'witness' (highlighted on a computer menu list) finally positing a direct link with the past. As he speaks of an extreme intensity experienced in combat during the Second World War, he makes several references to *facing* (he speaks in French): 'se faire face avec quelque chose' (facing up to something), 'face à quelque chose' (faced with something), while Chris (*l'as du montage* [the editing ace], as Laura has just dubbed him) intercuts Kenji's face with a larger-than-life grinning visage on an advertisement banner and an inflatable doll version of Edvard Munch's *The Scream*. Even more explicitly reminiscent of the O.W.L masks, the garish faces suggest a consumption-driven, mediatised façade, masking or screening out Japan's past. Inserted into the flow of the film, however, they frame Kenji's testimony with this context of popular amnesia, making all the more powerful the sense that any confrontation with that violent, traumatic part of the country's history will itself resemble the kind of intense, head-on struggle that Kenji associates with combat.

In *Pola à 27 ans*, a film which also 'faces up' to an impossibly difficult and violent moment in history, such a complex and self-conscious (not to mention self-reflexive) interplay of framing, masks and projections is avoided in favour of the simplicity of a series of unswerving visual encounters with the face and body of the witness, in the context of the various spaces of domesticity, city and concentration camp in which she takes up position. Once again, we as viewers are placed in an intimate relation to the remembering subject, for she is the filmmaker's grandmother, and since the filmmaker herself remains behind the digital video camera during their conversations, when Pola says 'you' she appears to be talking to the spectator. Before we ever see her face Pola addresses Natacha (and therefore the spectator) as 'ma chérie' (my darling). Inserted into the opening credits is a sequence of black leader where we hear Pola speaking and/or read the French subtitles.[3] Having explained that she was always the sweet, fragile one in the family and that none of her strong brothers survived the camps whilst she did, she says, 'tu ouvres de si grands yeux ma chérie' (you're looking so wide-eyed my darling). Addressed directly in this way by her voice, from the outset we look upon her (with widened eyes, like her granddaughter) from the perspective of a descendant, of someone for whom the traumatic survival she is recounting has a particular emotive resonance. From our first glimpse of her face it is framed by this emotional bond, on which we are allowed to trespass. However, unlike with Laura's face in *Level Five*, we are aware of the 'documentary' value of Pola's face, indicated to us in signs such as the interview format, the domestic setting and the photograph album she shows her granddaughter, as well as from extra-filmic material such as leaflets and posters. Samuel also allows lengthy moments of silence, in which Pola's face comes to stand in for the scene of memory. At one point near the start of the film, the camera rests on Pola in a drawn-out silence. She is sitting on a sofa, her chin cupped in her hand, which half-covers her face (Figure 3.1). When her granddaughter asks her what she is thinking about, she replies 'J'étais à Varsovie' (I was in Warsaw). The Warsaw of her memories is never reconstructed visually in the film; we as spectators cannot travel there. Samuel avoids including old footage of Warsaw, unlike Chris in *Level Five*, who has gathered and pieced together filmed images of Laura's past, or Yamina Benguigui, who in *Mémoires d'immigrés: l'héritage maghrébin*

Figure 3.1 Pola remembering Warsaw in *Pola à 27 ans* (2003). (Source: © Bizibi.)

(1997) weaves archival footage in among her subjects' testimony. Instead we simply watch Pola as she visualises the scene of this lost world from her past. Here, as in *Shoah*, the visceral reality of Pola's reserved, wrinkled face seems to anchor the truth of her testimony, while reminding the viewer that we can never have full access to her past. It is a screen that both reveals and conceals the experience of memory. However, the film ultimately offers a more complex vision of the relations between face, filming and testimony. In later scenes of painful, cumulative disorientation, we watch as Pola discovers that the Warsaw she remembers has vanished without trace, after intensive bombing and reconstruction. The strength of her memories, evidenced from her sense of 'being there' when thinking about Warsaw, foreclosed the possibility of such obliteration for her, even although she has qualified her dreams of return with 'si ça existe encore' (if it still exists). From this moment in Warsaw onwards (a sequence explored more fully in the next chapter), we observe with discomfort as the composure of Pola's face gradually disintegrates, as she realises that even she, the witness, does not have a full grasp on the reconstruction of the past. The spectator in turn comes to realise the import of Pola's clenched fist over her mouth, her immaculate care of her hair and make-up and constant reapplying of lipstick: feeling her face on camera, she keeps trying to appropriate the empty communicability that is her face, just as with her heartrending but

Figure 3.2 A moment of recognition in Birkenau, in *Pola à 27 ans* (2003).
(Source: © Bizibi.)

controlled narratives of the camps she appropriates her testimony as a site of unapproachable trauma. The film treads a delicate line as it pushes towards the disintegration of both, culminating in a scene that might at first appear cruel filmed by a granddaughter. When a spot behind a hut at Birkenau finally provides her with a moment of recognition, the camera slowly zooms in on her as she at last breaks down in tears, silently, and turns her head away from the camera's gaze (Figure 3.2). Immediately after this scene, however, Pola is shown carefully washing her hands and reapplying her make-up once more. The film ends as she turns towards the camera to smile, as if the film were allowing her to reappropriate her face before letting it become private again.

These two very different films both reveal the face as a site of pure communicability, a constantly framed boundary point between self and other where a struggle for appropriation takes place. In their different ways they grapple with the ways in which film frames the face and the gaze of the witness as they attempt to evoke traumatic events in the past. For if the very concept of eyewitness testimony frames the eyes of the witness with the weight of what they have seen, film can attempt to dismantle those projections, dislodging the viewer from a position of full sight and shielding the witness from the fantasy of full visibility.

In the next sections of this chapter, I want to take further this discussion of the filmed subject of testimony in order to develop two ways of thinking and exploring the relation between camera, subject, spectator and memory through the filming of the face. In both *Pola à 27 ans* and *Mimi* (Claire Simon, 2003), the evocation of memory takes place in a face-to-face situation between two women, a situation that is far from transparent, since, as we have seen, it is subject to an editing and framing process that has an impact both on the presentation of the women's faces (one shown, one hidden) and on the figuring of memory. Taking up Agamben's concept of the face as a locus of community and exploring in more detail the filming and framing of faces in these films, I hope to show how a space for collective memory is created in the encounter between subject, face and film. I shall suggest that such face-to-face filmic remembering could be described in terms of performative encounters, which 'invent new protocols of cohabitation and coexistence' (Rosello 2005: 6). The question of community becomes even more explicit in *Mémoires d'immigrés: l'héritage maghrébin*, a documentary trilogy that evokes the possibility of new communities through a shared remembering across generational and ethnic boundaries. The films give faces to the marginalised, even effaced, memories of postcolonial immigration, and in so doing ask viewers to face up to the historical forces that condition encounters in the present. In *Level Five* and *Histoire(s) du cinéma*, as I shall discuss in the final section of the chapter, women's faces are positioned as privileged *objects* of cultural, and particularly cinematic, memory. These latter two works seem to move away from the illusion of the filmed witness as entirely a *subject*, instead foregrounding the ways in which they inevitably become the object of the gaze once they appear on a screen. Notably these films are made by male filmmakers, raising the spectre of feminist critiques of the objectification or fetishisation of the female body in cinema. However, rather than constructing a diametrical opposition between the female face as 'faced' by the female filmmaker and the female face as objectified by the male filmmaker, I want rather to draw out the range of emphases and configurations of faces taken up by the different films and to explore the potency, as well as the problem, of the filmed face as memory object on screen.[4]

WOMEN FACE TO FACE

Both *Pola à 27 ans* and *Mimi* evoke memories through a conversation between two women, the filmmaker and her subject: grandmother and granddaughter, friend and friend. However, the dynamics of this joint remembering are not those of an ordinary conversation. The introduction of the camera means that one woman's face is revealed to an unknown spectator. The focus of the remembering is also trained on only one of the women in each case: it is this woman's past that is the object of the spectator's attention, as much as her physical person. So not only is there a third, invisible presence (the potential spectator) as the remembering and recounting of memories takes place, but also the processes of one woman's memory are shaped (as the narratives and images are selected, edited, angled) by the other – the filmmaker-interlocutor. These complex relations of faces, bodies and gazes belie the apparent simplicity of Samuel's and Simon's films, both of which eschew the recourse to archive footage that I shall examine in Benguigui's film, as well as the fragmentation, layering, accumulation and self-reflexivity of Godard and Marker's work. The visually straightforward style of these two films leads the eye to focus on the details of facial and physical expression as the women tell their stories, as well as on the materiality of the space and place that surrounds them (the latter will be developed further in the next chapter). Moving away from the notion of the face as direct communication of memory, I want to propose that it nevertheless plays a key role in these films, as the locus for the filmic encounter in which the potential for a shared, transmitted memory arises.

As I have suggested above, Pola's face (and by extension her clothes, her glasses, her hands which frequently move to touch her face in various ways) is the site of a struggle for control and composure in the passing on of her testimony to her granddaughter, and via the camera to the unknown, unseen spectator. She exemplifies Agamben's point that 'this is why appearance becomes a problem for human beings: it becomes the location of a struggle for truth' (2000: 90). Indeed our very first glimpse of Pola's face is in a shot with a hand-held camera that moves upwards from the photo album she is discussing into an extreme close-up on her painted mouth, then moves back slightly to reveal her ornate glasses, plucked and perfectly-arched eyebrows, shiny gold earrings and bejewelled fingers holding her black and gold cigarette holder. In the second scene of the film (immediately following this one) Pola is seated at a table before a fixed camera, carefully preparing a cigarette as she describes the experience of arriving in the camps. With precise gestures she cuts up and rolls a filter and inserts it into the cigarette holder. As is the case through most of the film, her hair is coiffed and set, her nails manicured, her lips perfectly coated with red lipstick. While we gaze upon this visible evidence of an elegant control of her appearance and possessions, she describes the stripping away of clothes and belongings by the Nazi guards, the gynaecological searches to prevent smuggling, the shaving of her head. She recounts how the female guards laughed at the deportees as they stood naked for inspection, making personal comments about their appearance. She explains that they were given any old clothes to put on, with complete disregard for size, shape or gender. Finally she tells of the time, early on before starvation set in, that she skipped the soup call to go and wash herself, and how she was whipped and made to kneel for hours holding bricks in the air because of this basic desire for hygiene and cleanliness. The scene reveals a danger in the filming of such testimony – the danger of forming a distant echo of the punishing gaze of the camps in which possession of one's own body is denied and in which the face is no longer one's own.

I have already sketched above how Samuel plays with this tension, allowing the camera to zoom in on her grandmother's face at her most vulnerable moment, but following this with a scene in which Pola reapplies her make-up and regains her composure. This moving and uncomfortable moment in Birkenau echoes an earlier scene in which tears come to her eyes as she tells of the deaths of her father, brothers and husband in the camps. Tears come to her eyes but she does not break down. Instead she takes control of this physical manifestation of her ongoing grief by carefully unfolding a handkerchief and wiping her eyes. As she carries on talking, she continues to fold and wipe first one eye then the other, methodically. Pola's calm voice and physical restraint give the impression that she has told these stories many times before, to others or to herself, and has mastered the narrative even down to her facial composure. I contend that the impact for the spectator of Pola's testimony lies precisely in the tension created by her granddaughter's probing camera and her own memory narratives. The full force of the past is felt *in between* Pola and her granddaughter, between Pola's face filmed (by Samuel) and her words. On the one hand Pola's gestures, make-up and appearance act as an inverted trace of the past, a negative imprint of the defacing process of the camps (becoming a number, having one's hair shaved off, having all marks of individuality removed by brutality and hunger). On the other hand this trace is only revealed as the result of a filmed and unequal encounter that not only juxtaposes her stories of the past with the physical presence of her face but also takes this act of juxtaposition further, showing the effect of a return to the sites where those past events took place.

Agamben's essay on the face ends with an exhortation to 'be only face. Go to the threshold. Do not remain the subjects of your properties or faculties, do not stay beneath them: rather, go with them, in them, beyond them' (2000: 99). This is because for Agamben the concept of 'face', in its pure communicability, suggests an outside, an encounter with exteriority. The face is thus the site of community and the collective: 'The face is the only location of community, the only possible city' (p. 90). Pola's face is the exterior, not only of her testimony but also of her granddaughter's postmemory, a memory mediated via the filming process to reach a generation which did not itself live through the events.

A face-to-face encounter through the camera is also experienced in *Mimi*, though it is inflected differently in this film's exploration of a woman's memories through locations in Nice and Saorge. As Mimi Chiola recounts her memories to friend and filmmaker Claire Simon (and by extension to the spectator), the camera observes the striking plasticity of her face and the dynamism of her hands, her gestures and even her hair. The face as 'the only possible city' is suggested in a very literal way by the mobile shots that often take in both face and environment, straying from one to the other and connecting the two through the continuity of Mimi's narration. Face and landscape are implicated in one another as locations of community, part of the intersubjective frameworks of memory. This would seem to evoke the notion of a *visage-paysage*, posited by Deleuze and Guattari in a chapter of *Mille plateaux* on the concept of *visagéité* (faciality). However, although for them, 'l'architecture place ses ensembles, maisons, villages ou villes, monuments ou usines, qui fonctionnent comme visages dans un paysage qu'elle transforme' (Deleuze and Guattari 1980: 211–12) ('architecture positions its ensembles – houses, towns or cities, monuments or factories – to function like faces in the landscape they transform' [1987: 172]), it is only because 'une machine abstraite de la visagéification' (1980: 206) ('an abstract machine of faciality' [1987: 168]) structures faces and landscapes according to a normalising Western-capitalist ideology, 'qui neutralise d'avance les expressions et connexions rebelles aux significations conformes' ('which neutralizes in advance any expressions of rebellious connections unamenable to the appropriate signification') (ibid., translation modified). Defined architecturally as a 'system' or 'process' of white wall and black hole (*mur blanc–trou noir*) the face, according to Deleuze and Guattari, is treated by cinema's close-up as a landscape, the zooming camera and flat screen of cinema mirroring the depth of orifices and 'flatness' of surfaces proper to *visagéité* itself (1980: 212, 1987: 172).

It is true that in the formal patterns of the film, Mimi's face and landscape (and especially cityscape) become part of a continuous texture. It is also true that the face-to-face encounter might be seen, since Simon's face (like Samuel's in *Pola*) is hidden 'behind' the camera, in terms of a meeting of screen and camera rather than one between two women. However, I would argue that Deleuze and Guattari's *visage-paysage* does not satisfactorily account for the filming of Mimi's face. Their vision of an inhuman system fixing both face and environment into a ghoulish mask, a controlled arena of holes and surfaces, is countered by the polyvalence of faces that inhabit the filmed environment. The slow mobility of Simon's camera, taking us close enough to observe every movement of Mimi's lips and smile lines or far away enough to see her face as part of the whole physical stance of her body (skinny, lithe and boyish, with restless hands), is mirrored by Mimi's own mobility. As we watch her remembering, her face seems to enter into a free play of gesture (pouting, biting or licking her lips, smiling) whose 'rebellious connections', to use Deleuze and Guattari's phrase, are not pre-neutralised but rather charged with the multiple possibilities of her past as pure virtuality. Moreover, as she delves into her past the faces of those she meets on her journey are included in the film. The strangers, friends and passers-by are of diverse ages, ethnicities and gender and more significantly can never be encompassed by Mimi's narratives or interaction with her. The intersubjective evocation of memory claims the environment as a collective, organic space that cannot be homogenised by commerce and politics. The face is revealed as a site of encounter in the intersubjective memory space of the city, a space whose evocation in the film will be explored in detail in the next chapter.

If for Pola the 'empty communicability' of her face makes it the site of a struggle, that is because the past she is facing (and which we face through her) is one of almost unimaginable pain and loss. This is the challenge taken up by the filmmaker and her courageous subject. Although Mimi's past has its share of difficulties and painful moments, the film inevitably provides a very different experience of remembering, one which spans many episodes of a life rather than one which returns to face the location of a particular, terrible, trauma. Between Mimi as subject and Simon as filmmaker the revelation of the face tends therefore to be one of play and open exchange, especially with her surroundings. The most frequent shots of her face show it in profile, looking out at the places that recall her past, a positioning that, in conjunction with contemplative pans across the surrounding environment, invites us to follow her gaze and move beyond her face and memories as an individual and into a collective domain. This reflects the vast difference between the kind of testimony she is transmitting and Pola's. For unlike Pola's testimony, Mimi's does not engage us in the specific ethical demand that the conditions of her experiences must never be repeated. Even the saddest moments of Mimi's past are seen in the context of a primarily happy life and a loved environment. This is not to diminish her courage in allowing us to participate in her memories, but to recognise the crucial differences that affect how these women, as subjects and makers of the films, respond to the challenges of facing both the camera and their pasts.

Facing up to the past

Like Samuel and Simon, the filmmaker Yamina Benguigui has a personal connection to her subjects' testimony in *Mémoires d'immigrés: l'héritage maghrébin*, making the film a further example of an intimate, face-to-face filmic encounter through which a remembering process takes place. In this three-part series of documentaries, her project was to create a space in French collective memory for the often untold experiences of North African immigrants, whose labour was a crucial part of the rebuilding of France after the Second World War. As the films show, labour was 'imported' from the colonies and protectorates of Morocco, Tunisia and Algeria (continuing during decolonisation and the Algerian war of independence) for economic ends, without consideration of the men as human beings who would have to make lives for themselves in a different society. It is evidence of a persistent colonial perspective, which construed North Africa in terms of a resource for France. Uprooted from their homeland, these immigrant labourers, and their families who mostly arrived later, during the *regroupement familial* (family reuniting) programme of the 1970s, not only had to cope with the emotional cost of displacement, but also with appalling living conditions, exploitation and racial prejudice. As she herself was born to Algerian parents in Lille in 1957, Benguigui's family history is implicated in this unearthing of marginalised memories. Unlike Samuel, however, Benguigui is not specifically filming her own relatives, but rather attempting to represent the common strands of experience shared by the community of North African immigrants living in France, a community which includes her own parents. Sylvie Durmelat notes the 'frequently cited figures – 350 interviews, two years of preparation, nine months of editing, 600 hours of rushes and a budget of fifty million francs' (Durmelat 2000: 171). In her work of postmemory, then, Benguigui has drawn on a wide range of testimony, as well as numerous archival sources, in order to distil something of a collective past that has an emotional resonance for her personally.

Benguigui's personal relationship to her subject-matter is kept implicit within the film but is emphasised repeatedly in extra-filmic material such as the interview included on the DVD of the film (MK2, 1997) and the book published by Albin Michel in the year the film was released (Benguigui 1997: 7–11). Durmelat's account of the film emphasises the absence and silence of Benguigui's father, with whom she broke off contact aged eighteen after infringing his strict rules about sex and marriage (Durmelat 2000: 172). According to Durmelat, Benguigui, 'has found a detour via a cultural artefact, the documentary, to create a heritage that her father [. . .] was either unable or unwilling to pass on' (p. 173). It has subsequently become clear, however, that it is not only her father's untold story that Benguigui was attempting to uncover for herself and a broader French public. In the filmed interview among the extras on the DVD of her later feature film, *Inch'Allah dimanche* (GCTHV, 2001), Benguigui explains that this more recent, fictional film in part represents an endeavour to visualise her mother's departure from Algeria and arrival in France: 'je suis sûre qu'elle est partie comme ça. [. . .] Je l'ai imaginé parce que je sais qu'elle ne peut toujours pas en parler' (I'm sure that was how she left. [. . .] I've imagined it because I know she is still unable to talk about it). In other words, at least at the time of the DVD's release in 2002, her mother's memories of the moment of immigration remained unspoken. By implication, *Mémoires d'immigrés*, which documents memories of immigration in three sections on fathers (*les pères*), mothers (*les mères*) and children (*les enfants*), is as much about the remembering of her mother's past as her father's. Devoting a section to the children of immigration, which includes children born in France as well as those who arrived with their parents, gestures towards her own position as the daughter of immigrants, and the desire of subsequent generations to bring to light their parents' experiences. Situated at the intersection of political statement, sociological inquiry and postmemory, the memories evoked in these films serve as an interface between a public engagement with the (post)colonial history of France, and a personal exploration of the shared memories of a marginalised community.

Benjamin Stora has said that 'les Français n'ont jamais voulu regarder en face la défaite de l'empire' (the French have never wanted to face up to the defeat of the empire) (Stora 2007: 24). The faces of the witnesses in *Mémoires d'immigrés* bring us literally face to face with France's colonial past and its postcolonial consequences for the lives of immigrant individuals and families. The question of facing the past is rendered particularly critical by the 'facial' character of prejudice and marginalisation, part of the legacies of colonialism.

Stora's discussion of the competing memories surrounding colonisation underscores this. He notes that 'un candidat d'aspect nord-africain a, par exemple, dix fois moins de chances d'obtenir un logement' (a candidate who looks North African, for example, is ten times less likely to get housing) (2007: 11), which highlights the importance of surface image in the racism which those of North African descent still regularly encounter in France. Stora later argues that 'les Français du métropole ont voulu se débarrasser du Sud pour ne plus à avoir à en parler. Il fallait que les hommes du Sud disparaissent, littéralement, de leur champ de vision' (the metropolitan French wanted to rid themselves of the South so as not to have to think about it anymore. They needed the people of the South to disappear, literally, from their field of vision) (p. 25). In other words it is precisely France's collective unwillingness to face its history of colonisation (and decolonisation) that has translated into an intolerance of the faces associated with former colonies. These are the very faces that Benguigui's films bring to the fore. As with *Pola à 27 ans*, the films' evocation of the past therefore entails an ethical demand, one that requires for its transmission the spectator's imaginative investment in the memories of others.

At a formal level, the *Mémoires d'immigrés* trilogy differs from both *Pola à 27 ans* and *Mimi* in the use of two elements, both of which can be considered relatively conventional features of documentary filmmaking. The first is the integration of what might be termed 'voices of authority' among those who give their testimony. These participants are distinguished from the North African immigrants who bear witness to their personal experiences by labels identifying their position of authority, as well as by the formal setting, in which they are frequently filmed sitting behind a desk. They also tend to speak from this position, rather than personally, using official discourses, facts and figures that contrast, at times disturbingly, with the immigrants' far more intimate address. The second key difference is in the films' recourse to archive footage, bringing images of the past into conjunction with faces and locations in the present. The spoken testimony and the faces of the witnesses are brought together with numerous images from sources including the Institut National de l'Audiovisuel (INA), the Centre National de Documentation Pédagogique (CNDP) and Pathé, which are supplemented by family photographs. While all of the film's *intervenants* (speakers, or contributors) are named in subtitles, these images from the past tend not to be attributed to named individuals or even places. Although the credits at the end of each part of the trilogy list the sources of the archive material, within the film the images circulate anonymously, often reappearing across the different sections. Even the family photographs depend on the spectator's recognition of faces marked by the passage of time. Photographs alternate with archive footage in illustrating the memories described on the soundtrack. This creates a persistent indeterminacy, in which particular images are detached from the specificity of their referents and participate in a more collective evocation of past possibilities. At the same time, the images are given meaning and specificity by the expressive power of the face-to-face testimony of named individuals. The archive images are frequently altered in their new context, shown in slow motion and divorced of diegetic sound, which is generally replaced on the soundtrack by popular Arab and North African songs about suffering, separation and exile. For Durmelat, the use of slow motion 'proceeds in part from a desire to pause on the anonymous faces that viewers have never really taken the trouble to look at before, with the hope of turning them into characters' (2000: 182). The use of slow motion certainly invites contemplation of the images and confronts the viewer with faces from the margins of French collective memory. Rather like the synthesised digital images in Chris Marker's *Sans soleil* (1983), though much less overtly and dramatically, the deceleration draws attention to the status of the footage as *image*, making the images unfamiliar and therefore catching the viewer's gaze. However, the silent, slow-moving faces from the archives do not become 'characters' as Durmelat suggests. In fact, it is in the unaltered archive sequences where individuals' speech is heard that a more humanistic sense of 'character' is brought to the fore, for example in a sequence where a young Algerian woman in the 1960s, sporting a fashionable Mary-Quant-style bob, is interviewed in a café and speaks frankly and eloquently about the conflict between her parents' expectations and her sense of identity as a young, independent woman who has grown up in France (*les mères*). By contrast, the faces in the mute, slow-motion images represent an elusive, almost frustrating anonymity, an empty communicability – expressive, yet indeterminate and uprooted – that is framed by the moving act of bearing witness to formerly unspoken memories of immigration. Lacking diegetic sound, they embody the silence surrounding the appalling living conditions, prejudice and marginalisation suffered by large numbers of North African immigrants in France. These shadowy figures, often shown moving through the muddy streets of shanty towns, do not speak directly to us. Instead they are given a voice through the individuals who do speak to camera, whose testimony crystallises fragments of a shared but heterogeneous experience. Frequently, as we watch the archive images, a collective experience is voiced on the soundtrack through the popular music of singers such as Dahmane El Harachi and Slimane Azem, whose songs in Arabic are given French subtitles at key moments to underscore the suffering and longing engendered by displacement.

Tracing the representation of the face of one of the immigrant mothers in *Mémoires d'immigrés*, Khira Allam, exemplifies this complex layering of image and sound. Music, archive images and photographs combine with Benguigui's own footage in order to reveal Khira's memories as an individual actualisation from a virtual realm of possible pasts. We first see Khira's face in the closing sequence of *les pères*, which is recapitulated in the opening credits of *les mères*, a montage sequence focusing on the women who, like the filmmaker's own mother, emigrated to France from North Africa. Each of the three films opens with a montage sequence accompanied by music (though this is much shorter for *les pères*, which moves more quickly into testimony in order to introduce the concept of the film), and both *les pères* and *les mères* end with linking segments that form a transition to the subjects (mothers, children) who will be the focus of the next film. Images from these closing brackets are then reprised in the montage sequences that open the following films. In this way, these sequences form a connecting thread of visual images that bind together the otherwise segregated family members, invoking cinematically a potential transmission across genders and generations. Significantly, the sequences also put faces at the forefront of the films.

Les mères opens with a series of women's faces interspersed with images that connote domestic space and the family, such as a woman standing with her husband in her home and a mantelpiece crowded with family photographs. The faces are shown in slow motion, echoing the films' archival sequences and thus making a visual connection between images from past and present. Moreover the women who will tell their stories in the film are placed alongside others (presumably drawing upon the 600 hours of initial rushes for the films) whose stories we do not hear, gesturing towards the virtuality of a collective past. The transition from image to image is made with a slow dissolve, so that faces overlap with other faces, photographs and scenes, which therefore briefly share the space of the screen. This gelling together of the images is reinforced at the level of the soundtrack by the melodic cadences and nostalgic lyrics of French-Egyptian singer Dalida's popular *Halwa Ya Baladi* (my beloved country), the French subtitles of which form haphazard inscriptions beneath the women's faces, reinforcing the envelope of sound with a textual connecting thread. So before we meet them as witnesses, these women are shown as part of a much wider sphere of memory, powerfully evoked in the blending of sound and image, and one that, through the visual emphasis on family, incorporates the postmemory of generations who have not lived through immigration.

In this sequence Khira is shown in close-up with one of her daughters by her side, both of them half-smiling as though aware of the slightly awkward artificiality of their silent pose in front of a moving camera. This filmed family portrait reappears twice later on in the section devoted to Khira's testimony, first as a group shot with the whole family – husband, children with their partners and a happy-looking grandchild – then in close-up again, the camera panning slowly across their faces. These filmed photographs echo the other family photographs that are shown in general throughout the films and in particular in Khira's section. This offers a visual bridge between past and present, but one which shifts between the specificity of a clear connection, for example the squinting gaze that identifies Khira's husband in an old photograph, and the indeterminacy described above, for example in the photograph shown as Khira speaks of her parents, showing an Algerian woman in rural dress sitting in front of a hut. In these circuits of images between past and present, as well as between institutional and family archives, I am reminded of Hirsch's emphasis on family photographs in her account of the aesthetics of postmemory, according them a privileged position in what she calls 'the particular mixture of mourning and re-creation that characterizes the work of postmemory' (1997: 251). She argues that artists who attempt to locate their own identity through an engagement with their parents' traumatic memories 'forge an aesthetics of postmemory with photographs as the icons of their ambivalent longing' (p. 246). In Benguigui's film, the use of family photographs to evoke the ambivalent longing of a desired connection to a problematic past is supplemented by animated photographs that bring these faces to life in the present. As the camera takes in the faces of Khira's family, each of them visibly attempts the particular composure and stillness of a pose: bringing the eyes to meet the camera, withdrawing a complicit smile or setting the mouth into a dignified line. This moment of posing is perhaps the most explicit and visual performance of Agamben's notion of the appropriation of the manifest openness of the face (2000: 92), yet that openness shines through in the tiny, uncontrollable, facial movements recorded by the camera. Like the still photograph coming to life in the blink of an eye in Marker's *La Jetée* (1962), each member of Khira's family blinks as the camera meets their gaze. For me, this moving scene suggests a desire to move beyond the mute stillness of the photograph, towards a dynamic mnemonic circuit in which the past's virtuality is constantly being actualised in the present, while the 'present' images constantly refer us back to the collective virtuality of the past.

The use of music in the film combines with these different forms of photography to enrich this effect. While Khira's family stage their 'photo', on the soundtrack we hear the start of *pied noir*[5] singer Enrico Macias' 'Non je n'ai pas oublié' (no I haven't forgotten). This song has a special significance, not only for its nostalgic evocation of Algiers, 'la ville blanche' (the white city), but also because Macias' music plays an important role in Khira's testimony. Indeed, as I shall show, talking about his music leads to a joyful disruption of the flow of her memory narrative that draws the viewer into the familial space of postmemory, a moment in which the expressive mobility of Khira's face plays a central role. She has explained how, left alone all day in her shabby, single-room lodgings with nothing to do except housework or chores for her Polish neighbours, she would listen to music. As she recounts this, a medium close-up shot of Khira cuts to a shot of an old-fashioned radio on an elaborate piece of furniture, carefully draped with white needlepoint fabric and topped with a whimsical, ornamental tea set. We then cut back to Khira, now in close-up, whose speech has moved into Arabic, asking, as French subtitles inform those of us who need them, 'comment s'appelle celui qui chante pour l'Algérie . . .?' (what is the name of the one who sings for Algeria . . . ?) Her face turns from the camera as she looks enquiringly towards a point beyond the frame, and from that off-screen space we hear a voice saying softly, encouragingly, 'mais dis-le toi maman: Enrico Macias. Redis-le!' (but say it yourself, Mum: Enrico Macias. Say it again!). As Khira's speech falters and she mispronounces the name, claiming she cannot say it in French, she breaks into a disarming smile, ultimately rocking back and forth with mirth so that the camera has to

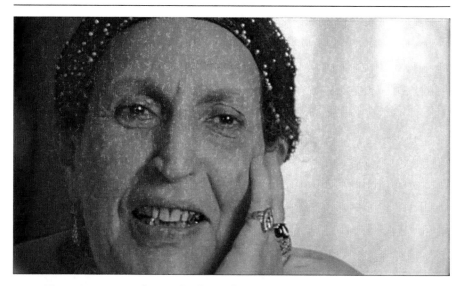

Figure 3.3 Face to face with Khira Allam in *Mémoires d'immigrés* (1997).
(Source: © Bandits Productions.)

zoom out slightly to keep her face in the frame. All the while fond laughter also rings out from the off-screen space, presumably coming from her daughter(s) and perhaps the film crew. This effectively frames the amusement on Khira's face with both the firm encouragement to speak, and then complicit laughter at the moment of struggle, from younger, French-speaking generations who share the off-screen space with the viewer of the film. The camera zooms in again to a close-up on Khira's face, capturing this moment of happiness as she returns to her memories of Macias' music and the song she loved about the prettiness of Algerian girls. Finally she repeats Macias' name clearly, with a certain firmness of purpose as though to prove she can, while the song's jaunty melody begins on the soundtrack (Figure 3.3).

This brief irruption of humour contrasts with the disturbing nature of Khira's testimony, in which she describes her childhood in Algeria, where she worked from the age of ten for exploitative colonial employers to support her family, and her arrival as a young woman in France to be faced with dismal living conditions and social isolation. Denied a proper education, she explains that 'mes enfants m'ont appris à signer' (my children taught me how to sign my name). This indicates a relationship between generations that is mirrored in the articulation of Enrico Macias' name, which takes place through the face-to-face encounter across the membrane of the screen, drawing the viewer into the relationship. The pleasure in remembering Macias' music includes the overcoming, through laughter and trans-generational dialogue, of a faltering of speech. It replays, and diffuses, the difficult negotiations between languages faced by those arriving in a new country, one where unequal power relations have accrued through a colonial history. It is therefore also a performance of

Khira's victory over the trauma of immigration: coping with a lack of education as well as loneliness and homesickness, while learning to make a home in a new country. The music's role in homemaking is highlighted in the cutting between Khira as she speaks and the 'still-life' shot of her radio, proudly displayed among the adornments of a carefully nurtured domestic space. Furthermore, while Khira may identify with Macias' nostalgic lyrics evoking the beauty of Algerian girls and the longed-for contours of the homeland, her focus on the memory of a song sung in the French language suggests the desire to bridge the two spaces of identity, housing her nostalgia for Algeria within her new home in France. Later, the animated family photograph, staged in Khira's domestic space and accompanied by Macias' music, testifies to the success of that family narrative of homemaking against the odds. It acts, woven as it is into a tapestry of cultural memory objects, photographs and faces, as a monument-in-motion to Khira and her generation of North African 'mères' who were flung, often reluctantly, into a difficult life in the country of former colonisers.

In her book *France and the Maghreb: Performative Encounters*, Mireille Rosello includes *Mémoires d'immigrés* in a list of examples of 'encounters between historiographies' (2005: 109).[6] It is a somewhat tantalising reference since she does not go on to examine *Mémoires d'immigrés* specifically. It does, however, suggest that it would not be too far-fetched to turn to Rosello's concept of 'performative encounters' to describe the model of testimony in Benguigui's film. For Rosello, a performative encounter is one which creates new positions for subjects, overcoming the 'long list of preexisting constraints' (p. 5) imposed upon subjects situated in historical narratives of conflict, preventing creative exchange. In this case, as I have previously discussed with reference to Stora's work, the interconnected historical narratives of colonisation, decolonisation and immigration produce ongoing conflict precisely because they have been repressed in national memory, producing the 'colonial fracture' described in the introduction to this book. In that sense, creating a face-to-face encounter where the viewer is invited to participate in the remembering of North African immigration offers 'new protocols of cohabitation and coexistence' (Rosello 2005: 6) in which the face acts, in Agamben's terms, as the 'location of community' (2000: 90). In my analysis of the representation of Khira's face in *Mémoires d'immigrés*, one among many possible threads that could lead us through the complex framing of faces in Benguigui's films, it is a moment of stuttering and laughter, drawing in off-screen dialogue, that acts as a focal point, drawing in other cultural memory objects and presenting us with the face as a radical opening. As Rosello says, 'the language of performative encounters will always be close to laughter or poetry. That is, it will always constitute some sort of translation within and between languages' (2005: 6). The fluid interweaving of face, testimony, photographs and music creates openings in the remembering process that position the viewer alongside the children of immigration (including the filmmaker herself), invoking an affective, imaginative investment in a problematic past.

Durmelat has argued persuasively that Benguigui takes on the role of 'memory entrepreneuse' in her *Mémoires d'immigrés* project, drawing on Gérard Noiriel's concept of 'memory entrepreneur': an individual who functions as a catalyst through which collective memories emerge in a formal process of naming and commemoration (Durmelat 2000: 173, see also Noiriel 1995: 380). My analyses of the films tend to support Durmelat's assertion that Benguigui's aim is 'to create a common ground at the heart of the community as well as between the community and the society in which it has established itself' (2000: 185). However, Durmelat's reading is intended as a more wide-ranging analysis of the three films and therefore necessarily stops short of delving into their formal complexity. She briefly argues that the 'aestheticisation' of the archive image lends the films a 'patina' (a term taken from Arjun Appadurai [1996: 75–85]) which, as she puts it, 'sparks in the children of migration, as well as in the non-Maghrebi audience, a certain nostalgia for the memory they have not lived firsthand' (Durmelat 2000: 183). However, I hope to have shown that these films create a richly textured audiovisual fabric that goes beyond the vague, nostalgic patina of archival footage in its evocation and transmission of (post)memory. Although not as densely layered as Godard's *Histoire(s) du cinéma*, and more conventional in its approach to documentary than Marker's *Level Five*, *Mémoires d'immigrés* arguably draws on similar formal techniques in the filmic rendering of a history: the recycling of filmed images, altered in their new context, the use of music as an emotive cultural memory object, and the interweaving of images of past and present to evoke a virtual realm of collective memory. Through these strategies, testimonial faces move beyond their specific documentary value and resonate with other images and sounds in order to engage the spectator's emotional investment in the community that is being created in this process of filmic remembering. Moreover, as in both *Pola à 27 ans* and *Mimi*, it is through a personal connection between filmmaker(s) and subject that the viewer is drawn into the process of communal remembering. An emotional link is tendered between the testimonial space of the screen and the off-screen space occupied by filmmakers and potential spectators, engendering a performative encounter. Such face-to-face encounters offer a fragile but powerful connection between past and present, one which encourages us, crucially, to experience the transmission of memory as a shared concern.

Faces in a Misty Light: Women as Cultural Memory

While the female filmmakers discussed in this chapter so far focus on the agency of faces as subjects engaged in a performative encounter, both Marker and Godard could be seen to privilege women's faces as *objects* of cultural memory. As early as 1962 Marker in *La Jetée* figured the woman's face as an embodiment (one should perhaps say *envisagement*) of the past moment. It is the image of a woman's face that imprints itself so powerfully on the visual cortex of the protagonist that it allows him to make physical contact with the past. In *Level Five*, it is Laura's face that acts as a prism through which the remembering of Okinawa can begin. Godard too has a long history of a visual fascination with women's faces. In *Histoire(s)* he draws iconic women's faces into the circulation of fragments and associative logic of remembering that make up the films. From Marguerite Duras, author of *La Douleur*, to the suffering face of Marguerite in F. W. Murnau's *Faust*, women's faces (still and in movement) return again and again as both intertextual and indexical links to the past. In both Marker's and Godard's films, as well as in Marker's *Immemory*, women's faces seem to act as a metonymic link to cinema. They thus represent a privileged means of access not only to the past but also to histories and memories of cinema itself. As Mulvey writes in 'Close-ups and commodities', 'Godard associates female beauty almost ontologically with the cinema' (Mulvey 1996: 40). In her volume on Marker, Catherine Lupton writes:

> The woman herself represents cinema as the object of the man's desire: it is the film that seems to wake up as she does. [. . .] The woman is also the sign of memory itself, the 'Madeleine' that, like the fragment of cake for Marcel Proust, unlocks the past and restores the hero to an intact moment of a previously lived life. The remembered image of the woman focuses the ambiguities of memory's nature and the role that memory plays in creating the identity of the hero (and by implication other human subjects). (2005: 95)

I have already noted in Chapter 2 how Marker develops the notion of 'Madeleine' in *Immemory* as a memory object able to set in motion a circuit of virtuality, a sphere of cultural memory. The choice of a signifier at once female, filmic (in Hitchcock's *Vertigo* [1958]) and culturally associated with memory (thanks to Proust) is not incidental. The whole of the *Immemory* CD-ROM is imbued with the idea of the inextricability of cinema, memory and images of women. This is made explicit in a striking description of a childhood memory that evokes visual pleasure, nostalgia and cinephilia in a powerfully emotive, cinematic experience of a woman's face. Taking a detailed analysis of the remembering of Simone Genevoix's face in *Immemory* as a starting point, I want to explore the role of women's faces – positioned as they are in the misty light of both memory and cinema – in Marker's and Godard's elaboration of cultural memory.

In the 'Cinéma' zone of *Immemory* we discover a formative experience (Marker's, we presume) of watching Marco de Gastyne's *La Merveilleuse vie de Jeanne d'Arc* (1927) as a 7-year-old child. The sequence begins with titles of the name of the star, Simone Genevoix, and her character, Jeanne d'Arc, framing a small, still image of a close-up of her face (thus emphasising from the outset the significance of both star and character). This image gives way to a blown-up version of this same image of her face, filling the rectangle of screen in which *Immemory* is viewed. Losing its sharpness of definition, the image recalls the obsessive enlarging of photographs in *Blow Up* (Michelangelo Antonioni, 1966), in which the photographer Thomas searches for clues in photographic images that become increasingly abstract and fluid. Visually, this blurred, enlarged female face also recalls a scene from the opening sequence of Ingmar Bergman's *Persona* (also 1966), in which a young boy (whom we later presume to be actress Elizabeth Vogler's abandoned son) presses up against and runs his hand across a vast screen on which are projected the blurred, merging faces of Alma and Elizabeth (Bibi Andersson and Liv Ullmann respectively), an image that also appears in transfigured form in chapter 2B of *Histoire(s) du cinéma*. In *Immemory*, the blurred close-up of Genevoix evokes the projection and vast enlargement of the star's face on the cinema screen, obsessively gazed upon by the filmmaker-spectator and blown up to even greater – though more fluid and less distinct – proportions by the nostalgic imaginings of memory. A text then scrolls down overlaying Genevoix's face, making these impressions more explicit as it describes 'cette image qui apprît à un enfant de sept ans comment un visage emplissant l'écran était d'un coup la chose la plus précieuse au monde' (this image which taught a child of seven how a face filling a screen was suddenly the most precious thing in the world). Three more, smaller images of the same close-up of Genevoix appear alongside the text, framed to give the impression of a film strip. The centre box is in fact a digitised movie clip and the image begins to move, with accompanying music – recalling the moment of 'animation' in *La Jetée*, when the woman's sleeping face is gradually propelled into a moment of movement as she awakens both literally and figuratively. We see Genevoix's head turn first right then left, a movement that takes about five seconds. It is a tiny fragment of De Gastyne's film, in both size and length, and the viewer can replay it over and over again (by navigating back one screen and letting the text and clip reappear), focusing on every small detail. The eye is drawn to a curl of hair on her cheek that is revealed as she turns her head to the left, a strand that has escaped being tucked behind her ear, and we are thus invited to share in the narrator's fixation with the sensual details of a face, 'un visage [. . .] dont se dire le nom et se décrire les traits devenait la plus nécessaire et délicieuse occupation' (uttering the name and describing to myself the features of that face [. . .] became the most necessary and delicious occupation). As in *La Jetée*, a *fixation* on a woman's face – in the 1962 film literally a fixed, still image with a fragment of movement, in *Immemory* the fixing of a moving fragment into a layering of words and images – is a means of relating memory to matter. However, in *La Jetée* it is the memory that leads the protagonist back to a tangible past world, whereas here it is the tactility of the memory object, a moving image fragment, that leads to the intangible world of cultural memory, a shared space of nostalgic cinephilia.

The enmeshing of images, text and clip assembles the traces of this childhood obsession, suggesting the different elements involved in it: the vastness of projection and close-up, the physical intimacy of a face in proximity, the compulsion to return repeatedly to the image 'qui revenait sans cesse, qui se mêlait à tous les instants de la vie' (which returned constantly, mingling with life's every moment). Once again a circuit of virtuality, a zone of potential memory, is spun from the juxtaposition of formal elements. But there are added elements of nostalgia and tactility that were not present in the layers of monuments discussed in Chapter 2 with relation to *Level Five*, elements which pertain particularly to the filmed female face and its mnemonic-metonymic link with cinema. As the text goes on to tell us, 'pour cet enfant devenu grand, le cinéma et la femme sont restées deux notions absolument inséparables' (for this now-grown-up child, cinema and woman have remained two absolutely inseparable notions). To return to *Level Five* in this line of inquiry, we see that here too the female face is integral to a cinephilic remembering. Once again an iconic female face is linked with a cherished memory of cinema, in the moment when Laura tells us (always addressing her beloved deceased, face to camera) how she came to be known as 'Laura':

> C'est à ce moment-là que tu as commencé à m'appeler Laura. On aimait le film. [. . .] J'étais tellement impressionnée qu'on puisse être amoureux d'une image et qu'ensuite une vraie dame vienne remplacer l'image . . . Est-ce qu'on peut être aussi belle qu'une image? Est-ce qu'on peut être aussi mémorable qu'une chanson? [. . .] J'ai peur de découvrir quelque chose qui peut naître là, comme ça, que je ne vois pas encore et qui d'un seul coup serait aussi fort qu'une chanson, qui d'un seul coup nous appartient plus, qui appartiendrait aux autres, comme la chanson de Laura nous appartient maintenant. [Sings:] 'Laura is a face in the misty light, footsteps that you hear in the hall'. Est-ce que tu entends mes pas?

> (That was when you began calling me Laura. We loved the film. [. . .] I was so struck that one could be in love with an image, and that afterwards a real woman could come to replace the image . . . Can one be as beautiful as an image? Can one be as memorable as a song? I'm afraid of discovering something which could spring up just like that, something I can't yet see and which would be suddenly as powerful as a song, which suddenly doesn't belong to us any more, and could belong to others, as Laura's song belongs to us now. [Sings:] 'Laura is a face in the misty light, footsteps that you hear in the hall'. Do you hear my footsteps?)

There are several strands to be teased out of this interlacing of faces and memories: the visual pleasure and romantic investment in gazing at a projected, screened and passive female face, a face that simultaneously connotes absence, mystery and loss, the merging of woman *and* cinema as objects of desire (as Lupton says, above) as well as of memory and the remembering of a cinematic experience that is at once private and collective. These strands are not distinct;

rather they form a complex web of relations that will ultimately lead the discussion back to the questions of witnessing and testimony with which I began this chapter. I want, however, to try to draw out these strands – drawing on theories from Mulvey and Aumont along the way – in order to explore more fruitfully how they are implicated in one another. It will be important to probe the problematic character of the nostalgic, cinephilic representation of women's faces, in order to see what is at stake in positioning the female face as memory object in films whose intention is to work against the amnesia surrounding a horrific outpouring of violence – an aim that is as important in Godard's *Histoire(s)* projects (the Holocaust and the Second World War) as it is in Marker's monument to Okinawa in *Level Five*.

In another link to the Simone Genevoix sequence in *Immemory*, the above scene in *Level Five* also turns on the notion of falling in love with the image of a face, a face at once mysterious and illuminated. In the film Laura describes, Otto Preminger's *Laura* (1944), a detective falls in love with the painting of a glamorous advertising executive (played by Gene Tierney) whose brutal murder he has been called in to investigate. As he sits in her flat mulling over the impenetrable case, drinking whisky and gazing at her beautifully lit portrait, whose pose and black dress place dramatic emphasis on her face, Laura suddenly returns, apparently unaware that she has supposedly been murdered. This plot mirrors a narrative thread running through *Level Five*: the relationship between Marker's filmmaker persona, Chris, and 'Laura' (not her real name, as the words quoted above inform us). It is suggested that images we see throughout the film have been gathered and assembled by Chris ('un jour je donnerai tout ce matériel-là en vrac à Chris pour qu'il essaie d'en tirer quelque chose. [. . .] on verra bien ce qu'il peut en tirer lui, l'as du montage') (one day I'll give this footage to Chris, all in a jumble, so that he can try to make something out of it [. . .] we'll see what he can draw from it, since he's the editing ace). In the final scene a hand-held camera wanders around the tiny room where we have watched Laura speak her 'log-ins' to camera; however, she is now absent from this space and only her possessions and audiovisual material remain. The room is deserted, *Marie Celeste*-style, with her computer still switched on and ready to connect to the Optional World Link. Chris's narration tells us:

Je n'ai jamais revu Laura. Quand je suis retourné à l'atelier, tout semblait normal, les machines étaient allumées, on aurait dit qu'elle venait de quitter la pièce. L'économiseur d'écran, le chat fidèle, faisait sa tournée, le programme était resté ouvert sur la page courrier d'O.W.L. Machinalement j'ai tapé son nom sur le clavier. [Computer screen: I don't know how to Laura]. Ça non plus, il ne savait pas.

(I never saw Laura again. When I returned to the studio everything seemed normal, the machines were switched on, you would have thought she had just left the room. The screensaver, the loyal cat, was doing his rounds, the programme was open on the message page of O.W.L. On autopilot I typed her name on the screen. [Computer screen: I don't know how to Laura]. It didn't know how to do that either.)

Laura's face mysteriously disappears, in a mirror image of the equally baffling reappearance of the original Laura in the Preminger film. However, there is also a parallel (as opposed to a mirroring) resemblance, for this final scene reveals that Chris has tenderly watched and pieced together Laura's last experiences. A fixation with a lost object, analogous to the detective's, is suggested in Chris's 'ace' editing together of her own mournful journey through bereavement and reconstruction of the events of Okinawa. The typing of the missing 'Laura' into the computer, which is unable to recognise it as interpretable code, literally designates Laura as an *object* by recalling an earlier scene in which Laura mocks the computer by entering a noun instead of a verb into the command line:

> J'ai envie de me moquer de l'ordinateur comme on faisait, [. . .] en logo par exemple: un mot à la place d'un verbe. 'Chien', et l'ordinateur est tout bête, il sait plus quoi répondre, et il avoue: 'je ne sais pas comment chien' [. . .] 'rhododendron', 'pelle à tarte', 'Tour Eiffel', 'soulier', 'je ne sais pas comment soulier'. Je me souviens d'un soulier qui avait été oublié, une nuit.

> (I feel like mocking the computer as we used to, [. . .] in logo for example: a word instead of a verb. 'Dog', and the computer is quite silly, it doesn't know what to reply and confesses: 'I don't know how to dog' [. . .] 'rhododendron', 'cake slice', 'Eiffel Tower', 'shoe', 'I don't know how to shoe'. I remember a shoe that had been forgotten one night.)

When Chris at the end of the film mimics this process using Laura's name, it aligns Laura with the 'volonté de moquerie permanente obstinée' (constant wilful and obstinate mockery) that she herself, in another context, attributes to objects. It also, however, subtly reinforces her status as *memory* object, evoking the process by which, in the extract above, Laura herself had been led from the object 'soulier' to the memory of a particular night.

Through the intertext of the film *Laura*, itself an object of cultural memory, Laura's face is figured as a screen, analogous to the cinema or computer screen as interface. Laura's face is the object upon which the desire for memory is projected but which at the same time represents the inscrutability of the past: a smoke screen. The last image we see of Laura is in a scene where she talks about time, loss and forgetting, whilst holding a video remote control that gradually enlarges and blurs the image of her face on the screen. Here one thinks once again of the enlargement of Genevoix's face and Marker's professed rapture at the 'visage emplissant l'écran' (face filling the screen). On the most overt level Laura's increasingly abstract face, out of focus and spilling over the edges of the screen, represents the way the process of forgetting gradually effaces the features of even the most cherished being. As she carries out this transfiguration of her own face (her hand holding the remote is clearly visible in the frame), Laura imagines what would have happened had her lover lived, allowing their romance to fade and, eventually, end: 'Un jour mon image aurait commencé à se brouiller, tu te serais aperçu que les bribes de mots, de vie, qui occupaient ta pensée et ton souvenir, ne raccordaient plus qu'avec une image floue' (one day my image would have begun to blur, you would have noticed that the scraps of words, of life, which occupied your thoughts and memories, were now attached to nothing but a hazy image). The implicit suggestion, however, when read in conjunction with the Genevoix sequence in *Immemory*, is that a woman's face is somehow unreadable, that, like Thomas in *Blow Up* with his crime scene photographs, the closer one gets the more the image seems to disintegrate and escape the gaze that would fix it. So the woman's face is a figure of the past as 'lost time', a concept perhaps rooted, for Marker, in Proust's depiction of the agonised analysis of Albertine's sexuality after her death, proleptically crystallised in the scene where Marcel first kisses her:

> D'abord au fur et à mesure que ma bouche commença à s'approcher des joues que mes regards lui avaient proposé d'embrasser, ceux-ci se déplaçant virent des joues nouvelles; le cou, aperçu de plus près et comme à la loupe, montra, dans ses gros grains, une robustesse qui modifia le caractère de la figure. Les dernières applications de la photographie [. . .] je ne vois que cela qui puisse, autant que le baiser, faire surgir de ce que nous croyions une chose à aspect défini, les cent autre choses qu'elle est tout aussi bien. (Proust 1988a: 66)

> (At first, as my mouth began gradually to approach the cheeks which my eyes had recommended it to kiss, my eyes, in changing position, saw a different pair of cheeks; the neck, observed at closer range and as if through a magnifying glass, showed in its coarser grain a robustness which modified the character of the face. Apart from the most recent applications of photography [. . .] I can think of nothing that can to so great a degree as a kiss evoke out of what we believed to be a thing with one definite aspect the hundred other things which it may equally well be. [Proust 2000: 420–1])

In likening the proximity of a kiss to the way photography reveals multiple hidden perspectives, Proust appears to anticipate Marker's cinephilic fascination with the mystery of the female face in close-up. For both Proust and Marker, the face seems to thwart the mastery of the gaze, yet it is precisely this slippery fluidity that provokes desire and lingers, so persistently, in memory.

This suggestion of a kind of blinding intermingling of woman and of memory is also present in *Histoire(s) du cinéma*, particularly in *2B fatale beauté*. We have seen above that Godard makes direct reference to Bergman's *Persona* in this chapter. The moment comes after Godard's narration describes the typical framing of men and women in cinema: the man positioned in the *plan améric-ain* (medium-long shot) to show his pistol, or sex, shooting from the hip, whilst women are framed in a medium shot to draw attention to their breasts: 'les femmes étaient toujours encadrées à hauteur de poitrine. Et au fond de chaque histoire d'amour se morfond une histoire de nourrice' (women were always framed from the breasts upwards, and beneath every love story lurks the story of a wet-nurse). After a photograph of silent film star Bessie Love with precisely this framing, hand on décolleté as though about to reveal a breast, comes an iconic still of Louise Brooks in close-up, recognisable from the film *Die Büsche der Pandora* (*Pandora's Box*) (Pabst, 1929): her trademark bobbed hair cutting across her check, her head tilted back and her eyes half-closed. A very slow cross-fade moves to the image from *Persona*, the boy's hand silhouetted against the vast, illuminated face on the screen. As in *Immemory* and *Level Five*, this sequence suggests a zooming in on the female face, as a series of iconic female figures are framed increasingly close to the face, with the *Persona* image finally suggesting the *image floue* (hazy image) where proximity becomes abstraction, underscored by the memory of the merging of the two female characters in the original Bergman film.

If for Godard in *Histoire(s)* the female face is a memory object, it seems to be one that suggests a cultural memory in which the face of the woman con-notes the mystery of an unattainable past. The notion of mystery implied by the screening of women's faces is significant, for if Godard, like Marker, asso-ciates women ontologically with cinema, he also attributes to both a profound *mystery*. As Aumont comments in his study of *Histoire(s)*, 'la beauté, ce sont des visages de femmes; ou, comme chez Malherbe [. . .] "ce qui se trouve sur le visage des belles femmes, que l'on y voit et que l'on ne peut définir"' (beauty is women's faces; or, as Malherbe would have it [. . .] 'that which is found in the faces of beautiful women, which one sees there and cannot define') (Aumont 1999: 70). This resonates with Godard's spoken and titled remark that cinema is 'ni un art, ni une technique mais un mystère' (neither an art nor a technique but a mystery). Cinema is a mystery embodied in the repre-sentation of a woman's face, and this is symbolised by the Proustian figure of Albertine. As Godard, seated at his desk, calls out 'Albertine', a cut takes us to a detail from Georges Seurat's pointillist painting, *Une Baignade à Asnières* (1883–4), of a young man calling, his hands cupped to his mouth. This is fol-lowed by a detail – a close-up of the face, in fact – of Auguste Renoir's luscious *Nue* (1882), overlaid with the title 'un mystère' (*2B fatale beauté*). 'Albertine disparue' (Albertine vanished) repeats Godard's voice, followed by, 'longtemps je me suis couché de bonne heure' (for a long time I went to bed early), well-known quotations from Proust's most famous work. The connection between the mysterious, 'disappearing' face of a beautiful woman and cinema is reinforced by a subsequent commentary on the nature of cinema. Godard distances cinema from literature as represented by Proust, by contrasting 'si c'était l'homme du cinéma? S'il fallait dire sans rien dire, par exemple, "longtemps je me suis réveillé de malheur"?' (what if it were the man of cinema, if he had to say without saying anything, for example, 'for a long time I woke up with unhappiness'?). Nevertheless, it is significant that Godard refers to À la recherche du temps perdu and in particular to the volume in which the search for lost time is intertwined with the mental and mnemonic search for the unknowable truth of Albertine's mysterious sexuality. The sequence is closely followed by a silent series of still, associative images, each one (thanks to the possibilities of video editing) opening or hollowing out from the last in an iris, as though each frame were burning through the previous one.[7] First we see Man Ray's photograph of Proust on his deathbed (22 November 1922) with the title 'Marcel', then this dissolves into a surreal painting of a featureless female face. Here the title 'Marcel' lingers (possibly referring to the dada artist Marcel Duchamp, although the painting is currently attributed to René Magritte)[8] before being replaced with 'Albertine'. Here we are returned to Albertine as mystery, the female face coded as human yet surreally effaced and blank. However, this very return suggests the extent to which she ('she' here representing the mystery of female beauty, the cinema) is key to the circuits of virtuality being extended by the accumulation of these intertextual memory objects.

The Albertine-like fluidity of the face, elusive to the point of disintegration or effaced to blankness, seems in line with Aumont's argument that contemporary culture in general and cinema in particular have acted destructively upon the human face. Moving from the face dévisagé (stared at) to the face dé-visagéifié (de-faced), Aumont claims that, 'le cinéma s'en est pris au visage' (cinema has taken against the face) (Aumont 1992: 192). Taking as a starting point Leos Carax's 1986 film Mauvais sang, Aumont moves through a diverse range of films (including Persona) to demonstrate the ways in which the 'humanity' of the human face was emptied out during the latter part of the twentieth century: 'Sa beauté propre, sa signification, son expression même sont évacuées. Dénué de sens, dénué de valeur, ce visage-là n'entre qu'à peine dans un échange quelconque, et interdit la contemplation' (its specific beauty, its signification, even its expression have been emptied out. Devoid of meaning, devoid of value, that face barely enters into any kind of exchange and forbids contemplation) (p. 149). Significantly for my arguments, Aumont also notes that the face has come to be treated as an object, rather than the expression of a subject: 'le visage est traité de façon appuyée comme ce que la tradition interdisait qu'il fût: un objet' (the face is insistently treated as that which tradition has not allowed it to be: an object) (ibid.). However, although for Aumont le flou (blurring) and l'agrandissement (enlargement) are two of the principal means of undoing the humanity of the human face in cinema, the kinds of enlargement and blurring or fluidity of the face as memory object that I have been describing with relation to Godard and Marker do not entirely fit Aumont's description of *le visage défait* (the distressed face). Rather than deny contemplation, these faces invite it, even if it is not the kind of humanistic contemplation Aumont associates with his other three 'types' of cinematic face: *le visage primitif* (the primitive face, associated with the circulation of signs and meaning), *le visage ordinaire* (the ordinary face, associated with physiognomy and *photogénie* (the aesthetic affinity with photography of specific faces)) and *le visage humain* (the human face, associated with the portrait and with expressivity). Moving beyond these classical modes of the cinematic face, *Level Five*, *Immemory* and *Histoire(s)* seek in the faces of women an interface between their memories and history, between self and other, subject and object. Rather than empty the face of meaning, female faces become imbued with an excess of multiple meanings and interconnections evoking a cultural and cinephilic memory and positing female beauty both as symbol of the mysteries of cinema and as a desired return to childhood, a remembrance of things past. It is perhaps surprising that Aumont leaves out of his otherwise wide-ranging discussion any reference to feminist theory, notably that of Laura Mulvey, whose work has often returned to questions of the female face on screen, particularly in close-up. In 'Close-ups and commodities' Mulvey traces the entangled histories of the close-up shot of the female star and the selling of images of sexualised female beauty as commodity (Mulvey 1996: 40–50). As the camera lingered on the face, suggests Mulvey, it introduced stasis into the movement and action of the narrative, thereby constructing the female face as an object upon which to gaze:

> The star close-up would hold the story in stasis, cutting her image out from the general flow of the narrative, emphasising her function as spectacle in its own right. Thus, a disjuncture appeared between the image of woman on the screen enhanced as spectacle and the general flow of narrative continuity organising the action. (p. 41)

Investigating in detail the implications of Mulvey's analyses of the strategies and effects of filming the female face for Aumont's theory of the *dévisageification* (defaceification) of the face in contemporary cinema constitutes a productive line of inquiry, but one that would lead me too far from my primary concern with memory and the moving image. I would nevertheless suggest that the *blowing up* (with its connotations of both enlargement and destructiveness) of the female face and the filmic presentation (in illumination and projection) of the female face as object of the gaze are connected to each other, as well as being bound up with the evocation of memory in the works by Godard and Marker under discussion. For both strategies figure the face as a memory object to be gazed upon and contemplated, allowing the viewer to make her or his own associations and connections. Female faces are presented as mysterious and inscrutable. But while on the one hand this fluidity suggests the mists of forgetting, on the other it represents a virtual cinematic zone where all our memories converge. The question then arises whether this self-reflexive deployment of women's faces as filmic monuments to cinema's past forms a closed circle, or whether it allows, as the films of Samuel, Simon and Benguigui do, an opening for the face in terms of what Agamben calls 'community'. In other words, how does this nostalgic attachment to the female face contribute to the circuits of cultural memory generated by *Histoire(s)*, *Level Five* and *Immemory*? Do they succeed in bearing witness to the past?

For Marker it would seem that the face acts as catalyst for 'participation in' the remembrance of the past of others, such as those who lived through the battle of Okinawa. The romantic investment in the face, with which we identify, draws us in to the mnemonic operations of the face. In this way, just as we saw for other objects in Chapter 2, the face as cinematic object creates a 'dream space' of mnemonic mediation, where individual memory (personal, emotive associations with the object) spills over into the collective sphere (shared cultural knowledge and commemoration). In Godard's case it is through faces of the past – among other objects of cultural memory – that *Histoire(s)* confronts history and cinema's role in it. By treating cinema as an archive-museum in which memory and meaning can be produced by the confrontation of fragments of its past, Godard turns cinema's obsession with (women's) faces back upon itself, springing them from their original contexts and thus creating a critical distance. These films and CD-ROM seem therefore to move away from Mulvey's and Aumont's models, while incorporating the aesthetic strategies of each. Both filmmakers attempt to go beyond and even subvert visual pleasure, transforming the beauty of the female face into a site of testimony to the horrors of violence. In this way films such as *Level Five* and *Histoire(s) du cinéma* offer an alternative form of witnessing that moves away from the face of the witness-survivor in the present as access to the past.

'Sois sûr d'avoir épuisé tout ce qui se communique par l'immobilité et le silence' (be sure to have exhausted all that can be communicated by stillness and silence) chants the soft voice of Julie Delpy in *2B fatale beauté*, citing a phrase that returns several times through the course of *Histoire(s)*. This quotation from Robert Bresson's *Notes sur le cinématographe*, spoken as the surreally blank female face of 'Albertine' fills the screen (as described above), takes on a significance that resonates with Mulvey's remarks about the passive stasis of the female star's face as filmed in classical cinema (Bresson 1995: 33). However, if classical cinema has exhausted the immobile and silent communication of the female face, as Aumont's argument would suggest, the films discussed in this chapter allow us to reconceive of women's faces on screen as conduits of memory. From Pola silently allowing her granddaughter to film her as she revisits the past in her mind's eye, to *Level Five*'s Laura, a phantom conversing with the deceased, these women offer the face as exteriority of their memory, as a site in which, through the framing of art, the pure, virtual communicability of the past is made manifest. It is uncomfortable and difficult to talk of the human face as a memory object, but only if one denies the fact that in film all subjects are also objects and that objects are one of the primary means of a mediation that makes cultural memory possible. As mediation between past and present, faces can 'screen' in both aspects of the word, presenting us with the problem of exposure versus the desirability of revelation. It is a tension with which moving image media must engage if they are to offer the spectator the possibility of facing the past.

Notes

1. In *Histoire(s) du cinéma: 2B fatale beauté*, Godard links the cinematic close-up to the practice of marking coins with the monarch's face: 'Et c'est un cinéaste, pas un historien, Marcel Pagnol, qui a découvert le secret du Masque de Fer, et en même temps l'origine du gros plan: le visage du roi sur la pièce de monnaie' (and it was a filmmaker, not a historian, Marcel Pagnol, who discovered the secret of the Iron Mask, and at the same time the origin of the close-up: the king's face on coins).
2. Kenji Tokitsu was born in Japan and has taught martial arts in Paris since 1971. He also holds doctorates in sociology and in Japanese language and civilisation. His status as witness is never clarified in the film; his own personal experiences are not explicitly recounted.
3. Although Samuel works in France, and the film was only distributed theatrically in France, having been produced by French production company Bizibi with funding from the Centre National du Cinéma, Natacha communicates with her grandmother in German throughout the film (Pola speaks Polish in Warsaw). We discover incidentally that Pola lived in Munich at some point after the war, but this remains unexplained. All quotations from the film are from the French subtitles.
4. This also relates to my discussion in Chapter 2 of the filmmakers themselves as both subjects and objects of memory in their films. Godard and Marker include themselves in this circuit and male faces are also drawn upon as memory objects in their work.
5. *Pied noir* is a term used in France to describe a person of European, or sometimes Jewish, heritage living in Algeria during French colonial rule; more specifically it refers to a person of French origin (though usually born in Algeria) repatriated after Algeria gained its independence in 1962.
6. Rosello is possibly referring to the book version of *Mémoires d'immigrés* rather than the film, since she refers in the chapter's introduction to 'writers whose interest in the French-Algerian conflict has led them to explore both the past and its difficult transmission' (2005: 109). However, she discusses Benguigui's film *Inch'Allah dimanche* in the following chapter, showing that on a more general level the kind of encounter she describes can be generated by film as well as written texts.
7. This form of transition recalls a shot in *Persona* where the film burns a hole through Bibi Andersson's face.
8. By Roland-François Lack (University College, London) in his unpublished list of sources for all the paintings in *Histoire(s) du cinéma*.

4. MEMORY MAPS AND CITY SPACE

Level Five (Chris Marker, 1997) opens with a vision of the contemporary city that implies a complex layering of temporalities and perspectives. The camera follows the circular motion of a hand moving a computer mouse then moves upwards to the monitor, zooming in on a video image of a city at night until it fills the screen and blurs out of focus, as if we are being sucked into that city image. Almost immediately there is a cut to a mobile shot where the camera moves along a road between high-rise buildings, illuminated with the lights of a city at night. This forward tracking shot is superimposed over another, still image of the calm, blank face of a statue. In Laura's voice we hear the following:

> Est-ce que tout ça peut être autre chose que les jouets d'un dieu fou qui nous a créés pour les lui construire? Imaginez un homme de Neandertal qui a la vision de cette chose-là; il a juste eu une vision poétique pleine de mouvements et de lumière, il a vu une mer de lumière. Il ne sait pas faire le tri entre toutes les images qui se posent à l'intérieur de sa tête comme des oiseaux, aussi rapides et irrattrapables que des oiseaux. Pensées, souvenirs, visions. Pour lui, tout revient au même: une espèce d'hallucination qui lui fait peur. C'est une vision du même ordre qu'a eu William Gibson en écrivant *Neuromancer* et en inventant le cyberspace.[1] Il a vu une espèce de mer des Sargasses, pleine d'algues binaires et sur cette image, les néandertaliens que nous sommes ont commencé à greffer leur propre vision, leurs pensées, leurs souvenirs, des misérables bribes d'informations. Mais aucun de nous ne sait ce qu'est une ville.
>
> (Could all this be anything but the playthings of a mad god who made us to create them for him? Imagine a Neanderthal man who has a vision of this; he has only had a poetic vision full of movements and light, he has seen a sea of light. He doesn't know how to sort out all the images which land inside his head like birds, as swift and ungraspable as birds. Thoughts, memories, visions. For him, it all comes down to the same

thing: a kind of hallucination that frightens him. It is the same kind of vision that William Gibson had when he wrote *Neuromancer* and invented cyberspace. He saw a sort of Sargasso Sea, brimming with binary algae, and onto this image, Neanderthals that we are, we began to graft our own vision, thoughts and memories, pathetic scraps of information. But none of us knows what a city is.)

The sequence posits the internet as the new modern city, but also implies that our experience as city-dwellers is precisely what is shaping our response to the new form of collective space that is cyberspace.[2] We are like the Neanderthal man who catches a surreal glimpse of a twentieth-century metropolis; we cannot grasp the meaning of this mass of connected technologies or understand what kind of space this is. All we can do is to try to comprehend it by imposing upon it our existing thoughts, visions and memories. We fit it into our current knowledge and frameworks for understanding the world and we construct it with these tools and forms of knowledge. Foremost among such frameworks is the city. The commentary, however, reminds us that our understanding of the concept of a 'city' is just as hazy as our comprehension of the internet. What exactly is a city? *Level Five*'s abstracted, blue-toned image of high buildings, motorways and electric lights may be an apt vision of the city as metaphor for the 'information superhighway', but it also returns us to the perspective of primitives: we see the city as 'une mer de lumière' (a sea of light), no less confusing and multiple than cyberspace itself.

For me this scene is a vivid and suggestive dramatisation of the interaction between contemporary media and our conception of space, most particularly of urban space. The suggestion that we in some way graft our memories, thoughts and visions onto intersubjective spaces, both physical and abstract, seems to be reflected in the filmic fabric of the sequence. On the superimposition of two images, a city and a primitive artefact, is in turn superimposed the two figures, of city space and cyberspace, in the commentary. Memories, thoughts and visions are grafted onto one another in the intersubjective space that is a film. In this chapter I want to explore the relation between the different kinds of spaces constituted by cities, media and memory and what film might reveal about such relations, drawing out some of the patterns of reflection as well as bearing in mind how each may affect the other. Cities, like objects and faces, can be positioned in film as points of intersection between past and present. As mobile spaces that are marked by the collective virtuality of memory, urban spaces provide a condensation of beings and buildings that, like memory itself, are a continual process of preservation, destruction and reconstruction. Cities seem to be particularly potent for the filmic exploration of memory's relation to space and location, although they are necessarily situated in a broader geography of lived space, which includes the virtual spaces of media and memory, as well as other physical environments such as rural areas. One might consider why Marker chose to begin *Level Five*, his investigation into memory and the remembering of the battle of Okinawa, with the meditation on cities and media technologies described above, a meditation which itself turns out to be from Laura's own memory of the writings of her dead lover ('voilà le genre de choses que tu écrivais' [this is the kind of thing you used to write], her narration continues). It is perhaps because for Marker memory itself is a kind of space. He theorises memory in specifically spatial terms in *Immemory*, as will be discussed below. Moreover, the CD-ROM is itself an example of the kind of evolving possibilities for mapping memory provided by contemporary forms of audiovisual media, creating new visions onto which the viewer's thoughts and memories can be grafted, through the intertextual, transversally signifying fabric of cultural objects. These works of Marker's figure memory as a space that can be charted through the visual and sonic textures of moving image media, revealing memory itself to be a palimpsest of inscription and reinscription, a mobile map that is continually being drawn and redrawn.

MEMORY AND PLACE

The link between memory and place has long been recognised, from classical philosophy to the present day. Ricœur emphasises this tradition when he takes the notion of *l'espace habité* (inhabited space) as a point of departure for his investigation into historiography as the inscription of memory. For Ricœur, memories of inhabited and visited places have a privileged status in human memory that makes them particularly important 'archives' for the historian:

> Le souvenir d'avoir habité dans telle maison d'une ville ou celui d'avoir voyagé dans telle partie du monde sont particulièrement éloquents et précieux; [. . .] dans ces souvenirs types, l'espace corporel est immédiatement relié à l'espace de l'environnement. (Ricœur 2000: 184)

> (The memory of having inhabited some house in some town or that of having travelled in some part of the world are particularly eloquent and telling. [. . .] In memories of this type, corporeal space is immediately linked with the surrounding space of the environment. [2004: 148])

This kind of memory that links body to environment has also been considered fundamental by Gaston Bachelard, who in *La Poétique de l'espace* figures the home (and most particularly the womb-like enclosure of the childhood home) as a primary site of memory, being a place where the body, and thus the self, is protected:

> Nous nous réconfortons en revivant des souvenirs de protection. Quelque chose de fermé doit garder les souvenirs en leur laissant leurs valeurs d'images. Les souvenirs du monde extérieur n'auront jamais la même tonalité que les souvenirs de la maison. (Bachelard 1957: 25)

(We comfort ourselves by reliving memories of protection. Something enclosed must conserve memories whilst allowing their value as images to remain. Memories of the external world will never have the same tonality as memories of home.)

The sense of the act of inhabiting as the formation of a protective shell is remarked upon in Walter Benjamin's notes on interiors and traces in *The Arcades Project*: '"to dwell" as a transitive verb – as in the notion of "indwelt spaces" – herewith an indication of the frenetic topicality concealed in habitual behaviour. It has to do with fashioning a shell for ourselves' (Benjamin 1999c: 221). For Paul Ricœur too, the power of memory of places comes from the act of inhabiting them, which is to say that inhabiting is active, or 'transitive' as Benjamin describes it. Ricœur conceives inhabiting as having as much to do with movement and routes through different spaces as it has to do with the desire for protection. He describes the act of inhabiting in terms of a series of structuring polarities: 'résider et se déplacer, s'abriter sous un toit, franchir un seuil et sortir au-dehors' (2000: 185) ('reside and displace, take shelter under a roof, cross a threshold and go out' [2004: 150]).

This leads me to return to Bergson's theories of memory discussed in Chapter 1. His concept of a motor-sensory, habitual memory implies that places are a particularly powerful means of remembering. The kind of memory that is ingrained in the body by repeated movements marks the routes and places through which we regularly move with such a strong sense of familiarity that after years of absence we can still return to a neighbourhood and navigate its pathways, or go straight to a secret hiding place in a house inhabited in childhood. It is my contention, however, that places are not only learnt by the body as a result of repeated movement through them; they are also privileged memory objects for the evocation of representational memory. We can vividly remember images of places we have known well, while a loved one's features fade into a blur over time, as Laura – the face in the misty light – reminds us in *Level Five*. This is a quality employed in the tradition that Frances Yates (1996) terms 'the art of memory': the classical mnemonic techniques of orators attributed to the poet Simonides of Ceos and passed down to us in Cicero's *De Oratore*, Quintilian's *Institutio oratoria* and the anonymous *Ad C. Herennium libri IV*. The story of Simonides' invention of the art of memory is recounted in Cicero's *De Oratore*. The poet chants a panegyric to his host at a banquet, dedicating a lengthy passage of it to the praise of Castor and Pollux. The host meanly pays him only half his fee, suggesting that he obtain the rest from the gods he has praised so highly. The poet is called away and informed that two visitors await him outside; as he leaves, the roof collapses, crushing the guests and leaving their corpses unidentifiable. Simonides finds no visitors but realises the two gods have amply rewarded him for his tribute by thus saving him. He is also able to identify the guests' bodies because he remembers where each was sitting, allowing the mourning families to find and bury their dead.

This experience is supposed to have inspired him to invent an art of memory based on the 'placing' of ideas. The first step of the mnemonic, Yates tells us in her authoritative study of this art, 'was to imprint on the memory a series of loci or places' (Yates 1996: 18). These places, such as streets or houses, are then furnished with images that stand in for parts of the speech to be memorised. When it comes to delivering the speech, the orator need only take an imaginary stroll through the rooms of the building or along a row of houses in order to remember the correct order of rhetoric. It is a highly visual art, for the orator must be able to create a vivid mental image of the space through which he navigates in his mind. This representational quality is underlined by Yates in her rejection of the term 'mnemotechnics' to describe the process:

> The word 'mnemotechnics' hardly conveys what the artificial memory of Cicero may have been like, as it moved among the buildings of ancient Rome, seeing the images stored on the places, with a piercing inner vision which immediately brought to his lips the thoughts and words of his speech. I prefer to use the expression 'art of memory' for this process. (p. 20)

Looking more closely at the process of this localised remembering suggests to me an apparent coming together of Bergson's apparently distinct two forms of memory: bodily, habitual memory and the visualising memory of representation. Yates highlights the vivid inner 'seeing' of the orator but also the automatic motor-sensory response to the vision, in the thoughts and words that are 'immediately brought to his lips'. For me this implies an interesting link between representation and habit. Is it not also possible that remembered places can be visualised or evoked in the mind's eye precisely because they can be associated mentally with that learned, physical habit that guides the body through familiar space?

Bergson's example of the learning of a schoolbook lesson differentiates between the repetitive action of memorising and repeating the lesson and spontaneous memories of the experience of the learning process.

> Le souvenir de la leçon, en tant qu'apprise par cœur, a tous les caractères d'une habitude. Comme l'habitude il s'acquiert par la répétition d'un même effort. [. . .] Au contraire, le souvenir de telle lecture particulière, la seconde ou la troisième par exemple, n'a aucun des caractères de l'habitude. L'image s'en est nécessairement imprimée du premier coup dans la mémoire, puisque les autres lectures constituent, par définition même, des souvenirs différents. (1939: 86)

> (The memory of the lesson, which is remembered in the sense of learned by heart, has all the marks of a habit. Like a habit, it is acquired by the repetition of the same effort. [. . .] The memory of each successive reading, on the contrary, the second or third for instance, has none of

the marks of a habit. Its image was necessarily imprinted at once on the memory, since the other readings form, by their very definition, other recollections. [1988: 79–80])

If we substitute the lesson for the orator's speech, it can be seen that the spatialisation of the lesson and its containment in localised images mean that remembering it draws on the imagination (in the sense of visualisation as opposed to fantasy, as discussed in Chapter 1) as much as on repetition. In fact, in making the distinction Bergson recognises that the two forms can work together: 'de ces deux mémoires, dont l'une imagine et dont l'autre répète, la seconde peut suppléer la première et souvent même en donner l'illusion' (1939: 87) ('of these two memories, of which the one imagines and the other repeats, the second may supplement the first and even sometimes be mistaken for it' [1988: 82, translation modified]). However, for Bergson the difference remains fundamental between memories acquired through repeated efforts and those evoking in a kind of flash a particular, datable and therefore unique, moment from the past. But his choice of wording here already alerts us to the complex relationship of these forms of memory. The relation is one of supplement in the Derridean sense: habitual memory both adds to and stands in for spontaneous memory. While it is difficult to avoid the conclusion that the memorisation of a text (or rhetorical structure of a text) is something quite different from the visualisation of a particular, non-repeatable event from the past, I propose that that the remembering of places troubles this clear distinction between habit and imagination. It is because we inhabit places, because we layer them with the embodied memory of repeated movement, that we so frequently remember (and envisage) them in the form of a condensation of similar episodes: not a particular moment in that stairwell but the many times we climbed the stairwell, condensed into a single image. This is rather like the Proustian imperfect tense of À la recherche du temps perdu, in which the narrator distils vivid images of the past from a myriad of similar moments, sometimes using the imperfect tense to convey a sense of recurring incidence over a duration of time, at other times using a variety of tenses and none the less alerting the reader to the condensation of episodes into a single description.[3] It is not that places can never be remembered in terms of specific, unique occasions, rather that certain kinds of place memory, including that involved in the classical art of memory, can reveal the complex entanglement of repeated bodily motion and inner representation or visualisation.

It is this entanglement that is pertinent for a study of 'motion pictures': films make possible a visual rendering of the movement of bodies through space. In addition, I would suggest, film holds the possibility of a descriptive mode or 'imperfect tense' which both crystallises duration into particular images and yet evokes the possibility of recurrent incidence. Benjamin speculated about this potential in The Arcades Project, imagining a montage of temporal condensation that would map a memory of Paris:

Couldn't an exciting film be made from the map of Paris? From the unfolding of its various aspects in temporal succession? From the compression of a centuries-long movement of streets, boulevards, arcades, and squares into the space of half an hour? (1999c: 83).

More recently, cultural studies has seen a burgeoning of interest in city space and its complex relations to lived experience, leading to rich seams of speculation about the affinities between film and the city. James Donald posits that 'the imagined landscape of the city has become, inescapably, a cinematic landscape (1999: 68), while Ackbar Abbas suggests that 'it is exactly the instability of the cinematic image that allows it to evoke the city in all its errancy in ways that stable images cannot (2003: 145). Clearly there is an increasing recognition of the effect of film on our experience of environment, as well as the particular possibilities of the filmic to capture the intricacy of urban spaces. In her dense and richly evocative 'atlas' of the mobile mappings of emotion in art, architecture and film, the theorist of visual culture Giuliana Bruno specifically posits film as a modern version of the art of memory, reconfiguring the art of Cicero and Quintilian as a proto-filmic invention:

> With respect to this rendering of location, the architecture of memory reveals ties to the filmic experience of place. Before motion pictures spatialized and mobilized discourse – substituting for memory, in the end – the art of memory understood recollection spatially. [. . .] it is precisely this experience of revisiting sites that the architectural journey of film sets in place, and in motion. (2002: 221)

Claire Simon's *Mimi* (2003) seems to support this assertion, and we can take it as an example of film's potential for the spatialisation of memory. In *Mimi*, we are taken on a journey around Nice that is also a journey into Mimi's past. Movement through various places triggers a series of memories; the film's architectural journey sets in place and in motion the architecture of Mimi's remembering. Though this journey takes Mimi to new places, it is clear that Nice is a city that she has inhabited. Its contours have become a physical habit that is none the less marked at specific places with unique moments or turning points, such as the church door, a site which marked a new opening for Mimi. For it was here that she entered into a reconciliation of her Catholic upbringing with her homosexuality, by means of a conversation with a kindly monk. This moment of particular experience and others like it are situated as if in relief, against a background in the imperfect tense that evokes Mimi's past as spatial duration, a layer of 'pastness' cloaking the city. The film opens with a slow, hazy panorama of Nice, intercut with credits that culminate in Mimi's name as the title of the film, followed by a medium shot of Mimi herself in profile, standing in a cloister of the Laghet monastery and apparently looking out over Nice. There is nothing especially surprising about this kind of establishing shot, but it comes to stand for this layer of Mimi's past that coats the city. It is the reverse of a point-of-view shot: we see Mimi's gaze only once the camera's gaze has wandered over the space she might be looking at. The city both contains her (just as it houses her memories) and is overwritten by her name.

Moving images are able to map inhabited space using editing and camera movement to house the individual's body in a place and suggest the temporal layers of inhabitation. But what of the city as a space of collective memory? *Mimi* explores Nice as the site of an individual's memories, but cities, of course, are by definition inhabited by thousands. How does film account for the city as intersection between subjective and collective pasts?

Memory and the City

Urban centres are shifting places where, as Ricœur points out, various different temporal layers are visible: 'une ville confronte dans le même espace des époques différentes, offrant au regard une histoire sédimentée des goûts et des formes culturelles' (2000: 187) ('a city brings together in the same space different ages, offering to our gaze a sedimented history of tastes and cultural forms' [2004: 151]). But these varying architectures and juxtaposed historical forms are only the visible sediment, to take up Ricœur's term, of myriad lives that have inscribed their habits into the city and have housed their memories there. These everyday movements of the masses that live in urban spaces, of which Mimi represents just one particle, are what interest Michel de Certeau, who opposes them to the overarching, panoptic viewpoint of authorities who theorise the city as a space to be made clean, orderly and functional (1990: 124–6, 1984: 93–5). This latter viewpoint he terms *la ville-concept*, a notion of 'city' with its own commanding rhetoric, which is always continually resisted by what he calls 'the semantic wanderings' of the masses.[4] Though he sees this in terms of a constant dispersal and rearrangement of narrative and therefore of the memorable, nevertheless traces, or sediments, do remain in what he calls 'legend', which one might also understand in terms of the cultural memory of the city:

> Il en sort [de la mémoire] des éclats dans les légendes. Les objets aussi, et les mots, sont creux. Un passé y dort, comme dans les gestes quotidiens du marcher, du manger, du coucher, où sommeillent des révolutions anciennes. (1990: 162)

> (Fragments of [memory] come out in legends. Objects and words also have hollow places in which the past sleeps, as in the everyday acts of walking, eating, going to bed, in which ancient revolutions slumber. [1984: 108])

That objects, words and gestures contain our memory is something I have discussed in detail in Chapter 2. What I find particularly significant, however, in this short excerpt from De Certeau is the connection between these material containers of memory and the mobile habits of the collective body. Recalling the etymology of the word *habit* (from the Latin *habitus* 'demeanour, appearance, dress', originally the past participle of *habere* 'to have, to hold, to possess'), it suggests a dual movement by which inhabitants of a city 'clothe' the space in memory at the same time as the city 'clothes' or contains them as the receptacle of their memories and therefore of a shared zone of identity.

> 'Les souvenirs nous attachent là . . . C'est personnel, ça n'intéresserait personne, mais enfin ça fait quand même l'esprit d'un quartier'.[5] Il n'y a de lieu que hanté par des esprits multiples, tapis là en silence et qu'on peut 'évoquer' ou non. On n'habite que des lieux hantés. (De Certeau 1990: 162)

> ('Memories tie us to that place . . . It's personal, not interesting to anyone else, but after all that's what gives a neighborhood its character.' There is no place that is not haunted by many different spirits hidden in silence, spirits one can 'invoke' or not. Haunted places are the only ones people can live in. [1984: 108])

I propose that this haunting, viewed in another way, can be seen in terms of the Deleuzian virtuality of the past. City space, like cultural objects, contains the virtual dimension of *passé en général* that is formed by the continual unfolding movement, or 'becoming' to use a more Deleuzian term, of everyday life and its gestures, objects and words. The reception of *Mimi* in the French press made much of Mimi's ordinariness, to the extent that *Figaroscope* dismissed the film as utterly banal: 'le portrait sans fard d'une femme à l'histoire plus que banale [. . .] Beaucoup de plans vides, sans intérêt, des lieux communs, de plates confidences' (the frank portrait of a woman whose story is incredibly banal [. . .] a lot of empty shots, lacking in interest, commonplaces and lacklustre confessions) (B.B. 2003). While more sympathetic reviewers saw this very ordinariness as a relationship of the particular to the universal, which has a long tradition in literary narratives, I find the visual and spatial emphasis in this brief, negative review especially revealing. The 'empty' shots (*plans vides*) of buildings, streets and vistas, and the commonplaces (*lieux communs*, a phrase with a double meaning in both English and French), describe precisely the haunted, mnemonic quality of sites in the film: personal and arguably 'uninteresting', just as De Certeau's Croix-Rousse inhabitant says in the quotation above, yet evoking a virtual realm of collective memory: *l'esprit d'un quartier* (the spirit of the neighbourhood).

More precisely, this virtual layer is evoked in two connected ways: the slow pan, tilt or tracking shot (in the ways I have already begun to explore above) and the intersubjective detour. I have already argued in Chapter 3 that the process of remembering in *Mimi* is intersubjective. It takes place in the space between the two women: the filmmaker and her subject. This is crucial to the remembering process as it relates to the city in the film. Although the film's promenade through Nice is certainly a means of drawing out narratives of the memories of an individual, Mimi, this promenade does not quite take the form one might expect. It is the filmmaker-camerawoman, rather than the inhabitant, who leads the way through the town. Simon takes Mimi to places she has not been to before and to sites that have changed beyond recognition; as Simon herself says, 'c'est moi qui ai choisi tous les lieux sauf le premier, le sanctuaire de Laghet où Mimi nous a emmenés' (It was me who chose all the places except the first one, the Laghet monastery where Mimi took us) (Simon 2003). So, for example, against a series of shots of an open-air sports complex, we see and hear Mimi begin to remember her intense infatuation with the neighbour's daughter who lived in Africa: 'je me souviens quand la fille de ma voisine arrivait d'Afrique [. . .]. Elle était très belle et j'ai été amoureuse, quoi' (I remember when my neighbour's daughter used to come back from Africa [. . .]. She was very beautiful and I was, well, in love). Mimi has never seen this sports complex before: 'je n'y suis jamais venue [. . .] quand j'étais môme ça n'existait pas. Il y avaient des cours de tennis, mais c'était pas pour nous quoi, c'était les riches qui allaient jouer au tennis' (I've never been here before [. . .] when I was a kid it didn't exist. There were tennis courts but that wasn't for us, it was the rich people who went to play tennis). However, it is the very absence of this place in her memory that triggers recollections of the attractive neighbour's daughter, since she was one of the lucky ones who did play tennis. The moment of remembering – 'je me souviens' – coincides on the soundtrack with a shot of a black female athlete running. Although we never know for certain the ethnic origin of the neighbour's daughter, only that her skin was a possibly North African but ultimately undecidable 'couleur de caramel' (caramel colour), the implication is that this athlete's black skin and physical beauty somehow contain the memory of a fascination with the exotic otherness of the object of Mimi's desire, who was rich, beautiful and from across the sea. When the camera returns to Mimi's face looking out across the people playing basketball and tennis, or running round the track, a cut between the two shots means we cannot know for sure whether she was looking at the black runner as she began to remember, or whether it was the filmmaker's (and editor's) eye that selected this figure as an appropriate 'Madeleine'. In either case, the runner is, in the film's juxtaposition of sound and image, a figure who suggests for the viewer the adolescent desire that Mimi is remembering, and yet exceeds and overflows that individual memory, opening up a gap between the Nice of Mimi's past and that of the filmed present.

The filmed images of Nice can be seen to function, then, as a kind of intersubjective detour in memory, whereby Mimi's remembering process passes through the filmic city tour and final editing process of her friend. As the filmmaker explains: 'Mimi avait un scénario, et moi j'en avais un autre: le plan de la ville de Nice' (Mimi had one script and I had another: the city map of Nice)

(Simon 2003). Simon's terminology is interesting here because the filmic city mapping in *Mimi* causes the term *plan de la ville* to take on a double meaning: 'plan' in French meaning both map and shot, something to which I will return in the next part of this chapter. The detour through Simon's filmmaking allows Mimi's personal memories to map onto a collective domain, because an inter-subjective gap is opened up in the film's dual movement through city space and Mimi's memory narrative. This creates a space for the ghostly presence of the memories of countless others, a virtuality suggested by the so-called *plans vides* (empty shots). These 'empty' shots mentioned in B.B.'s (2003) criticism of the film in fact refer to the slow wanderings of the camera over roof-tops, flyovers, paths, gardens, houses banked up in the hills, close-up shots of the texture of walls and stone, as well as the assimilation of passers-by into the frame. All of these lingering, roaming shots of the city open up a virtual space in the spatio-temporal disjunction between the place we are looking at and Mimi's narra-tive. But rather than leave this as an empty space, a pure virtuality, this sense of a collective past is actualised through chance encounters that are incorporated into the film: the scenes of Algerian musician Mohammed Mokhtari playing his violin, the Armenian tea-seller on the beach, the train-spotter who lets Mimi listen to his recording of steam trains on his Walkman, the sailor who imagines being reincarnated as a housewife with Mimi as his sailor husband (nationality unknown), young Arab men who perform an impromptu freestyle rap for the camera, and of course Mimi's Italian friend, Diego Origlia, who sings to her in Italian.

Such encounters illustrate the ways in which music can add to the mobile shots of the urban landscape as a memory object that also makes the collective fabric of the city's past resonate. Mohammed Mokhtari was brought over from Algeria to play the violin in the film and is seen, anonymously, playing in dif-ferent locations in the town. Simon's commentary reveals her intentions: 'son violon arabe disait l'exil et sa mélancolie. Disait que Nice est aussi une ville arabe, comme la Tosca dit que c'est une ville italienne et que ces identités sont merveilleuses mais amères' (his Arab violin told of exile and its melancholy, recounted that Nice is also an Arab city, just as la Tosca says it is an Italian city and that these identities are wonderful but bitter) (Simon 2003). But even without knowing this information about the musical sources and the direc-tor's intentions, the Italian opera and Arab music that underscore the images of Nice create the atmosphere of a port town and a border town, a place where different nationalities collide and where the social space is a palimpsest continually being inscribed with the comings and goings of different cultural identities. Music is therefore an important factor in the generation of the 'spirit of the neighbourhood' in *Mimi*: the shared music of collective memory. This is reminiscent of the functioning of music in Benguigui's *Mémoires d'immigrés* (1997), where music is seen to provide an emotive focal point for the memories of an uprooted immigrant community. Godard clearly had similar ideas about music when making his film *Notre musique* (2004), whose title translates as 'our music', and which also explores a city – Sarajevo – as a collective space haunted by a troubled past. In an interview, Godard explained:

> We went to Sarajevo and it was as if the tramways were making us hear a certain kind of music, so I called it *Notre musique*: theirs, ours, everybody's. It's what makes us live, or makes us hope. One could say 'our philosophy' or 'our life', but 'our music' is nicer and has a different effect. And then there's also the question of what aspect of our music was destroyed at Sarajevo? And what remains of our music that was there? (Godard and Witt 2005: 29)

In *Mimi*, music forms a mobile layer or sediment that, like the people Mimi meets, forms part of the texture of the cityscape and mingles with its sounds. Thus the 'music' that transports Mimi as she listens to a Walkman is the rushing sound of a steam train, recorded or obtained somehow by the train-spotter she and Claire meet by the railway tracks. The recording is not a part of the soundtrack. At this moment we are watching the remembering process, rather as we watch Pola revisit Warsaw in her memory's eye in *Pola à 27 ans* (Natacha Samuel, 2003). We watch as Mimi listens, sharing the headphones with the likeable fanatic. Responding to what she hears, Mimi describes her memory of a train and its great gusts of steam encountered on regular walks with her mother, as the ghostly train runs its course, conjured, imagined and remembered through the medium of recorded sound: 'et là il arrivait sous le pont [. . .] ma mère, sur le pont St-Philippe, elle me tenait la main, tu vois [. . .] et alors j'avais l'impression que ça m'emportait dans les nuages' (and there it would arrive underneath the bridge [. . .] my mother, on the St-Philippe bridge, she held my hand, you see [. . .] and then I had the feeling that it was carrying me away in the clouds). The sound allows Mimi to re-experience physically the habit of a repeated childhood journey, but it also forms a point of intersection between the city's past, as remembered by Mimi and recorded on a tape, and its present: the train-loving inhabitant encountered by chance.

The virtuality of the city's past, or its spirit, to pick up again on the term used by De Certeau, is conveyed in the film between the actual presences of Mimi, Claire and her camera, the others they encounter and the cityscape whose images and sounds, including the symbolic, extra-diegetic sounds of music, provide the framework of the film. Early on in the film a sequence shot pans slowly round a low-angle view of pine-tree tops, the sound of cicadas buzzing loudly. Finally the camera pans down and settles on a flight of stone steps leading through an archway into a walled corridor. We see Mimi in the archway disappearing into the corridor. Then the camera moves slowly downwards, following the zigzag pattern of the deep shadow cast on the steps by the bright Mediterranean sunlight. This is followed by a shot of Mimi in the corridor, between the white limestone walls, standing in a rectangle of light; we hear the following exchange:

Claire (from behind the camera):[6] Tu es déjà venue dans ce coin? (Have you been to this spot before?)

Mimi: Non. J'aimerais que tu viennes voir, Claire. (No. I'd like you to come and see this, Claire.)

Claire: D'accord. Qu'est-ce que tu vois? (Sure. What do you see?)

Mimi: Là je vois . . . je vois un portail. (Now I can see . . . I see a gate.) (Cut to a shot of Mimi standing in front of a large wooden gate.)

This once again illustrates the fact that Simon, rather than Mimi, is choosing the sites of Mimi's memory in the city. The extended shot of the sounds and sights of a corner of Nice on a hot day seems to engulf Mimi, framing her as just another part of the present and past of the city. However, Mimi's sighting of a gate creates a mental connection to a memory she has just been recounting. The previous sequence showed Mimi in profile, looking out across the bay, seeing a particular memory in her mind's eye, while we, the spectators, see only the panoramic shot of the bay. Her story began, 'là je vois un portail' (now I can see a gate). The intriguing thing about this memory is that it is not her own. It is the story of how her father was injured by a mine, and his commanding officer killed, stealing lemons from a garden during the war. She recounts it in the present tense as though she were witnessing it. The connection between the imagined memories – the postmemory – of family members and the present-day architecture of the city is finally made when Mimi discovers a real gate, a gate that may or may not be the same gate that led to the garden where the lemon tree tempted her father in the hunger of wartime. In a very concrete way, these two sequences reveal the city as a means of access to the memories of others. Rather like the 'dream space' of the museum, the filmed city can be sited at the intersection of the memories of viewer, filmmaker and subject and is haunted by those of many others.

Media and Mobile Mapping

In her 2003 book *La Mémoire saturée*, the historian and sociologist Régine Robin suggests that new media, such as the internet, DVDs and CD-ROMs, have led to new conceptions of memory. Extending back the lineage of such new media to the mechanical reproduction of photography and film, Robin seems, along with other contemporary cultural theorists, to fear that the limitless reproducibility and ceaseless multiplication of images could flatten out the contemporary experience of time into a kind of eternal present, in which 'une nouvelle logique de l'instant éliminerait de notre horizon le passé et le futur, l'épaisseur de l'historicité, donc la mémoire' (a new logic of the present moment would eliminate from our horizon the past and the future, the thickness of history and therefore memory) (Robin 2003: 415). However, Robin also recognises the possibility of navigation through such media in a way that resists the impositions of modern space, in what she calls a *détournement du non-lieu* – a diversion or hijacking of the non-place of visual media. She cites artists, writers and filmmakers who work with contemporary media in a way that incites the reader-spectator to become one of these new flâneurs, the nineteenth-century Parisian figure of the city wanderer. Robin suggests that such work makes us into new wanderers of space, taking our own paths through it and in doing so activating and encountering the mappings of memory. In conceiving such artwork in terms of *déambulation* (strolling or ambling), Robin moves towards a multidimensional, cartographic model of memory, evoked by the very media that had seemed to threaten a flattening out of the thickness of history and memory.

We have already seen how *Mimi* takes up this spatial conception of memory, particularly in terms of urban space. In other recent French films too, such as *Pola à 27 ans* and *Se souvenir des belles choses* (Zabou Breitman, 2002), the concrete, collective space of the city becomes a means of visualising the shifting inner space of an individual's memory. In the process, these films disrupt the linear, unitary character we like to impart to memory in common parlance. The workings of memory are revealed to be formed not as a linear trip down memory lane, but rather in the shape of a map – a map that is fragmentary, fluid and mobile. Such a memory map is hardly a stable guide for the tourist of the past's city, but it is none the less constitutive of the fragile experience we call identity, and deeply marked with feelings of desire, love, pain and grief. Departing from Robin's main proposition, I propose that contemporary media, rather than posing a threat to memory and history, provide us with new models and means of visualising the ways in which memory is always threatened from within, operating as it does in tandem with forgetting and with the continual flux of time. While this is absolutely necessary and profoundly creative, since it is what allows us to live, move, adapt and grow in our collective space, it can also be a source of suffering, as we will see particularly in *Pola à 27 ans* and *Se souvenir des belles choses*.

A cartographic model of memory can be found in one of the ambulatory works cited by Robin, discussed in Chapters 2 and 3 of this book: Chris Marker's CD-ROM *Immemory* (1998). As we have seen, *Immemory* creates a virtual memory space that, as the title *Immemory* suggests, allows for the fluidity and forgetting that are always bound up with remembering. The CD-ROM format allows the viewer-flâneur to travel and roam through the images, texts and sounds, taking bifurcations and short cuts and revisiting favourite places. It is precisely the kind of 'tender map' evoked by Bruno (2002) in relation to Mme de Scudéry's seventeenth-century *Carte de Tendre*, which lays out the emotional landscape of a love affair, for it too charts memory via the subjectivity of the map-maker. But *Immemory* is also an intersubjective map, drawing on cultural as well as personal associations to form its routes and layouts.

Wishing to move away from what he calls the 'megalomaniac tendency' of conceiving of our memories in terms of the overarching narratives of a classic novel, Marker theorises memory as spatial and remembering as a cartographic practice:

> Une approche plus modeste et peut-être plus fructueuse serait de considérer les fragments d'une mémoire en termes de géographie. Dans toute vie nous trouverions des continents, des îles, des déserts, des marais, des territoires surpeuplés et des terrae incognitae. De cette mémoire nous pourrions dessiner la carte. (Inlay cover of *Immemory*)

> (A more modest and perhaps more fruitful approach would be to consider the fragments of a person's memory in terms of geography. In every life we would find continents, islands, deserts, marshes, overpopulated territories and terrae incognitae. We could draw the map of this memory.)

The geography of *Immemory* creates in this way a fusion of historical time with lived space in its model of cartographic memory. As a point of intersection between a particular multimedia project and the wider sphere of memory in today's mediatised society, *Immemory* suggests that the vast, interconnected space of contemporary media – film, multimedia and internet – does not flatten out time into the two-dimensional space of the screen, but rather creates intertextual mnemonic spaces through which the viewing, and thinking, subject can browse, navigate or surf, to use internet terminology. Like the flâneur, the city wanderer moving through inhabited streets and architecture, the subject navigates through the contemporary landscapes of media, memory and the metropolis. But these representational zones rarely map onto one another perfectly. Rather, they fuse to create a multidimensional, mobile space where disorientation is a constant possibility. As we move through time and space, the mental maps we produce of our mnemonic, urban and media environments are constantly subject to redistribution and sometimes to complete disintegration and fragmentation. But rather than understanding this as a kind of growing threat to the spatiotemporal anchoring of the modern subject, I contend that the geography of our social representations has always held the possibility of dislocation, but that this can be reconceived and represented anew through contemporary artistic media, including film.

Film, like memory, may be conceived in terms of cartography. As we have seen, and as Bruno points out, it too maps space before the gaze of the spectator. I want to suggest that film's mapping processes resemble those of memory: they too are fragmentary, fluid and mobile, never giving a total picture, for even in the aerial view there is always something outside the frame. I am effecting here a slight *détournement* of some conventional notions of mapping and cartography. It might seem that the very concept of mapping is of a totalising, ordering function with relation to space: the kind of cartography that produces

Ordnance Survey maps and city guides for tourists. De Certeau distinguishes between 'cartes' (maps) and 'parcours' (tours) (De Certeau 1990: 175, 1984: 118). He aligns cartography with the god-like view from skyscrapers, and opposes the totalising view of the map-makers, in other words the authority figures and the town planners, to the everyday practices and movements of those at ground level. My notion of mapping goes beyond this binary opposition. Our existence in space draws on various different kinds of mapping, both the rigid cartography of *plans de ville* and, more importantly, the kinds of mental maps we constantly configure and reconfigure as we move through city space. Social psychologists such as Stanley Milgram have argued convincingly for a cartographic aspect of individuals' knowledge and memories of city space (Milgram 1984: 291), though of course these mental maps do not always fit those issued by authorities. In fact, in some ways they are more accurate, since they reflect the social representations individuals use to navigate their city, both physically and mentally. As Milgram puts it:

> The person's social identity is bound up with the neighbourhood in which he lives and the social connotations attached to that place. The social representations of the city are more than disembodied maps; they are mechanisms whereby the bricks, streets, and physical geography of a place are endowed with social meaning. Such urban representations, therefore, help define the social order of the city, and the individual's place in it. (p. 309)

This relates to the way in which Giuliana Bruno draws on Mme de Scudéry's seventeenth-century *Carte de Tendre* to elaborate her idea of 'tender mapping', an emotionally imaged geography. This kind of mapping, as Bruno puts it, 'does not reproduce the ordering principle of analytic knowledge, but rather tries to chart a movement. [. . .] In Scudéry's form of cartographic narration, as in film's own, there is no distinction between map and tour' (2002: 245).

In *Mimi* the virtuality of a city's past is evoked in the gaps and bridges between an individual's past and present, and in the intersubjective city space in which this is conjured. The narrative of Mimi's life is spatialised, mapped onto the contours of Nice, so that the *plan de ville* shown by the film is of the order of memory and emotion rather than the structured, totalising viewpoint of an official map. But while the small gaps between the filmed images of the present-day city and Mimi's memories fulfil the positive function of opening up an intersubjective, virtual space, in *Pola à 27 ans* and *Se souvenir des belles choses*, the moving image is used to convey the pain experienced in the disjunction between the mobile mappings of memory and the urban space that structures emotional landscapes. In this way, the vicissitudes of the individual's experience of time and space are brought together in a visual cartography, whose fragmentation reflects the instability at the heart of human memory.

Between Creativity and Disintegration

The two films to which I now turn could seem in some ways to be so different that it is difficult to compare them. *Pola à 27 ans*, a 2003 film by Natacha Samuel, is an hour-long documentary following Pola's return to Warsaw, and to the death camps of Auschwitz and Birkenau. *Se souvenir des belles choses*, a fictional feature by French actress-turned-director Zabou Breitman, released in 2002, charts the progressive disintegration of the world of a young woman, Claire, as her mind is overtaken by early-onset Alzheimer's disease, and the love affair that blossoms and suffers in the course of this. Despite their great differences it is notable that both films are haunted by the Holocaust. *Pola à 27 ans* is explicitly concerned with those events, while Breitman's film, on the other hand, touches fleetingly on that moment in history as part of a broader concern with troubled memory. Amongst the array of characters suffering from memory problems in *Se souvenir des belles choses* are two Jewish men, Léo Finkel and his friend. A brief flashback sequence, hovering on the periphery between fantasy and memory, shows them as young men in the uniform of camp detainees. As discussed in my introduction, the Holocaust clearly remains a significant part of French cultural memory, to the extent that it has become a reference point that potentially implicates all artistic inquiries into the nature of memory.

The films present two very different ways of showing the experience of spatiotemporal disorientation, but both do so in terms of the relation of the memory of the individual to the urban environment, a relation that in both cases is troubled by disintegration. Pola retains vivid memories of her time in Warsaw before the war and of her experience of the camps, but finds that her mental maps are unreadable in terms of the present-day space she encounters on her return. Time has swept away her childhood home in Warsaw and turned the horror and death of Auschwitz into a museum. On the other hand, Claire's memory mappings are disintegrating from the inside, whilst for those around her the town remains the same. Pola's memories fail to map onto a transformed space, Claire's memories are slipping away to such an extent that she can no longer map them onto any space.

Pola à 27 ans begins with a series of domestic scenes, filmed in long takes, where the filmmaker's grandmother poignantly answers her granddaughter's questions about survival and death in the extermination camps. Through the course of the film Pola passes through three kinds of place: the domestic space of home and hotel room, the city space of Warsaw and the domain of the camps at Auschwitz and Birkenau. Each has its role to play in the film's rendering of Pola's memory, but it is specifically the urban scenes on which I want to focus here. The first experience of urban space in the film comes in the scene already described in Chapter 3, where an image of her silently remembering is followed by the explanation, 'J'étais à Varsovie' (I was in Warsaw). In her memories she is transported there once again; she is in Warsaw. We watch her reinhabit the urban landscape where she had once been content, mapping happy memories onto the contours of the city. Sitting in her living room, she smiles almost girlishly as she revisits Warsaw in the imagination of her memory, and tells her granddaughter how glad she is they are able to return there together. Then, as the film makes the transition from the interview location to the return to Poland, we hear her continuing her tale, talking of Warsaw:

> La Varsovie était tout pour moi. Toute la famille vivait à Varsovie depuis des générations. C'était une ville sublime, 'le petit Paris', une vraie capitale – de belles femmes, une vie palpitante: des théâtres, des concerts, des expositions, des cafés, de grands restaurants, une vraie vie nocturne. C'était une belle ville. Et c'est là que je suis née.

> (Warsaw was everything for me. All my father's family had lived in Warsaw for generations. It was a sublime city: 'little Paris', a real capital – beautiful women, an exhilarating lifestyle: theatres, concerts, exhibitions, cafés, big restaurants, a real night-life. It was a beautiful city. And it's there that I was born.)

If Pola imagines the extent to which Warsaw has changed, it is chiefly in terms of the uprooting that she herself experienced and in the course of which almost all her family died. She explains that the reason she has never before returned to Warsaw is that she no longer knows anyone there: 'pas une âme que je connaisse' (not a single soul I know). She knows already, then, that Warsaw, bereft of her beloved parents, husband, brothers and friends, can no longer be the place it is in her memory. It seems, however, that in visiting Warsaw accompanied by her daughter's child, she hopes to reconnect the urban space of the past with the emotional landscape of the present.

It is then that we see the first image of the map. In a haptic image, an image that makes the tactile visible, we trace the city space visually through Pola's fingers as they seek out remembered places on the map. Her hands seem to know the city, and the image of her seeking fingers tracing over the map recalls the expression 'to know a place like the back of one's hand' (Figure 4.1). With a habitual sense of spatial outlines she confidently locates the street where she grew up, even though it is no longer on the map. We then cut to an image of Pola standing by a vast Warsaw highway, against a backdrop of skyscrapers and a crane that hints at the city's ongoing reconstruction. She looks around, no sign of recognition visible on her face. The gradual disintegration of Pola's mental map is revealed as we see her repeatedly asking for directions to Marianska Street, against an incoherent sequence of backgrounds of modern buildings and streets, ensuring that orientation is denied to the viewer as much as to Pola herself. We move from seeing Pola in the distance, dwarfed by the huge, concrete apartment blocks and the roar of the traffic, to an extreme close-up view, where the hand-held camera spins giddily round her, accentuating the

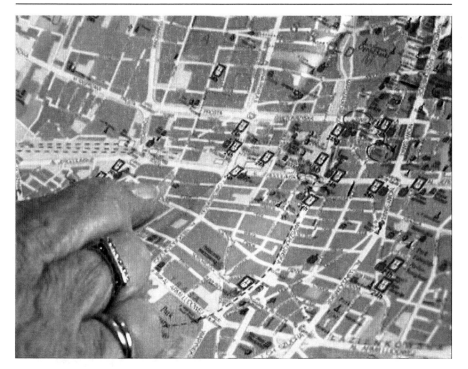

Figure 4.1 Pola searches for the Warsaw she knew in *Pola à 27 ans* (2003).
(Source: © Bizibi Productions.)

feeling of disorientation, with trams and cars whizzing past behind her head. The contradictory answers of those she asks for directions suggest, like the crane and diggers we have glimpsed in the background, a city of ever-changing contours, an Alice-in-Wonderland city where buildings, roads and streets shift and change shape. In a sense this is the archetypal city of forgetting, whose mnemonic map is constantly under erasure. However, it also seems eternally locked into a specific moment of trauma in its past, for it is as if the bombing and rebuilding have never stopped.

The sequence reaches a moving climax when Pola finally locates her childhood home, 3 Marianska Street: it has become an urban highway, ironically a place of unending transit and motion. Pola's search for the stable architecture of her past has led to a blunt reminder of the furious mobility of space and time. The more time she spends in Warsaw, the more her confidence in the stability of her memory's map crumbles. Her journey down memory lane has turned into a peculiar excavation, in which getting lost in a city repeatedly dug up and rebuilt comes to signify the pain of the past she has lost. This sense of both being lost and experiencing loss is emphasised later, in a heartrending scene where we again see Pola's fingers roving over the city map. 'Tu cherches quelle rue?' (What street are you looking for?), asks her granddaughter, and Pola replies, sadly, 'Je ne sais pas' (I don't know). The scene plays on the difference, discussed above with relation to De Certeau, between the image of a conventional city map and the mappings of memory. If, as Marker says, we can 'draw the map' of memory's geography, then it would have to be a cartography that could account for movement and change, for the virtual as well as the actual, as arguably Marker himself attempts with *Level Five* and *Immemory*. In Pola, both city and protagonist are suffering from disturbances of memory, and the close-up image of her fingers touching the map comes to signify the insufficiency of a flat, fixed image of the city to account for the fissures, both physical and emotional, that open up at sites of trauma.

Although post-war Warsaw represents an extreme instance of instability in the urban landscape, all cities exist in a state of constant flux, even if it can be slow moving. For Freud this was reason enough to demolish the analogy between city and memory that he constructs at the beginning of *Civilisation and its Discontents*, where he evocatively imagines the psyche's retention of the past via the mental superimposition of all the past incarnations of the city of Rome. He rejects the comparison on the grounds that 'even the most peaceful urban development entails the demolition and replacement of buildings, and so for this reason no city can properly be compared with a psychical organism' (Freud 2004: 10). But Freud here appears to envision cities purely in terms of bricks and stone, forgetting the human element of cities that constantly scrawls its 'semantic wanderings' over the cityscape, leaving ghostly trails to haunt the space in the form of memories and urban narratives, like the tracings on Freud's own mystic writing-pad model of memory (Freud 1991). As inhabited places, cities live as much as they are lived in; as with the psyche there is no demolition without a trace. City maps may seem to refuse this shifting urban fluidity, but they are of course periodically required to take account of it. Looking at different maps of one city throughout the ages reveals the secret temporal movement at the heart of all mapping. De Certeau comments on this changing nature of cities, locating the very essence of place in its 'shifting thicknesses':

> Frappe ici le fait que lieux vécus sont comme des présences d'absences. Ce qui se montre désigne ce qui n'est plus: 'vous voyez, ici il y avait . . . ', mais cela ne se voit plus. Les démonstratifs disent du visible ses invisibles identités: c'est la définition même du lieu, en effet, que d'être ces séries de déplacements et d'effets entre les strates morcelées qui le composent et de jouer sur ces mouvantes épaisseurs. (1990: 162)

> (It is striking here that the places people live in are like the presences of diverse absences. What can be seen designates what is no longer there: 'you see, here there used to be . . . ,' but it can no longer be seen. Demonstratives indicate the invisible identities of the visible: it is the very definition of a place, in fact, that it is composed by these series of displacements and effects among the fragmented strata that form it and that it plays on these moving layers. [1984: 108])

In *Mimi* too we are aware of the presence of absences in the mapping of city space. There are the absences of her father and mother, of her brother and of past lovers, which through Mimi's stories haunt the images of inhabited city space gleaned by Simon's camera. But this is also mirrored by the gap between perceived and remembered places, the changing shape of the city, which is constructed and reconstructed just as our memories of it are: the new sports centre that triggers Mimi's memories of the class divide that once denied such leisure activities to all but a few, the transformation of the bridge over the railway by the disappearance of steam engines. The opening panorama that frames the credit sequence is accompanied by the unmistakable rhythmic, mechanical creaking of a crane (quite literally a crane shot), again suggesting the continual rebuilding of the city even as it establishes Nice as the mnemonic home of Mimi's identity. Perhaps most emblematically, near the beginning of the film, a fixed camera shot shows Mimi leading her friend Diego over a motorway bridge in the neon-tinged light of dusk, pointing out roads below: 'Le Chemin des Collinettes, Pont St. Philippe – qui n'était pas comme ça – Avenue de Châteauneuf' (The Collinettes Path, St. Philippe's bridge – which wasn't like that – Châteauneuf Avenue). As she speaks she gestures with her hands, tracing out the familiar streets as she draws attention to their temporal transformation. She then asks Diego to sing 'her song' outside, near where her house used to be, pointing to a spot outside the frame: 'j'aimerais que tu me chantes ma chanson dehors . . . de ma maison, en fait, qui se trouvait là-bas' (I would like you to sing my song for me outside . . . of my house actually, which used to be over there). In the next scene we see Diego playing the guitar and singing to Mimi, as she has requested. The song he plays is called 'Il Ragazzo della Via Gluck', originally sung by Adriano Celentano in 1966, and popularised in France through Françoise Hardy's version, 'La Maison où J'ai Grandi' (the house where I grew up), released in 1967. By referring to it as 'my song', Mimi indicates the extent to which she has incorporated the song, making it a part of her inner cultural resources. It is a cultural memory object, possibly familiar to the viewer, and it is one which Mimi invests with her own memories of place. The lyrics tell the story of a young man who leaves the countryside for the city but who never forgets his childhood home, by now absorbed by the tar and cement of the city itself. It is a song about places, streets and houses known and lost, as well as memory, departure and return. We cannot tell whether, like Pola, Mimi has lost her childhood home under a concrete strip of road, or whether it has become absorbed by the breeze-block buildings across which the camera also pans during the song. What is clear is that somehow her house is no longer there. This scene both expresses the melancholy of that loss and evokes the virtual presence of remembered dwellings in the changing cityscape. The rhythmic rushing noise as each of the constant stream of cars goes past becomes a part of the song. The noise intrudes, overlaying the words and harmonies of the song. In doing so it mirrors the way that in the song's own story the city covers what used to be grass ('ma dove c'era l'erba, ora c'e una città' [but where the grass once was there is now a city]). Like the city, the filmic text is made up of overlapping visual and sonic layers, each of which intersects individual and collective memory: the sounds and images of the city in motion, which also once held Mimi's home; a popular, nostalgic song, which seems to Mimi to be in some way her own. In this way the scene becomes a commemorative moment shared between the two friends, the filmmaker and the viewer; a monument-in-motion that expresses the mnemonic and physical movement of urban space.

Although 'shifting thicknesses' may be an essential feature of both cities and memory, in Pola's case the moving strata are marked with such a powerfully traumatic sense of loss that the kinds of creative commemorative interaction we see in Mimi seem foreclosed. When she finds the road that covers the absence of her childhood home, there is no song to mediate between past and present and the inevitable losses entailed by the passage of time. This is of course because Pola's memory mapping is haunted by the horrifying collective trauma of the Holocaust. Her memory narratives turn on her identity as a survivor of the camps. As its title (*Pola Aged 27*) indicates, the film aims at a very particular moment in Pola's life story; its evocation of memory is of a traumatic memory, and the city space it explores is devastated by the same trauma that devastates Pola's memory. The sequence immediately following her discovery of the disappearance of 3 Marianska Street (an interview in her Warsaw hotel room) makes the connection between the present-day experience of loss and the assault on the Jews' inhabiting of Warsaw in the early days of German occupation: 'on a tout de suite fait de nous des sous-hommes. On n'avait plus de chemise, plus d'oreiller, plus de maison, plus de chez nous' (they immediately rendered us sub-human. We no longer had shirts nor pillows, no house any more, no home). After Pola points to the road where her home used to be, we cut to a shot that frames her hands tucking away her map of Warsaw into her bag, suggesting the failure of both mnemonic and city mapping to act as a reassuring guide in this confrontation with the past. However, in providing a testament to this, the film itself becomes a kind of trace. The subsequent 225-degree pan of the road, with its roaring traffic where her house used to be, comes to rest on Pola, whose expression of restrained confusion and disappointment itself signifies the presence of an absence. The creativity of the film is in the starkness with which it reveals disintegration in the face of trauma, allowing absences to haunt the filmed space without filling in the gaps.

Se souvenir des belles choses is a fiction film; unlike *Mimi* and *Pola à 27 ans* it avoids allowing the viewer to place the town as a specific location. Here there is no Warsaw or Nice to take position as a cultural, historical object. This is significant, for while Warsaw and Nice in the former two films are shown as having elements common to all contemporary cities, such as concrete and graffiti, roaring traffic and road works, they are also, as we have seen, inscribed with specific mnemonic textures: Warsaw as disorienting site of trauma, excessively scarred by history, and Nice as multi-ethnic port and border city with a rich and difficult history of arrivals and departures. Breitman's film on the other hand posits the urban (and rural) landscapes of roads, town centres, cemetery, hospital, abandoned warehouses and so forth as 'any-places' which function both as a spatial backdrop to the fictional narrative of the film and as recognisable sites (to a European viewer) through which the protagonist Claire's disorientation takes on the quality of realism. The deterioration of Claire's own memory is situated in a world where the imperfections of human memory are constantly revealed. The film opens with a frantic monologue by Claire's sister Nathalie, who is talking to Claire as she drives her to a clinic for disturbances of memory, ironically unable to remember her route through the bland, suburban landscape we glimpse through the car's front window as she talks: 'écoute, je reconnais pas du tout là [. . .], évidemment il n'y a plus aucune indication, ce serait trop beau, [. . .], mais dis-donc il n'y avait pas un Mammouth là avant?' (right, well I don't recognise this at all [. . .], naturally there isn't a single sign, that would make it too easy, [. . .], but hang on, wasn't there a Mammouth supermarket there before?). Perhaps even more than the difficulties of the bewildered patients at the humorously named memory clinic Les Écureuils (The Squirrels), it is the everyday perturbation of memory, such as Nathalie's inability to navigate or Dr Licht's failure to retain dates or remember meetings, that forms a framework for Claire's more complete loss of functional memory.

Like *Pola à 27 ans*, *Se souvenir des belles choses* makes use of a close-up of a city map as a point of connection between the experience of getting lost and the emotional sense of loss produced by disturbances of memory. The film's female protagonist, 32-year-old Claire Poussin, is suffering from symptoms that increasingly resemble the Alzheimer's disease that afflicted her late mother: she is forgetting words and places and finding it difficult to concentrate. In order to see what can be done for her, she moves into Les Écureuils, a clinic and residential community for people suffering from memory disturbances. At the clinic she meets and falls in love with Philippe, who is suffering from localised amnesia surrounding a tragic accident in which his wife and son were killed. As Claire progressively becomes more disoriented, Philippe's traumatic memories begin to return. The narrative of their encounter was itself conceived in spatial terms by the director, who explains that 'l'idée était de faire croiser les deux personnages dans leurs parcours respectifs' (the idea was for the two characters to cross each other on their respective routes).[7] The spectrum of spatial disorientation resulting from the failure of habitual memory is unobtrusively evoked throughout, from Nathalie's monologue as she drives to the clinic, to the striking close-up shots of Claire's feet following the coloured lines that function like Ariadne's thread, guiding the patients of Les Écureuils through the buildings to different rooms and areas. When the couple move into a flat together, the issue of mapping that has been developing in the film finally comes to the fore. In the new flat Philippe surrounds Claire with post-it notes, white-board messages and alarm clocks to help orient her in time and space

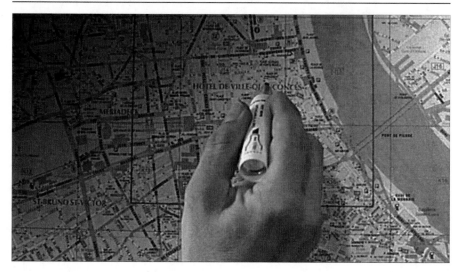

Figure 4.2 Claire's memory map in *Se souvenir des belles choses* (2001).
(Source: © SND Groupe M6.)

as the illness takes over. A large map of the provincial town where they live is plastered onto the kitchen wall and a close-up shows Philippe circling places on it with a marker: first the house, then the hospital, to which Claire must make daily visits (Figure 4.2). But it soon becomes clear that Claire is no longer able to map two-dimensional pathways onto a three-dimensional environment. To use De Certeau's terms, the *carte* and the *parcours* of her bodily memory become disconnected and disintegrate. Even the confined space of their own flat becomes a confusing jumble of walls and doors, which she tries desperately to remember, in a scene that shows her rushing from room to room, repeating out loud 'chambre, cuisine, couloir' (bedroom, kitchen, corridor) and trying to make a map of it in her notebook. Philippe makes her an audiotape to guide her on simple routes through the town, and one scene shows her walking past houses, a chemist's and a café, following Philippe's instructions on the machine held to her ear, until his voice tells her to look up to the window where she will see him wave. For a time they have found a mapping prosthesis, a device that supplements her memory and makes the town navigable physically and emotionally. The sound and sight of her lover temporarily create a protective 'tender map'.

Later, when Claire becomes lost in the back streets and warehouses behind the hospital, we see her laughing gaily as she listens to taped instructions that do not match the townscape that surrounds her. The mobile camera follows her, cutting from a shot facing her to one from behind her head and finally moving into slow motion as she spins round and round, apparently liberated by a sense of complete disconnection from her environmental mapping. At this point, each time she looks upwards, we cut to a point-of-view shot of tree-tops viewed from below, spinning round as we have seen Claire doing to indicate the connection between her gaze and this image. The grey buildings of the town and derelict warehouses behind the hospital have become an autumnal wooded glade in Claire's mind's eye. In forgetting where she is she seems to have returned to the natural landscapes where, as we see in previous scenes, she and Philippe celebrated their love. In Bergsonian terms, Claire's memory here is pure, fragmentary visualisation. The motor-sensory habitual memory that connects past experience to the present perception of space has disappeared and the space she now inhabits seems to be an entirely mental, remembered vision. Though in these scenes we see Claire smiling and untroubled, free at last from the anxiety of her gradual loss of a memory able to function in the present, the slippage between space and mnemonic mapping is painful none the less. For in dislocating from perception, Claire's memory has become dislodged from its social frameworks at the very moment when a deep emotional attachment has been formed with Philippe.

The film's cartography of Claire's mental and lived space presents us with a series of disarticulations: of sound and image, of remembered landscape and moved-through townscape. The film has a conventionally linear structure, making its narrative trajectory, that is, the crossing of two characters' memory journeys, relatively simple for the viewer to map. At the same time, however, the film accumulates small formal disorientations for the spectator, as though drawing the spectator into a perceptual world where spatiotemporal orientation is no longer a given. The movement between scenes, and indeed shots, is often ambiguous in terms of elapsed time or movement through space, with jump cuts breaking up the flow of action within scenes. As the film's narrative and Claire's illness progress, the editing makes increasing use of sonic and graphic mismatches across the cut. For example, a cut takes us from a shot of Philippe opening a bottle of wine to a close-up shot of hands pouring it into a glass, hands revealed by an upward tilt of the camera to be those of Dr Licht. The sound match of a cork popping at the instant of the cut creates a sound bridge that leads us to expect the glass to be Philippe's. Instead this small jolt provides a first clue to a bond between Philippe and Dr Licht: their shared love of fine wine. This is an important part of the depiction of Les Écureuils as a place where social bonds are formed through a shared sense of disorientation and memory troubles: a reconfiguration of the conventional notion of community as bound by shared memories and the group identity that arises from these, and a reminder that communities are equally founded in disturbances of memory. But these formal disruptions also echo Claire's mounting confusion. By the time we reach the final scenes, we experience the full force of the disintegration of space in Claire's world, but this process exceeds Claire's subjectivity, permeating the fabric of the film. As Philippe hastens worriedly between the empty warehouses he bends down to look through a jagged hole in a broken window. A cut takes us to a close-up of the hole, as though following his point of view, but to our surprise we then glimpse Philippe rushing past the opposite window. This shattering of perspectives culminates in the last scene of the film where Philippe finally finds Claire. Apparently seated in a beautiful forest she beckons Philippe to come and sit beside her, but the shot–reverse-shot exchange between them is disjointed and takes us from a radiant, articulate Claire listening in confusion as Philippe appears to mumble, to a drenched, lost Claire, sitting on a crate amongst the ruined warehouses, incoherent and failing to recognise her lover. The subtle disintegration in the form of the film is significant because rather than simply showing or telling the spectator what Claire sees and feels, it generates a filmic world of multiple perspectives where the entire space becomes inhabited by Claire's disorienting loss of spatial memory. Although the space therefore becomes refracted through Claire's subjectivity, by the same movement it takes the disintegration outwards beyond her body, making it inextricable from the places and people that surround her. In our inhabiting of places there is an interpenetration of inside and outside, a flow of exchange which always carries the risk of fragmentation and arrest.

Focusing on two such moving films as *Pola à 27 ans* and *Se souvenir des belles choses* reveals that the movement of film – images, camera and narrative – is a powerful medium for revealing the emotion of movement. This is what Giuliana Bruno describes in her concept of *e*motion, 'that particular landscape which the "motion" picture itself has turned into an art of mapping' (2002: 2). While this motion, as Bruno's exhilarating atlas of films, art and architecture suggests, may present a wealth of creative, erotic and imaginative possibilities, these films remind us of the pain that may also be caused when time and space dislocate in an encounter between shifting maps. The wealth and variety of contemporary media open up the possibility of a mobile, multidimensional cartography, but have also served to reveal the potential for dislocation rendered so movingly in these two films. It is pertinent too that it should be the city that provides a conceptual focus for the subjective disintegration portrayed in these films. Although it may be placed in relation to a broader geography, the city, as a mobile and inhabited landscape, a place of transit and a locus of intersubjective communication, is perhaps an even more appropriate figure of memory than Marker's deserts and valleys. As the protagonists move through the city on film, we are reminded that the city, like memory, is a continual process of construction and reconstruction, inscription and reinscription. It is the place where we find ourselves, but also where we most intensely experience the feeling of being lost.

HIDDEN IN THE CITY

The discussion so far has shown how the accretion of collective memory is as shifting as the material fabric of the city itself, arising as it does at the intersection of media representation, individual attachment and the city's physical geography. Films can reveal the fractures at sites where these layers diverge and our mental memory maps come into conflict with the environment. Yet, while emphasising the flux of both cities and memories, we must not forget that fixity can also pose a problem. As we have seen with relation to *Pola à 27 ans*, traumatic memory can become caught in the past, making it difficult to reconcile past and present. As discussed with reference to Ricœur and Nora in Chapter 1, this operates on a collective level too: 'que de violences par le monde qui valent comme *acting out* "au lieu" du souvenir!' (Ricœur 2000: 96) ('how much violence in the world stands as acting out "in place of" remembering!' [2004: 79]). Likewise, the city's geography can be experienced as too rigid, consolidating historical social divisions through the segregation of space.

Didier Lapeyronnie has examined this with relation to the *banlieue*, those spaces at the margins of the city which tend to be inhabited by socially marginalised groups (2005: 209–18).[8] Representations in the mass media in France have typically tended to define the *banlieue* in terms of 'an explosive cocktail of unemployment, poor housing, racial discrimination and lawlessness from which there appears to be no escape' (Hargreaves 1999: 117), an image which reinforces the sense of claustrophobic segregation associated with these marginal areas. For Lapeyronnie the *banlieue* can be seen as a 'théâtre colonial' (colonial theatre) in which the drama of colonial inequalities is constantly reiterated:

> Le vécu de la discrimination et de la ségrégation, et peut-être plus encore le sentiment d'être défini par un déficit permanent de 'civilisation' dans les discours du pouvoir, d'être soumis à des injonctions d'intégration au moment même où la société vous prive des moyens de la construire, évoquent directement la 'colonie' et donc, pour nombre d'habitants issus d'immigration, un 'passé qui ne passe pas'. (2005: 210)

> (The lived experience of discrimination and segregation, and perhaps even more so the feeling of persistently being defined in terms of a deficit of 'civilisation' in the discourses of the powers-that-be, of being subjected to the command to integrate at the very moment society is depriving you of the means of constructing that integration, directly evoke the 'colony' and, therefore, for many inhabitants with origins in immigration, a 'past which does not pass'.)

Lapeyronnie acknowledges that there can be no direct analogy with a colony, for of course the *banlieues* are not territories that have been conquered and occupied by armed forces, and there are no colonials who come to live in and exploit the territory and its population (p. 210). None the less, France's colonial past inhabits social representations of the *banlieue* and its relation to the centre, incarnating in spatial terms the inequalities and injustices of the colonial system. If this past seems to haunt the topography of the city, it is in part because, as discussed in my introduction, French society has yet to confront fully the connections between the history of colonisation and the present-day difficulties of a multi-ethnic society. Thus the past cannot 'pass'; instead it is caught in the repetition compulsion that is played out in the structures of urban geography and the mental mapping of its inhabitants.

This collectively repressed colonial past is precisely what is 'hidden' in Michael Haneke's film of the same name. Moreover *Caché* (2005) dramatises this resistance to confronting the past and its resulting ethnic and class tensions in terms of the interweaving spheres of city space and filmic images. I want now to turn to this film in order to consider a different kind of mobile mapping, in which the city and the moving image come together to confront the viewer with a past that is disavowed, yet refuses to pass. It is a confrontation in which the viewer is himself or herself profoundly implicated. The film's protagonist, Georges Laurent, is a television presenter who lives in a comfortable, bourgeois neighbourhood in the thirteenth arrondissement of Paris. When he receives a mysterious two-hour videotape of a fixed camera view of his house, followed by what appear to be a child's drawings of possibly violent images, Georges begins to suspect that an Algerian man, Majid, who lived with his family briefly when they were children, is responsible for these unnerving interventions in his life. This is Georges' own assumption and it is never confirmed for the viewer: at the close of the film the source of the videotapes remains a mystery. Georges, however, draws this conclusion because his boyhood jealousy of the orphaned Majid, whom Georges' parents were planning to adopt, led him to tell lies that resulted in Majid being sent away and consequently deprived him of the family support and better opportunities in life this adoption would have provided. The simplistic drawings in crayon and paint Georges receives, showing a face spewing red streaks and a cockerel with a cloud of red paint about its neck, remind Georges uncannily of the tales he told his parents about Majid: that he was coughing up blood and, when that failed, that the Algerian child had deliberately decapitated a cockerel in order to frighten him (something which Georges had in fact persuaded Majid to do by saying it would please his father). Georges is convinced that Majid is seeking to terrorise him and his family as revenge for these childhood acts of cruelty and their subsequent impact on his life. The two men's respective dwellings, situated in two quite different urban environments, might appear to reinforce this assumption that Majid would envy Georges and desire vengeance. Georges' elegant and comfortable family home in central Paris is contrasted with Majid's suburban neighbourhood and dingy flat, a contrast that confirms that Georges' family's decision to send Majid away did indeed exclude him from the world of socio-economic privilege enjoyed by Georges. In other words, the past actions of Georges and his family return to haunt the present in the visible evidence of Majid's urban and domestic existence. As we shall see, ultimately this uncanny return implicates not only an individual family but also a wider collective sphere, including the viewer of *Caché*.

Georges' house in the thirteenth arrondissement exudes, if not opulent wealth, at least refined luxury. The home he shares with his wife Anne, who works in publishing, and their 14-year-old son Pierrot is self-contained, spacious and tastefully decorated, centred on a stylish open-plan living area with cream walls and sleek furniture in glass, chrome and polished wood. In the sitting and dining areas the walls are lined with custom-built shelves crammed with books. Their large, flat-screen television provides a focal point for the capacious cream leather sofa and is surrounded by videos, DVDs and reference books. Georges' first hypothesis about the provenance of the tape reinforces the visual impression made by his home, which is that the Laurents would most probably be classed as 'Bobo', a portmanteau term derived from bourgeois and bohemian:[9] 'c'est peut-être un copain de Pierrot, un de ces abrutis, qui veut se moquer des parents Bobo de son pote' (maybe it's a friend of Pierrot's, one of those idiots, who wants to make fun of his mate's Bobo parents). The comfort of a lifestyle in which it is taken for granted that material needs will be met is expressed in the persistence of Georges and Anne's habits even in moments of crisis: throughout the film they continue to entertain friends, open bottles of wine and sit down at a properly set dining table for meals with their son, Pierrot. On the night they receive the first tape, Georges and Anne are unnerved and querulous; they are destabilised and threatened by the idea that they are being watched by an unknown and potentially malevolent observer. Yet this does not prevent them from sitting down to their pasta and salad ('pas terrible ce soir' [no great shakes tonight], says Anne), drinking red wine from smart claret glasses. The relative ease of their lifestyle provides a buffer of normality in which taste, choice and abundance, rather than want and deprivation, are the unquestioned norm.

Georges and his family are the primary focus of the film and we see far more of their domestic life than we do of Majid's. Yet Georges' defensive reaction to the return of this repressed episode from his past leads him, along with the film's viewers, out of his comfort zone in the affluent neighbourhoods of central Paris and into the working-class *banlieue*, with its drab tower blocks and ordinary-looking streets marked by petrol stations and cheap cafés. Before he visits Majid, Georges is seen drinking coffee in one such café, a poster behind him declaring in huge letters 'oui aux prix bas!' (yes to low prices!) It is in this area, somewhere on the Avenue Lénine in Romainville (a suburb northeast of Paris), that Majid occupies a modest flat, with a quite different interior to that of the Laurents' designer residence. His is a cramped space, with a mismatched series of stained and dated wallpapers, a zip-up fabric wardrobe, green formica doors, net curtains and cheap 1970s-style kitchen units. Oddly, Majid's home appears as a distorted and diminished mirror image of Georges' house, which only serves to exacerbate the contrast. Whereas the Laurents' central living area is fashionably open plan, Majid's living space appears forced into the confines of one room, with a faded sofa and unmade bed both visible in the same frame as the tiny kitchen area. While the Laurents' shelves are heaving with a dramatic display of cultural wealth in the form of books, videos and DVDs, Majid's wall of shelving is piled up with a higgledy-piggledy array of old boxes, plastic containers, bags and suitcases. In front of this is an old cathode-ray television and aerial, recalling the smartly shelved flat-screen version on which Georges and Anne watch the strange videotapes. Even the tacky formica and chrome chairs around Majid's kitchen table are a distant and poor relation of the Laurents' chic, similarly shaped versions in wood and chrome.

It is an environment that is entirely foreign to Georges and yet at the same time it is a strangely familiar one, at which he barely needs to glance in order to decipher it. On his first visit it is Majid who appears taken aback by the encounter, while Georges steps blindly into the flat as though he had always known it would be like that. This is not surprising: perhaps the predominantly middle-class arthouse audience of *Caché* reacts in the same way.[10] I am reminded here of the doily Macha Makeïeff finds in Agnès Varda's *Deux ans après* (2002), the object of cultural memory that contains her past as part of a virtual, collective realm (see Chapter 2). Social inequalities are embedded into the very fabric of our homes and environments: they materialise the lingering cultural memories of old injustice, even as we conveniently forget them. Majid's Romainville location and home are indeed a *théâtre colonial*, in which the drama of a threatened French aggressor and a peaceful yet resistant Algerian is replayed, as the openly hostile Georges accuses Majid of terrorising his family and angrily threatens harsh consequences if the situation continues. It is a scenario repeated more dramatically later in the film when Pierrot goes missing and Georges shortly has the police pounding at Majid's door, demanding to know what he has done with the boy. Of course, this pseudo-colonial dynamic mirrors the brutal French repression of the peaceful demonstrations of 17 October 1961, alluded to in the film as the cause of the disappearance of Majid's parents. This non-violent march supporting the FLN (the *Front de Libération Nationale*, a revolutionary body fighting for independence in Algeria at the time) took place just six months before the end of the war, when De Gaulle had already recognised the inevitability of Algerian independence (Stora 1992: 383). Yet faced with the appearance of between 20,000 and 30,000 primarily Algerian demonstrators in the streets of Paris, breaking the 'recommended' 8.30 p.m. curfew for North Africans, the French authorities (perhaps afraid of a destabilisation of the delicate negotiations with the FLN and military retreat from Algeria) opted for severe repression. The violence of the police was pitiless and completely unjustified: the unarmed demonstrators were fired upon with machine guns, beaten with truncheons and thrown into the Seine. Up to 200 were killed and many thousands were seriously injured. Nearly 12,000 were arrested and beaten (Stora 1992: 307–8). It was not until the prefect of police at the time, Maurice Papon, was tried in 1997–8 for crimes against Jews during the Occupation that the state officially acknowledged the events as a massacre (Stora 1991: 93–100). In case one should forget the prevailing colonial attitudes and discourses surrounding these horrific events, it is helpful to turn to a sample reaction from the newspaper *Paris-Jour* (18 October 1961), cited by Stora in his account of the events, which has disconcerting resonances with the feelings of indignant threat experienced by Georges in *Caché*:

> C'est inouï! Pendant trois heures, hier soir, 20,000 musulmans algériens auxquels s'étaient mêlés un certain nombre d'Européens, ont été les maîtres absolus des rues de Paris. Ils ont pu défiler en plein cœur de la capitale, en franchir les portes par groupes importants sans avoir demandé l'autorisation de manifester et en narguant ouvertement les pouvoirs publics et la population. (cited in Stora 1992: 309)

> (It's unheard-of! For three hours last night, 20,000 Muslim Algerians, amongst whom mingled a certain number of Europeans, were the absolute masters of the streets of Paris. They were able to march right into the heart of the capital, to pass through its gates in large groups, without having asked for permission to demonstrate and thus openly disrespecting public authority and the general population.)

The rhetoric of outrage here is used to portray the demonstrators, rather than the police, as a menacing force, while the space of central Paris is envisaged as a fragile enclave unable to defend itself sufficiently against the uncontrollable invaders (positioned as 'other' for the writer and addressees of the article by the religious marker of difference 'Muslim'). It is a scenario of inverted logic whereby the colonised and oppressed are seen as an invasive threat, thereby retrospectively justifying the oppression which has led to this menacing appearance. Similarly, in *Caché* Georges enacts in the present his childhood fear of the invasion of his home and family by the Algerian boy, responding to his fears by anticipating them with his own aggression and intrusions. It becomes apparent that his first invasion was an unwitting one, taking place through his role as presenter of a literary television programme, where Majid recognised him thanks to a 'disagreeable sensation' in his stomach on watching the show. Television is perhaps the most insidious and pervasive intrusion into private domestic space, so it is significant that Georges has already penetrated Majid's home via the cathode ray some years before doing so in person. Since they both deny it convincingly, we never discover whether it was Majid, his son or neither of them who sent the videotapes and drawings. But it is notable that neither Majid nor his son enters Georges' home, while Georges not only enters Majid's but threatens him with violence there, later bringing reinforcements in the form of the police, who arrest both father and son.

Several critics have picked up on the themes of intrusion and domestic space in Haneke's films generally and *Caché* in particular. Ranjana Khanna, in her comparative essay on *Caché* and Edgar Allen Poe's short story 'The Murders in the Rue Morgue' (1841), argues that 'both story and film document the fear of intrusion into dwelling' (2007: 243). Michael Cowan elaborates this with relation to Haneke's cinematic oeuvre:

> Haneke's films of the past two decades are all about the horror of private interiors: both the fear that leads to the fortification of space and the horror that ensues when the violence expelled in the process makes its uncanny return. (2009: 117)

This notion of an 'uncanny return' resonates with David Sorfa's discussion of 'uneasy domesticity' in Haneke's films. Sorfa draws on Freud's definition of the uncanny (*Unheimlich*) as 'that class of the frightening which leads back to what is known of old and long familiar' (Freud 1985: 340). On examining the intriguing etymology of *Unheimlich*, Freud discovered that it can come to mean the same thing as its opposite, *Heimlich*, which means not only 'homely', or what is familiar and agreeable, but also 'what is concealed and kept out of sight' (p. 345), thus slipping into *Unheimlich* as this secret interiority comes to light. In other words, 'the frightening element can be shown to be something repressed which recurs' (p. 363). With this in mind, Sorfa argues that the very notion of 'home' in Haneke's films is constituted by a hidden violence which destabilises it from within: 'the surface of domestic ease does not only hold within it a disturbing element, but is also brought into existence by that very factor' (2006: 98). Sorfa refers only briefly to *Caché*, focusing on the unnerving effect on the viewer of the ambiguous status of the videotapes rather than on the depiction of domestic and urban space. It is therefore useful to read his essay alongside Cowan's analysis, which reminds us that the 'horror' of the private dwelling is part of a larger-scale system of control at the level of the city itself. Cowan suggests that Haneke's films 'illustrate a transformation of urban space in the era of immigration, in which private space is treated as a defensive shell against the outside world' (2009: 118). Taken together with reference to *Caché*, these essays reinforce my argument that the film's engagement with the past emerges precisely through the uncanny functioning of urban topography, interiors and thresholds. The real intruder in the film is the (un)homely past; not only Georges' dirty secret but the collective colonialist ideology surrounding the violence of 17 October 1961, which remains ingrained in an urban environment still conceived and experienced in terms of centre and margin: a civilised centre whose gates are always in danger of succumbing to the disorderly menace of the *banlieue* (see the quotation from *Paris-Jour* above). This is reminiscent of James Donald's concept of the uncanny city, which draws once again on De Certeau's contrast between the *ville-concept* and the disordered dispersal of the inhabitants' lived experience: 'the uncanny specific to the modern metropolis arises in the disquieting distinction between the city as object of government and the city as frame of mind' (Donald 1999: 73). This is true at both an individual and a collective level. One of the things that *Caché* helps us to envisage is the way our lived environment functions in between the amnesiac repression of past violence and the correlative potential for the violent re-emergence of that past, lurking as it does at the virtual juncture of physical geography and mental representations.

Furthermore, in *Caché* moving image media are shown to be an integral part of the uncanny city's disquieting oscillation between the familiarity of a space fortified against confrontations with the past and the dread of a site permeated with spectral mnemonic traces. This arises in part through the film's disconcerting representation of space, defying the normal cinematic rules that allow the viewer to imagine a coherent totality beyond the space of the frame. In her analysis of the relation between on-screen and off-screen space in *Caché*, Libby Saxton observes that the film 'enlists both its protagonists and its viewers in a quest to make sense of off-screen space' (2007b: 5). Placing the camera in seemingly impossible viewpoints for the videotapes' recordings of Georges' house and the interior of Majid's flat frustrates our ability to piece together the film's narrative and field of vision as a unified whole. Moreover, the frequent use of relatively static shots, or shots placed at a distance from the characters, has the effect of troubling our perception of the status of the image, making us wonder whether we are watching through the anonymous observer's lens, a tape viewed on the Laurents' television or through the extra-diegetic camera of the film's real makers. The film's opening scene alerts us to this problem from the outset, with a very long static take of a street scene over which the credits appear at one point. It is only when we hear Georges' and Anne's voices on the soundtrack, discussing the image, that we understand we are watching a tape within the diegesis. This effectively thrusts us into the same off-screen space as the fictional characters, or brings them into our space. Either way the borders of the diegesis are crossed and the film's spectators are implicated in the anxiety and guilt evoked by the tapes. The accumulation of uncertainty and ambiguity in the images of the present is heightened in the few brief scenes depicting 'the past' in the film. Situated somewhere in the interstices of fantasy and memory, as well as somewhere in between Georges' interiority and the filmmaker's or viewer's imagination, the images of a boy wiping blood from his mouth and, later, decapitating a cockerel before turning menacingly towards the camera brandishing the axe, are crystalline time-images, exceeding any rational motivation (for example Georges remembering or dreaming) in the surrounding scenes. It would appear that Haneke, as Martine Beugnet puts it, 'revels in exploring the ambiguity of the moving image: the medium of presence is also the medium of absence' (2007: 229). Both on-screen and off-screen space are made indeterminate and inconclusive. Saxton is led to conclude that, 'rather than containing and reappropriating unseen space through continuity editing, rather than rendering it navigable and comprehensible and thereby defusing its threat, the film prompts the permanent suspicion that we are missing something' (2007b: 15). I would add that while the film's unwavering gaze upon interiors and exteriors reveals the reification of cultural stereotyping and the ideological segregation of urban space, its self-reflexive examination

Figure 4.3 Venturing into the *banlieue* in *Caché* (2005). (Source: *Caché/Hidden* by Michael Haneke © Les Films du Losange 2005.)

of the moving image reveals the potential of interpenetration and exchange. If moving images mediate our cultural memory, then, as *Caché* and the other works discussed in this book show us, they have the (highly ambivalent) potential to introduce a destabilising fluidity into the striation of our environments and the traumatic disavowal of the past.

Georges is led to Majid's home by the fourth tape he receives, of which we are shown two sequences. The first, apparently shot through the windscreen of a car, travels down a street towards a tower block before turning right along the main avenue (Figure 4.3). The second tracks down a dingy corridor of identical, cheap-looking blue doors, coming to a halt at number 47. The scenes in which we watch these videotapes with the Laurents afford us a good view of the two men's contrasting social status and lived environments. Filling the screen, these images are navigated for us by Georges and Anne, who rewind certain sequences and pause on specific frames in an attempt to decipher these curiously indeterminate and anonymous images. For example, when Georges is seen leaving the house and walking down the Rue des Iris past the spot where the camera must have been, he pauses the tape, mystified by his failure to notice anything at the time. Later Georges and Anne locate the Romainville tracking shots described above by pausing on the frame which shows the street sign, advancing step by step until the lettering is almost in focus. Using a map of Paris and the half-guessed street and district names on the signpost, they are able to pinpoint the place that appears on the anonymous tape. For all their anxious deciphering, however, they, like us, are unable to elucidate the mystery of the tapes. The explanatory thread of narrative that would map out a teleological history, connecting image with source, sign with meaning and past with present, remains hidden. Yet it is precisely that which is hidden in the city, and in the image, that intrudes.

Film has long provided a means of travelling without moving, from early city symphony films such as *Rien que les heures* (Alberto Cavalcanti, 1926) to contemporary global travel films like *Baraka* (Ron Fricke, 1993). But as we have seen, the spatial movement created by editing and camera motion can also provide strategies for exploring subjective and intersubjective temporal movement, revealing the multiple ways in which place is inhabited by memory. If I have focused on the mobile mappings of the city in this discussion it is because the city, as we have seen, forms a conceptual locus for visualising the spatial conglomeration of memory.

Certainly, all of the films discussed in this chapter contain movements between the city and other types of place: the rural isolation of Mimi's Saorge home, where the film ends, the haunted, grassy emptiness of the camps revisited by Pola, the sheltered gardens of Claire's memory clinic, and Georges Laurent's rural family home in *Caché*. In each case, however, the city is a central paradigm through which other spaces are envisioned, whether in contrast or in parallel. In *Se souvenir des belles choses*, for instance, the disorientation created by memory impairment reveals supermarkets, clusters of old warehouses and even the layout of rooms in one's own flat to be structured like cities. For all of these are spaces where social frameworks must be negotiated and physical pathways navigated, and where a failure of recognition inevitably results in the anxiety of a threatened sense of self. In *Pola à 27 ans*, Auschwitz is all but unrecognisable to Pola without 'la masse humaine' (the human mass) that defined it, or as Pola puts it, 'faussait l'image des lieux' (distorted the image of the sites). Her remark reveals how a death camp may be seen as a perverted, obscene distortion of a city, with its map of buildings, pathways and districts and, when functioning, its flows of human life and death. 'Death in the camps', in this sense, is the horrific, unthinkable correlative of 'life in the city', the imposing authority of De Certeau's *ville-concept* taken to a terrible extreme, a connection implicitly made in Godard's vision of a dystopic city in *Alphaville* (1965). Now empty and turned into a memorial, the camps have, unlike Warsaw, been preserved intact. But apart from the bunk-lined interior of one hut they are equally difficult to align with Pola's memories. It too is a city-site of trauma, but one where the obliteration and destruction have left the ghostly absences of human beings rather than buildings and neighbourhoods. At the same time, it matches Warsaw as its correlative, figuring Pola's own deportation from one place to the other, both in the film's journey and in its conceptual mapping between city and camp.

The city as conceptual locus also suggests a very different kind of parallel, one called forth by Marker in the 'Musées' zone of *Immemory*:

> Heures passées à marcher dans les musées comme dans les villes, oubliant
> les villes qui les abritaient, conférant à chacun sa souveraineté de ville, à

la recherche de ce qui fait une ville, la couleur d'un quartier, le style des habitants, découvrant de visite en visite un air de famille entre ces habitants, fussent-ils séparés par des siècles ou des mers.

(Hours spent walking in museums as though through cities, forgetting the cities sheltering them, conferring upon each one the sovereignty of a city, in search of what constitutes a city, the colour of a neighbourhood or the inhabitants' style, discovering from visit to visit a family resemblance between these inhabitants, even if they were separated by centuries or seas.)

Marker here reconfigures the flâneur as museum visitor, seeking the 'spirit of the neighbourhood' in the collection and juxtaposition of memory objects. Recalling the experience of the visitor who wandered through Varda's *L'Île et elle* (2006), the mapping engendered by such ambulation through the museum as city, or, conversely, the city as museum, is three-dimensional and mobile. As Sheldon Annis says of the dream space, 'the symbolic landscape [. . .] is three- rather than two-dimensional. The visitor can move into, through and past. He can slow down images, speed them up, or hold them steady' (Annis 1987: 169). As I have shown in this chapter, filmic representation can enact such three-dimensional wanderings, evoking the temporal layering of places inhabited by the virtuality of the past.

NOTES

1. Published in 1984, William Gibson's cult book *Neuromancer* is often credited with having invented the concepts of cyberspace and virtual reality. It was also an inspiration for the Wachowski brothers' 1999 film *The Matrix,* since it describes cyberspace in terms of 'The Matrix', a graphic representation of the databanks of every computer in the human system, into which individuals can plug their nervous systems electronically (Gibson 1984).
2. When *Level Five* was released in 1997, this kind of reflection was particularly cutting-edge, since internet use in France was less ingrained in everyday social experience than in the UK or the USA. In this it seems that Marker's experience as a global traveller is informing his understanding of space and time.
3. For an insightful analysis of the temporalities of the Proustian sentence, see Bowie (1998: 30–67).
4. De Certeau is citing Jacques Derrida's notion of an 'errance du sémantique' at work in metaphor in *Marges de la Philosophie* (Derrida 1972b: 287).
5. A footnote explains that De Certeau is here quoting an inhabitant from the Croix-Rousse district in Lyon.
6. I refer to her as Claire here as she is a character in the film at this point, albeit an invisible one. 'Claire Simon' or 'Simon' refer to her as film director.
7. Zabou Breitman, interview with the author, 18 March 2009.
8. The word *banlieue* can be translated as 'suburbs'. However, as Carrie Tarr notes, 'by the end of the 1980s the *banlieue* had come to refer not just to the suburbs, but more precisely to those *cités* (housing estates) linked with poor-quality social housing and high densities of immigrant and other disadvantaged populations' (Tarr 2005: 17).

9. The term 'Bobo' was originally coined in English in David Brooks' *Bobos in Paradise* (Brooks 2000), referring to the rise in the USA of an intellectual, liberal and wealthy elite. In France it has taken on a rather pejorative connotation of superficial left-wing politics and trendy, consumerist environmentalism (D'Epenoux 2003).
10. For a discussion of the demographics and expectations of the arthouse film audience in relation to Haneke's films, see Sorfa (2006: 93–6).

CONCLUSION

In his exploratory analysis of the subjective experience of remembering films, Victor Burgin remarks that, 'in a scene equally available to us all, that means the same to us all, there is an opening onto a destination towards which only one of us will be drawn' (2004: 65). I believe Burgin is right to emphasise film's ability to create an intimate connection with the spectator, in which filmic signs bond with fragments of personal memory in unpredictable and potentially unique ways. Burgin gives the term 'sequence-image' to the fragment of remembered film and illustrates the concept with a description of two scenes from different films that have become inextricably linked in his memory:

> The narratives have dropped away, like those rockets that disintegrate in the atmosphere once they have placed their small payloads in orbit. Detached from their original settings each scene is now the satellite of the other. Each echoes the other, increasingly merges with the other, and I experience a kind of fascinated incomprehension before the hybrid object they have become. (p. 59)

Like Burgin's choice of the term 'sequence-image', which echoes film terminology (the 'sequence shot'), the above passage suggests that the remembering of film itself takes on a filmic form. Reminiscent of creative gleaners, as I suggested in Chapter 2, our minds pick up fragments and bring them together in ways that resemble montage, whether in the form of its traditional cutting and pasting, the pulsing oscillation of the Godardian video suite, the selection of a sequence of video windows in a postcard, or the digital fusion of Chris Marker's *musée imaginaire*. Commenting on the structure of montage in *Histoire(s) du cinéma* (Jean-Luc Godard, 1989–98), Aumont makes a comparison between the network of memory traces in the brain and the network of images in a film: 'de la pensée, les anthropologues comme les physiologistes ont su que le premier stade est la capacité de souvenir, fixer les traces, des "grammes", et en même temps fixer les réseaux de ces traces, les monter' (where thought is concerned, anthropologists and physiologists alike have recognised that the first step is the capacity to remember, to fix traces or 'grammes' and at the same time to fix networks of these traces, editing them together) (Aumont 1999: 18). Burgin creates a material manifestation of this by performing it in his own experimental filmmaking, but for each of us the editing together of moving images, narratives and lived experience is a part of the labile and dynamic functioning of memory. Different forms of mnemonic experience may resemble different kinds of moving image text. Simon says of Mimi Chiola, the 'star' of her 2003 film *Mimi*, that she has 'une salle de montage dans la tête' (an editing suite in her head) (2003). She is able to visualise her memories in filmic scenes and evoke these images as though they were shots. However, unlike Burgin's description of a hybrid constellation of fragmentary images from which narrative has 'dropped away', Mimi's memory editing is ordered like a narrative film, the images brought together to describe a series of events. These two examples of 'filmic remembering' do have something in common. They are both in accordance with my argument that not only do we quite literally incorporate the films we view, making them (or fragments of them) into a part of our neurochemistry, but the way we do so bears a resemblance to the operations of film itself. However, while our memory montages may become something unique, individual and intimately private, they are mediated through common ground.

Burgin's book, with its coda on the 'Possessive, pensive and possessed' (2004: 109–10), forms part of a growing interest in questions of possession in relation to spectatorship. Laura Mulvey takes Raymond Bellour's (1987) concept of the 'pensive spectator', which relates to the contemplation of the photograph, and redefines it for the filmic image in the era of DVD. She argues that the possibilities of pause and repetition provided by DVD allow a new kind of contemplative, 'pensive' viewing. Such watching can also become 'possessive', with the viewer fetishistically seizing upon and obsessively revisiting frames, or even elements within the frame since DVD can provide a 'zoom' option: 'as the film is delayed and thus fragmented from linear narrative into favourite moments or scenes, the spectator is able to hold on to, to possess the previously elusive image' (Mulvey 2005: 161). Godard, so often ahead of the game, wove questions about possession and the filmic into the conceptual framework of *Histoire(s) du cinéma*. In the sequence on infamous producer-director Howard Hughes in *1A toutes les histoires* we repeatedly see a drawing of Hughes (either in full or in detail) as he became most known in his later years: an obsessive-compulsive recluse, unable to cut his hair or nails and refusing to leave one room where he would watch his own films over and over again. 'Tout lui appartenait' (everything belonged to him), reads the inscription printed over the sketch in one of its manifestations, 'mais [. . .] l'important était de démêler à qui il appartenait, *lui*' (but [. . .] the important thing was to work out to whom *he* belonged). A fragment of these words reappears as a title in *2B fatale beauté*. 'À qui il appartenait, lui' (to whom did *he* belong) is positioned to follow a frame bearing the title 'Cinéma' and is inscribed over a play on the films' title, 'Histoire(s) du cinémoi' (history/-ies of cine-me).

The notion of a *cinémoi*, a 'cine-me', suggests a self refracted through cinema but also the presence of the not-me, the *n'est moi*. In posing the question of cinema's belonging, Godard proposes a fusion of self and cinema, reinforcing this with the visual mingling of the words within the frame. This resonates in the viewer's memory, recalling other word-play in *Histoire(s)*, such as the highlighting of 'toi' (you) in 'histoire(s)' and the phrase intoned in the commentary in *2B*: 'Toutes ces histoires qui sont maintenant à moi, comment les dire?' (All these stories which are now my own: how to tell them?). But if all this belongs to us, as individuals, if we make cinema and history our own, what of the 'not-me' that we therefore incorporate through our imaginative investments in the objects, faces and places of cinema? Throughout this book, I have been arguing that film is part of a cultural memory, a memory that exceeds the individual body. This raises questions about ownership: to whom do our memories belong? The answer I propose is that filmic remembering is a means by which our memories are constituted through and with those of other people. Our memories therefore belong neither solely to us nor to others, but rather are constitutive of a shared reality in which each of us participates in a continual dynamic exchange, mediated through cultural interfaces such as film. This perspective is of vital significance in a world of continual migration and instantaneous global communications, for it shows us that our collective habits are always already inhabited by others. Whether in the museal accumulation of objects, an engagement with the human face as a site of testimony or the affective mapping of the temporal layers of urban space, the filmic strategies discussed in this book all offer ways of traversing the boundaries between interior worlds and social spaces. Potentially, moving images help us to recognise our common ground in the radical otherness of the past and the mnemonic encounters of the present.

In examining the interrelation of memory and the filmic, this book aims to meet a need in film and media studies to move beyond the consideration of memory purely in terms of a subject within films, or of history as reflected in cinema. It also aims to move beyond a rigid distinction between the 'inside' and 'outside' of film, just as memory is both inside and outside the individual subject. The audiovisual material I have discussed consists primarily of objects that are still called 'films', and I have continued to use the term 'filmic' to refer to their spatiotemporal representation and audiovisual juxtaposition of words, sounds and images. However, the inclusion of a CD-ROM and a multimedia exhibition here provides a point of departure for exploring these questions of cultural memory with relation to other kinds of screen media, such as the internet, video games and television, all of which draw on the filmic operations described above in different modes and contexts. Scholarship devoted to the 'new media' has long since recognised that digital creativity rehearses, revitalises and expands upon the aesthetic legacy of cinema, incorporating and reconfiguring its forms in spite of (or perhaps because of) the growing uncertainty about what cinema 'was'. Timothy Murray, for example, has argued that 'the cinematic code as hallucination haunts the interface of digital multi-media' (1999: 10). Stephen Barber has signalled the continued importance of the filmic in the collective imaginary of the city: 'alongside its powerful web of media screens, the digital city is assembled from the delicate visual and emotional projections of its inhabitants, and that often hallucinatory apparition of the city is pre-eminently rendered and narrated in filmic style' (2002: 156). The concept of hallucination in these statements, used to designate the feverish fantasies we sustain of both cinema and the mediated space of the city, reminds me of the opening of *Level Five* (Chris Marker, 1997) described in Chapter 4, where media and city spaces of the future are envisaged as unintelligible visions of light, which we make comprehensible through recourse to our memories. It is inevitably through visions of past forms that we navigate the present and construct the future: such 'hallucinations' are thus constitutive of our socio-cultural lives, rather than simply illusions to be dispelled. By analysing the mnemonic role of film in the digital era, I hope to have shown that so-called 'new media' can be understood productively as part of an ever-evolving continuum of cultural memory.

Of course, the scope of this is necessarily broader than a French context. The works I have discussed show that, where memory is at stake, national boundaries are no less permeable than those of our individual identities. To engage with the past is to recognise the memories of elsewhere that participate in the constitution of what is 'here'. In this sense, the transition from the twentieth century into the twenty-first in France has proved particularly fertile ground for the exploration of these questions, as the nation continues to contend with the violent conflicts that are implicated in the constitution of its collective identity. As the past continues to make itself felt in the present of French social and cultural life, film and other moving image media have the potential to make visible the dynamic relations between past and present, as well as the potential stasis of traumatic collective amnesia. In closely analysing French material in relation to these questions I have also aimed to offer new approaches to the study of recent French film. I have discussed the work of much-studied auteurs in relation to other contemporary moving image texts, including less well-known and first-time filmmakers, as part of a cultural context, whilst also exploring how such work feeds back into the cultural context from which it arises, expanding and contributing to the continual evolution of cultural memory. At the same time, I hope that the theoretical strands of this book might also be usefully taken up in other contexts and with other examples, which will no doubt in turn reveal further possibilities and perspectives.

I believe that the positing of a multidirectional flow between individuals, culture and collective memory, and the dynamic co-constitution of memory that this implies, is not only a theoretical premise worth bringing to the study of cultural objects. It also entails a methodological recognition of the interrelation between individual, culture and society, between interiors and exteriors, between faces, communities, cities and museums, as well as between all these things and their filmic representation. The process of researching and writing this book has shown me the extraordinary richness of potential encounters in the shared zone of memory.

FILMOGRAPHY

Alphaville, Jean-Luc Godard, 1965, France, 99 min.

À Propos de Nice, Jean Vigo, 1930, France, 25 min.

Bande à part, Jean-Luc Godard, 1964, France, 97 min.

Baraka, Ron Fricke, 1993, USA, 96 min.

Belle de jour, Luis Buñuel, France/Italy 1967, 100 min.

Blow Up, Michelangelo Antonioni, 1966, UK/Italy, 111 min.

Büsche der Pandora, Die (*Pandora's Box*), Georg Wilhelm Pabst, 1929, Germany, 100 min.

Caché (*Hidden*), Michael Haneke, 2005, France/Austria/Germany/Italy, 99 min.

Chagrin et la pitié, Le, (*The Sorrow and the Pity*), Marcel Ophüls, 1969, France, 251 min.

Chats perchés, Chris Marker, 2004, France, 59 min.

Créatures, Les, Agnès Varda, 1966, France/Sweden, 105 min.

Daguerréotypes, Agnès Varda, 1975, France, 80 min.

Deux ans après, Agnès Varda, 2002, France, 63 min.

Dites caryatides, Les, Agnès Varda, 1984, France, 13 min.

Éloge de l'amour, Jean-Luc Godard, 2001, France, 97 min.

Fabuleux destin d'Amélie Poulain, Le (*Amélie*), Jean-Pierre Jeunet, 2001, France, 129 min.

Fängelse (*Prison*), Ingmar Bergman, 1946, Sweden, 98 min.

Festen, Thomas Vinterberg, 1998, Denmark/Sweden, 105 min.

Glaneurs et la glaneuse, Les (*The Gleaners and I*), Agnès Varda, 2000, France, 82 min.

Good Morning Vietnam, Barry Levinson, 1987, USA, 119 min.

Hiroshima mon amour, Alain Resnais, 1959, France/Japan, 90 min.

Histoire(s) du cinéma: 1A toutes les histoires, Jean-Luc Godard, 1989–98, France, 52 min.

Histoire(s) du cinéma: 1B une histoire seule, Jean-Luc Godard, 1989–98, France, 42 min.

Histoire(s) du cinéma: 2A seul le cinéma, Jean-Luc Godard, 1989–98, France, 26 min.

Histoire(s) du cinéma: 2B fatale beauté, Jean-Luc Godard, 1989–98, France, 28 min.

Histoire(s) du cinéma: 3A la monnaie de l'absolu, Jean-Luc Godard,1989–98, France, 26 min.

Histoire(s) du cinéma: 3B une vague nouvelle, Jean-Luc Godard, 1989–98, France, 27 min.

Histoire(s) du cinéma: 4A le contrôle de l'univers, Jean-Luc Godard, 1989–98, France, 27 min.

Histoire(s) du cinéma: 4B les signes parmi nous, Jean-Luc Godard, 1989–98, France, 34 min.

Immemory, Chris Marker, 1998, France, CD-ROM.

Inch'Allah dimanche, Yamina Benguigui, 2001, France/Algeria, 98 min.

Indigènes (Days of Glory), Rachid Bouchareb, 2006, France/Morocco/Algeria/Belgium, 128 min.

Jacquot de Nantes, Agnès Varda, 1991, France, 118 min.

Jetée, La, Chris Marker, 1962, France, 28 min.

Julien Donkey-Boy, Harmony Korine, 2000, USA, 94 min.

King Lear, Jean-Luc Godard, 1986, Bahamas/USA, 90 min.

Laura, Otto Preminger, 1944, USA, 88 min.

Level Five, Chris Marker, 1997, France, 110 min.

Matrix, The, Andy and Larry Wachowski, 1999, USA, 136 min.

Mauvais sang, Leos Carax, 1986, France, 116 min.

Memento, Christopher Nolan, 2000, USA, 113 min.

Mémoires d'immigrés: l'héritage maghrébin: les enfants, Yamina Benguigui, 1997, France, 55 min.

Mémoires d'immigrés: l'héritage maghrébin: les mères, Yamina Benguigui, 1997, France, 50 min.

Mémoires d'immigrés: l'héritage maghrébin: les pères, Yamina Benguigui, 1997, France, 51 min.

Mépris, Le (Contempt), Jean-Luc Godard, 1963, France/Italy, 110 min.

Merveilleuse vie de Jeanne d'Arc, La, Marco de Gastyne, 1927, France/Germany, 125 min.

Mimi, Claire Simon, 2003, France, 105 min.

Mon colonel, Laurent Herbiet, 2006, France, 111 min.

Notre musique, Jean-Luc Godard, 2004, France/Switzerland, 80 min.

Novo, Jean-Pierre Limosin, 2002, France, 98 min.

Nuit noire, 17 Octobre 1961, Alain Tasma, 2005, France, 106 min.

Parapluies de Cherbourg, Les (The Umbrellas of Cherbourg), Jacques Demy, 1964, France, 91 min.

Persona, Ingmar Bergman, 1966, Sweden, 85 min.

Plages d'Agnès, Les (The Beaches of Agnès), Agnès Varda, 2008, France, 110 min.

Pola à 27 ans, Natacha Samuel, 2003, France, 55 min.

Quatre cents coups, Les (*The 400 Blows*), François Truffaut, 1959, France, 93 min.

Rear Window, Alfred Hitchcock, 1954, USA, 112 min.

Rien que les heures, Alberto Cavalcanti, 1926, France, 45 min.

Sans soleil (*Sunless*), Chris Marker, 1983, France, 100 min.

Se souvenir des belles choses, Zabou Breitman, 2001, France, 110 min.

Shoah, Claude Lanzmann, 1985, France, 566 min.

Trahison, La, Philippe Faucon, 2006, France, 80 min.

Urgences, Raymond Depardon, 1988, France, 105 min.

Vertigo, Alfred Hitchcock, 1958, USA, 123 min.

Vivre sa vie, Jean-Luc Godard, 1962, France, 80 min.

BIBLIOGRAPHY

Abbas, Ackbar (2003), 'Cinema, the city, and the cinematic', in Linda Krause and Patrice Petro (eds), *Global Cities: Cinema, Architecture and Urbanism in a Digital Age*, New Brunswick, NJ, and London: Rutgers University Press, pp. 142–56.

Agamben, Giorgio (2000), *Means Without End: Notes on Politics*, trans. Vincenzo Binetti and Cesare Casarino, Minneapolis: University of Minnesota Press.

Annis, Sheldon (1987), 'The museum as staging ground for symbolic action', *Museum*, 151, pp. 168–71.

Appadurai, Arjun (1996), *Modernity at Large: Cultural Dimensions of Globalization*, Minneapolis: University of Minnesota Press.

Arnoldy, Edouard (2005), *À perte de vues: images et nouvelles technologies d'hier et d'aujourd'hui*, Paris: Éditions Labor.

Aumont, Jacques (1992), *Du visage au cinéma*, Paris: Éditions de l'étoile.

Aumont, Jacques (1999), *Amnésies: fictions du cinéma d'après Jean-Luc Godard*, Paris: P.O.L.

Austin, Guy (2007), 'Drawing trauma: visual testimony in *Caché* and *J'ai 8 ans*', *Screen*, 48:4, pp. 529–36.

Bachelard, Gaston (1957), *La Poétique de l'espace*, Paris: Presses Universitaires de France.

Bal, Mieke (1999), 'Memories in the museum', in Mieke Bal, Jonathan Crewe and Leo Spitzer (eds), *Acts of Memory: Cultural Recall in the Past*, Hanover, NH, and London: University Press of New England, pp. 171–90.

Bancel, Nicolas, Pascal Blanchard and Sandrine Lemaire (2005), 'La Fracture coloniale: une crise française', in Pascal Blanchard, Nicolas Bancel and Sandrine Lemaire (eds), *La Fracture coloniale: la société au prisme de l'héritage colonial*, Paris: Éditions La Découverte, pp. 9–30.

Barber, Stephen (2002), *Projected Cities: Cinema and Urban Space*, London: Reaktion Books.

Barthes, Roland (1970), *S/Z*, Paris: Seuil.

Barthes, Roland (1977a), 'The death of the author', in *Image Music Text*, trans. Stephen Heath, London: Fontana Press, pp. 142–8.

Barthes, Roland (1977b), 'From work to text', in *Image Music Text*, trans. Stephen Heath, London: Fontana Press, pp. 155–64.

Barthes, Roland (1980), *La Chambre claire: note sur la photographie*, Cahiers du Cinéma, Paris: Gallimard.

Barthes, Roland [1968] (1984a), 'La mort de l'auteur', in *Le Bruissement de la langue: Essais critiques IV*, Paris: Seuil, pp. 63–9.

Barthes, Roland [1971] (1984b), 'De l'œuvre au texte', in *Le Bruissement de la langue: Essais critiques IV*, Paris: Seuil, pp. 71–80.

Barthes, Roland (1990), *S/Z*, trans. Richard Miller, Oxford: Blackwell.

Barthes, Roland (2000), *Camera Lucida*, trans. Richard Howard, London: Vintage.

Baudelaire, Charles [1857] (1972), *Les Fleurs du mal*, Paris: Gallimard.

Baudrillard, Jean (1991), *La Guerre de golfe n'a pas eu lieu*, Paris: Galilée.

Baylac, Marie-Hélène and Jean Garrigues (eds) (2000), *Les Objets racontent l'histoire*, La Mémoire de l'Humanité, Pairs: Larousse/HER.

Bazin, André (1958), 'Ontologie de l'image photographique', in *Qu'est-ce que le cinéma I: ontologie et langage*, Paris: Éditions du Cerf.

Bazin, André (1967), 'The ontology of the photographic image', in *What is Cinema? Volume 1*, trans. Hugh Gray, Berkeley and Los Angeles: University of California Press, pp. 11–19.

B.B. (2003), '*Mimi* de Claire Simon: insipide', *Figaroscope*, 9 April, p. 16.

Bellour, Raymond (1987), 'The pensive spectator', *Wide Angle*, 9:1, pp. 6–7.

Bellour, Raymond and Laurent Roth (1999), *Qu'est-ce qu'une Madeleine? À Propos du CD-ROM Immemory de Chris Marker*, Paris: Éditions du Centre Pompidou.

Benguigui, Yamina (1997), *Mémoires d'immigrés: l'héritage maghrébin*, Paris: Albin Michel.

Benjamin, Walter [1936] (1999a), 'The work of art in the age of mechanical reproduction', in Hannah Arendt (ed.), *Illuminations*, trans. Harry Zorn, London: Pimlico, pp. 211–44.

Benjamin, Walter [1950] (1999b), 'Theses on the philosophy of history', in Hannah Arendt (ed.), *Illuminations*, trans. Harry Zorn, London: Pimlico, pp. 245–55.

Benjamin, Walter [1982] (1999c), *The Arcades Project*, trans. Howard Eiland and Kevin McLaughlin, Cambridge, MA, and London: Belknap Press of Harvard University Press

Bergson, Henri [1896] (1939), *Matière et mémoire*, Paris: Félix Alcan.

Bergson, Henri (1988), *Matter and Memory*, trans. Nancy Margaret Paul and W. Scott Palmer, New York: Zone Books.

Berlant, Lauren (1997), *The Queen of America Goes to Washington: Essays on Sex and Citizenship*, Durham, NC, and London: Duke University Press.

Beugnet, Martine (2007), 'Blind spot', *Screen*, 48:2, pp. 227–31.

Borges, Jorge Luis [1944] (1998), 'Funes, his memory', in *Fictions*, London: Penguin, pp. 91–9.

Bowie, Malcolm (1998), *Proust Among the Stars*, London: HarperCollins.

Bresson, Robert [1975] (1995), *Notes sur le cinématographe*, Paris: Gallimard.

Brooks, David (2000), *Bobos in Paradise: The New Upper Class and How They Got There*, New York and London: Simon & Schuster.

Brophy, John (1963), *The Face in Western Art*, London: Harrap.

Bruno, Giuliana (2002), *Atlas of Emotions: Journeys in Art, Architecture and Film*, London and New York: Verso.

Burgin, Victor (2004), *The Remembered Film*, London: Reaktion.

Catinchi, Philippe-Jean (1997), 'Mémoire d'une nation', *Le Monde*, 13 June, p. 10.

Cooper, Sarah (2008), *Chris Marker*, Manchester: Manchester University Press.

Cowan, Michael (2009), 'Between the street and the apartment: disturbing the space of fortress Europe in Michael Haneke', *Studies in European Cinema*, 5:2, pp. 117–29.

Csikszentmihalyi, Mihaly (1993), 'Why we need things', in Steve Lubar and David W. Kingery (eds), *History from Things: Essays on Material Culture*, Washington, DC, and London: Smithsonian Institution Press, pp. 20–9.

Dall'Asta, Monica (2004), 'The (im)possible history', in Michael Temple, James S. Williams and Michael Witt (eds), *For Ever Godard*, London: Black Dog, pp. 350–63.

De Baecque, Antoine (2004), 'Godard in the museum', in Michael Temple, James S. Williams and Michael Witt (eds), *For Ever Godard,* London: Black Dog, pp. 118–25.

De Certeau, Michel (1984), *The Practice of Everyday Life*, trans. Steven Randall, Berkeley and Los Angeles: University of California Press.

De Certeau, Michel (1990), *L'Invention du quotidien: 1. arts de faire*, Folio Essais, Paris: Gallimard.

Delbo, Charlotte (1961), *Les Belles lettres*, Paris: Éditions de Minuit.

Deleuze, Gilles (1985), *Cinéma 2: l'image-temps*, Paris: Éditions de Minuit.

Deleuze, Gilles (1998), *Le Bergsonisme*, Paris: Presses Universitaires de France.

Deleuze, Gilles (2005), *Cinema 2: The Time-Image*, trans. Hugh Tomlinson and Robert Galeta, New York: Continuum.

Deleuze, Gilles and Félix Guattari (1980), *Mille plateaux: capitalisme et schizophrénie*, Paris: Éditions de Minuit.

Deleuze, Gilles and Félix Guattari (1987), *A Thousand Plateaus: Capitalism and Schizophrenia*, trans. Brian Massumi, London: Athlone Press.

D'Epenoux, François (2003), *Les Bobos me font mal: bourgeois bohèmes: minorité mal intégrée à qui l'on doit une droite un peu gauche et une gauche maladroite*, Paris: Anne-Carrière.

Derrida, Jacques (1972a), *La Dissémination*, Paris: Éditions du Seuil.

Derrida, Jacques (1972b), *Marges de la philosophie*, Paris: Éditions de Minuit.

Derrida, Jacques (1981), *Dissemination*, trans. Barbara Johnson, London: Athlone Press.

Derrida, Jacques and Bernard Stiegler (1996), *Échographies de la télévision: entretiens filmés*, Paris: Galilée/INA.

Donald, James (1999), *Imagining the Modern City*, London: Athlone Press.

Durmelat, Sylvie (2000), 'Transmission and mourning in *Mémoires d'immigrés: l'héritage maghrébin*: Yamina Benguigui as "memory entrepreneuse"', in Jane Freedman and Carrie Tarr (eds), *Women, Immigration and Identities in France*, Oxford: Berg, pp. 171–88.

Ekman, Paul, E. Richard Sorenson and Wallace V. Friesen (1969), 'Pan-cultural elements in facial displays of emotion', *Science*, n.s. 164:3875, pp. 86–8.

Ekman, Paul, E. T. Rolls, D. I. Perrett and H. D. Ellis (1992), 'Facial expressions of emotion: an old controversy and new findings', *Philosophical Transactions: Biological Sciences*, 335:1273, pp. 63–9.

Elsaesser, Thomas (2009), 'Freud as media theorist: mystic writing pads and the matter of memory', *Screen*, 50:1, pp. 100–13.

Ezra, Elizabeth (2004), *European Cinema*, Oxford: Oxford University Press.

Ferro, Marc [1977] (1993), *Cinéma et histoire*, rev. edn, Paris: Gallimard.

Freud, Sigmund [1925] (1985), 'The uncanny', in *Art and Literature*, trans. James Strachey, Penguin Freud Library, vol. 14, London: Penguin, pp. 336–76.

Freud, Sigmund [1925] (1991), 'A note on the mystic writing pad', in *On Metapsychology*, trans. James Strachey, Penguin Freud Library, 2nd edn, vol. 11, London: Penguin, pp. 428–34.

Freud, Sigmund [1930] (2004), *Civilisation and its Discontents*, trans. David McLinktock, Great Ideas, London: Penguin.

Gibbons, Joan (2007), *Contemporary Art and Memory: Images of Recollection and Remembrance*, London: I. B. Tauris.

Gibson, William (1984), *Neuromancer*, London: Victor Gollancz.

Godard, Jean-Luc and Youssef Ishaghpour (2005), *Cinema: The Archeology of Film and the Memory of a Century*, trans. John Howe, Oxford and New York: Berg.

Godard, Jean-Luc and Michael Witt (2005), 'The Godard interview: I, a man of the image', *Sight and Sound*, June, pp. 28–30.

Halbwachs, Maurice (1925), *Les Cadres sociaux de la mémoire*, Paris: Félix Alcan.

Hargreaves, Alec (1999), 'No escape? From "cinéma beur" to the "cinéma de la banlieue"', in Ernstpeter Ruhe (ed.), *Die Kinder der Immigration/ Les Enfants de l'immigration*, Würzburg: Konigshausen and Heumann, pp. 115–28.

Hargreaves, Alec (2007), '*Indigènes*: a sign of the times', *Research in African Literatures*, 38:4, pp. 204–16.

Hirsch, Marianne (1997), *Family Frames: Photography, Narrative, and Postmemory*, Cambridge, MA: Harvard University Press.

Hobsbawm, Eric [1987] (1994), *The Age of Empire: 1875–1914*, London: Abacus.

Huyssen, Andreas (1995), *Twilight Memories: Marking Time in a Culture of Amnesia*, London and New York: Routledge.

Joyce, Mark (1999), 'The Soviet montage cinema of the 1920s', in Jill Nelmes (ed.), *An Introduction to Film Studies*, 2nd edn, London and New York: Routledge.

Kavanagh, Gaynor (2000), *Dream Spaces: Memory and the Museum*, London: Leicester University Press.

Khanna, Ranjana (2007), 'From Rue Morgue to Rue des Iris', *Screen*, 48:2, pp. 237–44.

Kosselleck, Reinhart (1985), *Futures Past: On the Semantics of Historical Time*, trans. Keith Tribe, Cambridge, MA, and London: MIT Press.

Lalande, André [1912] (1932), *Vocabulaire de la philosophie*, Paris: Félix Alcan.

Lapeyronnie, Didier (2005), 'La banlieue comme theatre colonial, ou la future coloniale dans les quartiers', in Pascal Blanchard, Nicolas Bancel and Sandrine Lemaire (eds), *La Fracture coloniale: La société française au prisme de l'héritage colonial*, Paris: Éditions La Découverte, pp. 209–18

Le Goff, Jacques (1988), *Histoire et mémoire*, Paris: Gallimard.

Le Grice, Malcolm (2001), *Experimental Cinema in the Digital Age*, London: BFI.

Ligget, John (1974), *The Human Face*, London: Constable.

Lupton, Catherine (2003), 'Terminal replay: Resnais revisited in Chris Marker's *Level Five*', *Screen*, 44, pp. 58–70.

Lupton, Catherine (2005), *Chris Marker: Memories of the Future*, London: Reaktion.

Malraux, André (1952–4), *Le Musée imaginaire de la sculpture mondiale*, 3 vols, Paris: Gallimard.

Marks, Laura U. (2000), *The Skin of the Film: Intercultural Cinema, Embodiment, and the Senses*, Durham, NC, and London: Duke University Press.

Marratti, Paola (2003), *Gilles Deleuze: cinéma et philosophie*, Paris: Presses Universitaires de France.

McCrone, John (2003), 'Not-so-total recall', *New Scientist*, 3 May, pp. 26–9.

McNeill, Isabelle (2008), 'Transitional spaces: media, memory and the city in contemporary French film', in Andrew Webber and Emma Wilson (eds), *Cities in Transition: The Moving Image and the Modern Metropolis*, London: Wallflower, pp. 205–15.

McNeill, Isabelle (2009), 'Agnès Varda's moving museums', in Peter Collier, Anna Elsner and Olga Smith (eds), *Anamnesia: Private and Public Memory in Modern French Culture*, Oxford: Peter Lang, pp. 283–294.

Megay, Joyce N. (1976), *Bergson et Proust: essai de mise au point de la question de l'influence de Bergson sur Proust*, Essais d'art et de philosophie, Paris: J. Vrin.

Metz, Christian (1971), 'Le cinéma: langue ou langage?', in *Essais sur la signification au cinéma*, 2 vols, Paris: Klincksieck, vol. 1, pp. 39–93.

Miles, Adrian (1998), *O.W.L*, http://www.cyberbohemia.com/o.w.l./wel.html, accessed March 2009.

Milgram, Stanley (1984), 'Cities as social representations', in Serge Moscovici and Robert M. Farr (eds), *Social Representations*, Cambridge: Cambridge University Press, pp. 289–309.

Minnis, Stuart (1998), 'Digitalization and the instrumentalist approach to the photographic image', *Iris*, 25, pp. 49–59.

Mulvey, Laura (1996), *Fetishism and Curiosity*, Bloomington and Indianapolis: Indiana University Press and BFI.

Mulvey, Laura (2005), *Death 24x a Second*, London: Reaktion.

Murray, Timothy (1999), 'By way of introduction: digitality and the memory of cinema, or, bearing the losses of the digital code', *Wide Angle*, 21:1, pp. 2–27.

Murray, Timothy (2008), *Digital Baroque: New Media Art and Cinematic Folds*, Minneapolis: University of Minnesota Press.

Musil, Robert [1936] (1986), 'Monuments', trans. Burton Pike, in Burton Pike (ed.), *Selected Writings*, New York: Continuum, pp. 320–3.

Nader, Karim (2003), 'Memory traces unbound', *Trends in Neurosciences*, 26, pp. 65–72.

Nichols, Bill (1993), '"Getting to know you. . .": knowledge, power, and the body', in M. Renov (ed.), *Theorizing Documentary*, AFI Film Readers, London and New York: Routledge, pp. 174–91.

Noiriel, Gérard (1995), 'Immigration: amnesia and memory', *French Historical Studies*, 19:2, pp. 367–80.

Nora, Pierre (1984), 'Entre mémoire et histoire', in Pierre Nora (ed.), *Les Lieux de mémoire*, Paris: Gallimard, vol. 1, pp. xvii–xlii.

Nora, Pierre (ed.) (1984–92), *Les Lieux de mémoire*, 7 vols, Paris: Gallimard.

Nora, Pierre (1992), 'L'ère de la commémoration', in Pierre Nora (ed.), *Les Lieux de mémoire*, Paris: Gallimard, vol. 5, pp. 977–1012.

Nummenmaa, Tapio (1992), *Pure and Blended Emotion in the Human Face: Psychometric Experiments*, Annales Academiae Scientiarium Fennicae Ser. B. 261, Helsinki: Sunomalainen Tiedeakatemia.

Pourvali, Bamchade (2003), *Chris Marker*, Paris: Cahiers du Cinéma.

Proust, Marcel [1921] (1988a), *À la recherche du temps perdu*, vol. 2: II, ed. Jean-Yves Tadié, Bibliothèque de la Pléiade, Paris: Gallimard.

Proust, Marcel [1921] (1988b), *À la recherche du temps perdu*, vol. 4: II, ed. Jean-Yves Tadié, Bibliothèque de la Pléiade, Paris: Gallimard.

Proust, Marcel (2000), *In Search of Lost Time: III: The Guermantes Way*, trans. C. K. Scott Montcrieff, Terence Kilmartin and D. J. Enright, London: Vintage.

Rabinovitz, Lauren (1998), 'Introduction: film theory and the digital image', *Iris*, 25, pp. 3–5.

Ricœur, Paul (2000), *La Mémoire, l'histoire, l'oubli*, Paris: Seuil.

Ricœur, Paul (2004), *Memory, History, Forgetting*, trans. Kathleen Blamey and David Pellauer, Chicago and London: Chicago University Press.

Robin, Régine (2003), *La Mémoire saturée*, Paris: Stock.

Rodowick, D. N. (1997), *Gilles Deleuze's Time Machine*, Durham, NC, and London: Duke University Press.

Rodowick, D. N. (2007), *The Virtual Life of Film*, Cambridge, MA, and London: Harvard University Press.

Rose, Stephen (1993), *The Making of Memory: From Molecules to Mind*, New York: Doubleday Anchor.

Rosello, Mireille (2005), *France and the Maghreb: Performative Encounters*, Gainesville: University Press of Florida.

Rothberg, Michael (2006), 'Between Auschwitz and Algeria: multidirectional memory and the counterpublic witness', *Critical Inquiry*, 33:1, pp. 158–84.

Rousso, Henri (1987), *Le Syndrome de Vichy*, Paris: Seuil.

Saxton, Libby (2007a), *Haunted Images: Film, Ethics, Testimony and the Holocaust*, London: Wallflower.

Saxton, Libby (2007b), 'Secrets and revelations: off-screen space in Michael Haneke's *Caché* (2005)', *Studies in French Cinema*, 7:1, pp. 5–16.

Simon, Claire (2003), 'Mimi: secrets de tournage', *Allocine*, www.allocine.fr/film/anecdote_gen_cfilm=49489.html, accessed April 2009.

Sobchack, Vivian (2004), *Carnal Thoughts: Embodiment and Moving Image Culture*, Berkeley: University of California Press.

Sorfa, David (2006), 'Uneasy domesticity in the films of Michael Haneke', *Studies in European Cinema*, 3:2, pp. 93–104.

Sotinel, Thomas (2002), 'Fou et souverain, Godard règne sur Lear', *Le Monde*, 3 April, p. 31.

Stora, Benjamin (1991), *La Gangrène et l'oubli: La mémoire de la Guerre d'Algérie*, Paris: Éditions La Découverte.

Stora, Benjamin (1992), *Ils venaient d'Algérie: l'immigration algérienne en France 1912–1992*, Paris: Fayard.

Stora, Benjamin (2005), 'Quand une mémoire (de guerre) peut en cacher une autre (coloniale)', in Pascal Blanchard, Nicolas Bancel and Sandrine Lemaire (eds), *La Fracture coloniale: la société française au prisme de l'héritage colonial*, Paris: Éditions La Déouverte, pp. 57–65.

Stora, Benjamin (2007), *La Guerre des mémoires: la France face à son passé colonial: entretiens avec Thierry Leclère*, La Tour d'Aigues: Éditions de l'Aube.

Taranger, Marie-Claude (1991), 'Une mémoire de seconde main? Film, emprunt et référence dans le récit de vie', *Hors Cadre*, 9, pp. 41–60.

Tarr, Carrie (2005), *Reframing Difference: Beur and Banlieue Filmmaking in France*, Manchester: Manchester University Press.

Temple, Michael, James S. Williams and Michael Witt (eds) (2004), *For Ever Godard*, London: Black Dog.

Varda, Agnès (1994), *Varda par Agnès*, Paris: Cahiers du Cinéma.

Varda, Agnès (2006), *L'Île et elle*, Arles: Actes Sud.

Vigne, Eric (1997), *L'Essai*, Paris: adpf-publications.

Yates, Frances (1996), *The Art of Memory*, London: Pimlico.

Zittoun, T. (2005), *Transitions: Development Through Symbolic Resources*, Greenwich, CT: InfoAge.

INDEX